ROUTLEDGE · ENGLISH · TEXTS

GENERAL EDITOR · JOHN DRAKAKIS

THE TALES OF THE CLERK AND THE WIFE OF BATH

ROUTLEDGE · ENGLISH · TEXTS

GENERAL EDITOR · JOHN DRAKAKIS

GEOFFREY CHAUCER

The Tales of the Clerk and the Wife of Bath

Edited by Marion Wynne-Davies

LONDON AND NEW YORK

First published 1992
by Routledge
11 New Fetter Lane,
London EC4P 4EE

Simultaneously published in the USA and
Canada
by Routledge
a division of Routledge, Chapman and Hall,
Inc.
29 West 35th Street, New York NY 10001

Introduction, critical commentary and
notes © 1992 Marion Wynne-Davies

Typeset in 9/11½ pt Bembo and Times by
Florencetype, Kewstoke, Avon

Printed in Great Britain by Clays Ltd,
St Ives plc

British Library Cataloging in
Publication Data
Chaucer, Geoffrey
   Tales of the Clerk and the Wife of Bath.
   – (Routledge English Texts Series)
   I. Title II. Wynne-Davies, Marion
   III. Series
   821.1

Library of Congress Cataloging in
Publication Data

Chaucer, Geoffrey. d. 1400
   [Clerk's tale]
   The tales of the clerk of the wife of
Bath / Geoffrey Chaucer ;
   edited by Marion Wynne-Davies
      p. cm. — (Routledge English
texts)
    Includes bibliographical references.
    I. Wynne-Davies, Marion. II.
Chaucer, Geoffrey, d. 1400. Wife of Bath's
tale. 1992. III. Title. IV. Series.
PR1868.C62W96 1992
821'.1—dc20 91–46368

ISBN 0-415-00134-X

Contents

Acknowledgements

I would like to thank my friends and colleagues working on medieval literature, especially the Medieval Feminist Seminar, for their unfailing encouragement, and my editor John Drakakis for sustained belief in this project. I would also like to thank Geoff Ward for his warm and loyal support throughout the writing of this book.

Abbreviations

Ars	Ovid, *Ars amatoria*
Rem.am.	Ovid, *Remedia amoris*
Meta.	Ovid, *Metamorphoses*
RR	*Roman de la Rose* by Guillaume de Lorris and Jean de Meun
Val.	Valerius Maximus, *Facta et dicta memorabilia*

BOOKS OF THE BIBLE

Cor.	Corinthians
Eccles.	Ecclesiastes
Ecclus.	Ecclesiasticus
Eph.	Ephesians
Matt.	Matthew
Tim.	Timothy

Introduction

The lives of medieval writers often remain obscure to us since we lack the primary sources to build a credible picture. This is not entirely true of Geoffrey Chaucer, whose political employment and attachment to the court serve to provide us with a considerable amount of documentary evidence. The nature of this source material is, however, nugatory in all but monetary and legal terms. Although we may compute his various salaries and official duties, Chaucer's personal life and artistic interests remain a matter for conjecture. What is possible is a highlighting of some points in Chaucer's life through a correlation of documentation and social history.

We know that Chaucer was born in Thames Street, London c.1343, since in the Scrope Grosvenor trial of 1386 he stated that he was a little over forty years old. His father, John Chaucer, was a vintner and belonged to the increasingly prosperous group of merchants congregating in the capital. It is assumed that Chaucer received a formal Latin education at St Paul's school and a grounding in legal scholarship at the Inns of Court. From these initial experiences of middle-class wealth and clerical learning, Chaucer entered the world of the court as a page to Elizabeth, Countess of Ulster and wife of Prince Lionel. In 1357 we have a record of the clothes purchased by Elizabeth for her page.

It is interesting to note the importance of a female patron in Chaucer's early career and, when he later became attached to the Lancastrian faction of John of Gaunt, this bond was formed through another woman, his wife. Chaucer married Philippa Roet in approximately 1366; she was a lady-in-waiting to Queen Philippa with the respectable annual salary of 10 marks. When Queen Philippa died in 1369 Philippa Chaucer became a lady in waiting to John of Gaunt's second wife, Constance of Castile and received several payments and gifts while serving there. The network of feminine associations extends further, however, for Philippa's sister, Katherine Swynford, became Gaunt's mistress in 1371–2 and his third wife in 1396. These links with the Lancastrian household were to persist for both Chaucers. In 1386 Philippa was admitted to the fraternity of Lincoln Cathedral with Henry Earl of Derby – Gaunt's son – and two of her nephews, one of whom was Gaunt's illegitimate child. In the same year, Chaucer's two controllerships were awarded elsewhere and this may have happened because of his close association with the increasingly unpopular Lancastrian group. It is peculiarly fitting that Chaucer's *Book of the Duchess* (1369) should acknowledge the debt to John of Gaunt through an elegy to another woman, Gaunt's first wife, Blanche.

Apart from the records relating to Philippa and the Gaunt household we also have documents attesting to Chaucer's growing public duties. In 1374 he was appointed Controller of Customs and Subsidies of Wools, Skins and Hides in the port of London and was given a rent-free house in Aldgate. All his posts and annuities were renewed at the accession of Richard II in 1377. In 1386, as has been mentioned, he lost these posts, but in the August of that year became a Knight of the Shire of Kent and was able to attend Parliament. He had probably moved to Kent in 1385 and we may assume that Philippa died in 1387 since her annuities cease in this year.

After Philippa's death Chaucer seems to have been poorer and was sued for debt in 1388 and 1398. His official duties continued, however; he was appointed Clerk of the King's Works in 1386 and sub-forester for the King's park in North Petherton, Somersetshire, in 1391. In 1399 Chaucer was given an annuity of 40 marks by Richard and he finally returned to London and the tenement of a house in the garden of Westminster Abbey. He died on 25 October 1400 and, in acknowledgement of his literary stature, was buried in the Abbey itself.

Just as it is problematic to fix any details of a medieval author's life, so it is similarly difficult to determine an accurate list of the works which he/she wrote. In Geoffrey Chaucer's case most of our information comes from his own poetry where he refers to his canon three times: once in *The Legend of Good Women* (Prologue 417–30), and twice in *The Canterbury Tales*, in the introduction to 'The Man of Law's Tale'

(45–76) and in 'The Retraction' (1085–7). Even though we possess extant copies of most of these works, the lists call our attention to the precarious nature of a medieval canon, for it is clear that some of Chaucer's writing is lost to us, *The Book of the Leoun* for example.

The tales of the Wife of Bath and Clerk are two stories contained within one of Chaucer's most famous works, *The Canterbury Tales*, which he wrote in the last twenty years of his life. The wide variety of narratives contained within this late work is reflected by Chaucer's literary career. He wrote dream poems (*The Book of the Duchess*, *The House of Fame* and *The Parliament of Fowls*), courtly romances (*Troilus and Criseyde*), literary and philosophical translations (*The Romaunt of the Rose* and *Boece*), and even astronomical treatises (*A Treatise on the Astrolabe*). These broad scholarly interests permeate all his texts, and ideas drawn from earlier works are frequently referred to in *The Canterbury Tales* as a whole, as well as in the narratives of the Wife and Clerk. As such it is important to be aware of Chaucer's major textual productions and their place in his canon.

Date	Text
1368–72	*The Book of the Duchess*
	The Romaunt of the Rose
1372–80	*The House of Fame*
1380–87	*Troilus and Criseyde*
	The Parliament of Fowls
	Boece
	The Legend of Good Women
	Early versions of some of *The Canterbury Tales*
1388–92	Begins *The Canterbury Tales*
	A Treatise on the Astrolabe
1392–1400	The remainder of *The Canterbury Tales*

THE WIFE OF BATH'S TALE AND THE CLERK'S TALE

The Canterbury Tales is a collection of stories framed by the motif of a pilgrimage to the shrine of St Thomas à Becket. The original plan was for each pilgrim to tell two stories on the way to Canterbury and two on the return journey, making a total of one hundred and twenty tales altogether. This target was never achieved and it is clear that Chaucer was modifying his first conception even as he wrote; for example it is clear from 'The Parson's Tale' that the stories for the return to London were abandoned. The tellers of these tales are introduced in 'The General Prologue' which provides a series of cameo portraits of the pilgrims detailing their characters, occupations and groupings.

Variety is the key theme in *The Canterbury Tales*. The pilgrims represent a broad cross-section of medieval society from the nobility, through the servitors in the feudal structure and the different echelons of the Church hierarchy, to the growing numbers of independent, self-employed tradesmen and women. Indeed, Chaucer places himself amongst them. While the pilgrims are often stock literary types, most have strong individual characteristics, and the direct colloquial language of the tales adds to our impression of verisimilitude. In keeping with their different personalities they tell diverse tales such as romances, fabliaux, sermons and parables, so that the work as a whole is as much a catalogue of literary genres as it is a collection of social portraits.

Such heterogeneity has continued to puzzle editors and critics, especially as we have no authorial record of the tales' sequence, but eighty-five surviving manuscripts with no consistent order whatsoever. While this attests to the contemporary popularity of *The Canterbury Tales* it does little to offer the modern reader a chronological way of looking at the stories, even though several critics have imposed their own structure on the text. Instead, perhaps we should abandon our demands for a linear development of the narrative and look for thematic parallels and similarities throughout the work, providing an alternative kaleidoscopic pattern. If we look at contemporary collections of tales, such as John Gower's *Confessio Amantis* (1390) and Giovanni Boccaccio's *Decameron* (1335), we can see that medieval authors privileged the individual tales and their correlations, rather than the overall linking device. An example of this thematic patterning can be found in the 'Marriage Group' and Chaucer's broader interest in the relationships between men and women.

The theory of the Marriage Group was developed by G.L. Kittredge and is generally accepted as one of the fairly accurate ways of trying to order the tales. The linking themes are those of authority in marriage, the association between genders, the theory of 'gentilesse' and the position of women in society. The tales of the Wife of Bath and of the Clerk both focus upon who is dominant in marriage, the Merchant's tale mocks the marriage between an old man and his much younger wife, and the Franklin's contribution provides a happy conclusion of an ideal marriage in which both partners are equal. This manner of ordering the tales is set out in the table.

Manuscript Fragment	Marriage Group	Other tales
III	Wife of Bath	
		Friar
		Summoner
IV	Clerk	
	Merchant	
		Squire
V	Franklin	

From this it is clear that even in this case there can be no direct lineal ordering, for although the Clerk's tale answers the Wife's, the stories of the Friar and the Summoner intervene, and similarly the Squire interrupts the connection between the Merchant and the Franklin. Moreover, the Marriage Group tales are not complementary in themselves but confrontational, more a case of incompatibility than association. It is no surprise then that the Wife refers to the conventional antipathy between clerks and wives – 'it is an impossible / That any clerk wol speke good of wyves' (688–9) – and that the Clerk names her personally at the end of his tale (1170–2).

The Wife of Bath's character is intimated in the 'General Prologue' and amply augmented in her own introduction to the tale. On the one hand, she may be related to the literary stereotype of old bawd, and more specifically to the aged prostitute, La Vieille, in the French work *Roman de la Rose*, a text which Chaucer had translated. However, on the other hand, small personal details have led critics to believe that she might have been based on a real woman: for example, Chaucer had visited Bath in an official capacity, the city was well known for its cloth manufacture, and there were several women residing there at that time with the same name as the Wife, Alison. This sort of identification, while intriguing, always remains insubstantial, especially from such a temporal distance. Certainly she cannot be contained within a misogynist archetype, for although her prologue contains many references to the traditional antifeminist literature of the time, the confessional and remarkably honest tone of her quasi-autobiography lends her character a sense of human and individualistic failings, rather than unredeemable transgression.

The Wife's tale is a conventional Arthurian romance with an inserted homily on the importance of individual 'gentilesse' or nobility of character, as opposed to inherited status or quality. Although we know from manuscript evidence that she was originally intended to tell the Shipman's Tale, this narrative is particularly fitting for her since it offers an old woman a young lover and affirms that what all women desire most is sovereignty over their husbands. Again the hag of the tale is a stock medieval character, the Loathly Lady, as for example in Gower's *Confessio Amantis* which has a similar story. Yet uniquely in Chaucer's tale the woman is old and ugly through her own personal desire to test the knight rather than through the imposition of a malignant spell.

Both the character and tale of the Clerk are appropriate antitheses to those of the Wife. In fourteenth-century England a clerk was a man of learning who was either a student or a man in holy orders; however, as, often, they did not become ordained, a specific ecclesiastical reading of the Clerk's persona is not demanded. As an individual he is an idealised figure, who is poor, humble, devoted to learning, and concise in his speech. These characteristics are evident in the straightforward manner in which he tells his tale and in the simple message which advocates patience, faithfulness and humility. The Clerk has a very short prologue in comparison to the Wife and, moreover, concentrates on the source of his poem – Petrarch's *A Fable of Wifely Obedience and Faithfulness* – rather than upon his own experiences.

His tale concerns the marriage of a peasant woman, Griselda, to a nobleman, Walter, who proceeds to test her loyalty in a series of cruel ordeals, in which she believes her children to be murdered. It concludes with the revelation to Griselda that all her sufferings have been a way in which to prove her inner nobility and she is reunited, at last, with her husband and children. The tale's moral message of patience in the face of adversity is equally applicable to Christian doctrine, obedience to feudal authority, and a lessoning of rebellious women.

Literature is not produced in a literary or social vacuum and the prologues and tales of the Wife and Clerk are no exception. Other works influence the writing of a text, indeed several writers and titles, such as Gower, Boccaccio and *Roman de la Rose* have already been mentioned among Chaucer's sources. Moreover, an author's own experiences affect what he or she wishes to say, Chaucer's life as a public employee for example means that it is equally important that we understand his political and economic background. European literature in the fourteenth century existed partly in a state of paradox, for while access to texts was severely constrained by the lack of printing processes and general illiteracy, at the same time those people who could read were far more familiar with works written outside of their own country than we are today. Hence, Chaucer's primary contemporary influences in 'The Clerk's Tale' are Italian and French. The story of Patient Griselda was placed in a literary context by Giovanni Boccaccio, who included it as his last tale in the *Decameron*. This however was not Chaucer's direct source. Instead he used Francesco Petrarch's retelling of Boccaccio's narrative in *De obedientia ac fide uxoria mythologia* (*A Fable of Wifely Obedience and Faithfulness*, 1373), and an anonymous French translation of Petrarch's rendition, *Le livre Griseldis* (1380s). Chaucer did not follow his sources slavishly but altered certain aspects of the tale to suit his own purpose: for example his poem introduces far more sympathy for Griselda and emphasises Walter's irrational cruelty.

In keeping with his own preference for the vernacular over Latin, Chaucer also used English sources. In 'The Wife of Bath's Tale' he draws upon 'The Tale of Florent' in John Gower's *Confessio Amantis*; although Gower's work was not finished until 1390, we may assume, because he was a friend, that Chaucer had seen an early version of the manuscript. Each of the works mentioned so far has a distinctly scholastic appeal, but Chaucer's eclectic tastes enabled him to draw equally on less elevated English sources. The Wife's tale is an Arthurian romance and there are two very similar tales of transformation and marriage which, although they were not Chaucer's direct source material, both clearly belong to the same tradition. The two parallel texts are the *Weddynge of Sir Gawen and Dame Ragnell* and the ballad *Marriage of Sir Gawaine*, although again Chaucer introduced distinctly original features, such as the hag's control over her own appearance and the knight being won over by her arguments and not her beauty.

The emphasis on the hag's power makes the tale a fitting one for the Wife, who is herself determined to be sovereign in her own marriages. As such, Chaucer draws upon another romance context, the French allegory of courtly love, *Roman de la Rose* (thirteenth century), where the confession of the bawd, La Vieille, serves as a basis for much of the Wife's character and prologue. This, often misogynistic, text was begun by Guillaume de Lorris (c.1237) and completed by Jean de Meun, or le Clopinel as Chaucer sometimes names him (c.1277). It is also possible that Chaucer knew of the original for La Vieille, that is the old bawd, Dipsas, in Ovid's *Ars amatoria* (first century BC). These are, however, but two of the antifeminist works either used or cited in 'The Wife of Bath's Prologue'.

The catalogue of texts warning of the evils of physical love, marriage and women, which are referred to by the Wife of Bath and collected in Jankyn's *Book of Wikked Wyves*, are not esoteric but some of the most commonly known works of the medieval period. The Christian Church's antagonism towards the desires of the flesh and its dissuasion against marriage is summed up in St Jerome's *Epistola adversus Jovinium* (*Letter Against Jovinian*, c.393), which contains within it the only known copy of another popular antifeminist piece, Theophrastus's *Liber aureolus de nuptiis* (*Golden Book on Marriage*, third century BC). Chaucer also draws, less completely, upon two other texts attacking marriage: Walter Map's *Epistola Valerii ad Rufinum* (*Letter from Valerius to Rufinum*, c.1181) and Eustache Deschamps' *Le Miroir de Mariage* (not in circulation until 1406, but Chaucer probably saw an early manuscript version).

The interplay of influences on the two tales examined here ranges more lightly over other cultural areas of productivity; for example, the Platonic Christianity of Boethius's *De Consolatione Philosophiae* (*Consolation of Philosophy*, 522–4), which was translated by Chaucer as *Boece*. This infuses 'The Clerk's Tale' with its sense of patient human suffering, and contributes to the hag's discourse on 'gentilesse' in the Wife's tale. On a less intellectual level the Wife attributes her character to the astrological influences present at her birth, invoking a whole panoply of medieval astrological lore. Finally, both narratives are grounded in the more socially pervasive structure of folktales; the peasant girl's marriage to a lord has clear overtones of Cinderella, and the transformation of an ugly creature into a beautiful spouse reminds us of the tale of the Frog Prince.

8

What seems outstanding about Chaucer is the heterogeneous eclecticism of his own works and those he used as source material, from folktale, through romance, to scholarly treatises. He is never exclusive or hierarchical in his choice of subject matter, character or theme. No doubt this was partly due to his own receptiveness. But the age in which Chaucer lived experienced a period of such upheaval that in many ways his textual mutability may be seen as a literary enactment of those changes which were taking place about him. Chaucer alerts us to the importance of social context when the Wife of Bath begins her prologue with the words 'experience thogh noon auctoritee', by which she implies that a personal evaluation of material events is equally as important as the written account of some learned authority. Although not as prolific with social references as some of his contemporaries, John Gower for example, Chaucer does include in the discourses of the Wife and Clerk material which has a specific relationship to the cultural and political events of the late fourteenth century.

The Marriage Group was written in the late 1380s, a decade which had begun with one of the most serious social upsets England had ever seen, the Peasants' Revolt. The grievances which culminated in this collapse of social order had, however, their origins in the events of the previous fifty years. The fourteenth century endured several major outbreaks of the Black Death: in 1349 and again in the 1370s and 1380s. Indeed, Chaucer's elegy *The Book of the Duchess* was written to commemorate Blanche of Lancaster who died in the plague of 1369. This resulted in a population reduction of 40 to 50 per cent which left vast tracts of land uninhabited and a population demoralised by the plague's hideous physical symptoms and the apparent randomness of the contagion. As a result of the subsequent labour shortage, the demand for land tenancies dropped and the manorial landowners had to introduce incentives, such as a reduction of rent and an increase in wages, to ensure that their farms were worked. This led to a general drop in profits for the nobility who retaliated by enacting the Statute of Labourers (1351), which was intended to keep wages down. In addition to wage restraints, the commoners were also faced with rapidly increasing prices and crippling taxes, which ran at their highest in 1377–87.

Some of the taxes were levied in order to finance the military campaigns against France, which in the 1370s and 1380s were less successful than any before them in the Hundred Years War. This led to an outcry against the folly of continuing the war and wasting England's wealth in its support. Concurrently there was a general disillusionment with the traditional knightly values of chivalry, which is reflected in the beginning of the Wife's tale where a knight wantonly rapes a maiden. Disastrous foreign policy was coupled with inadequate government, for in 1377 the crown had been passed from the powerful kingship of Edward III to the youthful and ineffectual dominion of Richard II. In 1399 Richard was eventually deposed and murdered.

While social disruption fermented, the Church hierarchy fared little better, as it was being challenged by the growing claims of Lollardism. The late fourteenth century saw a gradual breakdown of the Catholic Church's authority and a widespread condemnation of its corrupt practices; the friars and pardoners being especially popular targets. The Wife commences her tale with a commonplace attack on the lechery and greed of friars, which Chaucer repeats in the 'Summoner's Tale', also part of the Marriage Group. Lollardism offered an attractive alternative, particularly to the more scholarly person, for it challenged the domination of the Church and advocated individual worship based upon a Bible translated into English. This appeared to relegate as worthless the Church's role as intermediary between man and God, as well as its emphasis on a Latin Bible and the consequent need of ecclesiastical translation. Moreover, Lollards stressed the importance of using this direct Biblical knowledge in order to reform the corruptions of the Church. We are aware that Chaucer knew several Lollard knights and that, until 1381, John of Gaunt, Chaucer's patron, also offered his protection to the most prominent Lollard, John Wycliffe. The hag's speech on 'gentilesse' in the Wife's tale seems to offer up a Lollard interpretation since it emphasises the importance of individual moral value and denies the notion of hereditary worth, 'gentilesse cometh fro God allone' (1162). The possible subversiveness of Lollardism in the social and political spheres was evident and the Peasants' Revolt of 1381 saw the banishment of Wycliffe and the disbanding of his followers, intriguingly, to the cloth-weaving towns around Bristol.

Considering this catalogue of adverse events it's hardly surprising that the country erupted in a challenge to the authorities who had so mismanaged affairs, social and religious. Still in hindsight, it is difficult to realise the dramatic impact of the Peasants' Revolt. Imagine those four revolutionary days in June 1381. On the 10th a large group of people, led by Wat Tyler, marched on Canterbury, took the city and, declaring loyalty to the Commons and King, called for the execution of Archbishop Sudbury. On the 11th they walked to London, arriving at Southwark on the 12th. On the 13th they captured London, extracted Sudbury from the Tower and beheaded him; they also burnt the Savoy, the palace of the all-powerful and hated John of Gaunt. On the 14th the young King Richard met the peasants in a field outside the city; he agreed to their demands and offered them all pardons. Touchingly naive and loyal to the idea of kingship, they accepted. Several weeks later the pardon was withdrawn and the peasants hunted down and executed, a sad and ignominious defeat. But for three days London had been in the hands of commoners and the experience was not one that could be easily dismissed.

The personal effect on Chaucer must have been considerable, for he was intimately connected with the Gaunt faction, had familial and legal connections with Kent, the origin of the revolt, and his lodgings in London's Aldgate could have made him an eyewitness to the peasants' entry into the city. He mentions civic rebellion and unrest in 'The Clerk's Tale', 'O stormy peple!' (995), and *The Canterbury Tales* itself follows the course of the peasants' march, only in reverse. The importance of this social unrest to Chaucer's poetry has recently become the focus of materialist critics, such as David Aers and Stephen Knight, the latter of whom writes in his book *Geoffrey Chaucer*,

> The world of *The Canterbury Tales* is the world of conflict that generated the Peasants' Revolt, and one of the major forces of the long poem is to realise the unrest and the quest for freedom and individual rights that were all central to this historically potent period. (Knight, 1986, p. 69)

The radical growth in the importance of individual determinism can be seen in the Wife: in the uniqueness of her character, in her social role as a self-employed manufacturer, and in her quasi-Lollard sermon on 'gentilesse'. Alternatively, the Clerk and his tale can be seen as a paean to authority and the humble submission of women and peasants alike, embodied in the person of Griselda. However, Walter's relationship with his tenants is more complex, since it is they who demand that he should marry in the first place, and he respects their requests; more like contractual than absolute rule. Still these readings mostly constrain the social and cultural contextualisation to the experiences of men. The nature of the Marriage Group, the presence of the Wife as narrator, and the feminine location of submission in 'The Clerk's Tale' also necessitate an examination of those experiences particular to women in the late fourteenth century.

WOMEN IN THE MEDIEVAL PERIOD

The Wife of Bath and Patient Griselda provide, even allowing for a certain degree of literary licence, two very different exemplars for how women lived in the late fourteenth century. Which character then is the more valid portrayal? There can be no simple answer to such a question, because the minimal evidence which we can excavate is often of a conflicting nature. In the first instance, however, we must accept that it is the Clerk who paints the more accurate picture. The official role of women in medieval society was essentially subservient; they had no rights in government and little education, and they were suppressed by the law, the Church and, more immediately, by their fathers and husbands.

Although education was offered equally to both sexes at the beginning of the medieval period, by the late fourteenth century there were clear divisions in the training offered to girls and boys of the noble and merchant classes. Peasants of both sexes received no education whatsoever. Women were trained, from prescriptive books written by men, in good manners, domestic duties, religious observances and, occasionally, household medicine. The book most commonly owned by women was the devotional *Book of Hours*, but we also know of didactic texts written by men for their wives and daughters. One such book of instruction is *The Goodman of Paris* (c.1393) which was written by a sixty-year-old man for his fifteen-year-old wife. It is interesting for us in that the Goodman cites the tale of Patient Griselda as an example of how all women should behave; he writes, 'it behoves them of need to submit them in all things to the will of their husbands and to suffer patiently all that those husbands will' (*Goodman of Paris*, 1928, p. 136). The expectations of Walter in 'The Clerk's Tale' appear less unreasonable when compared to this reading of the same narrative by an actual husband of Chaucer's period. Similar submissiveness is demanded of women in another contemporary instruction manual, *The Book of the Knight of La Tour-Landry* (c.1371), which was written by a father for his daughters.

Women of the nobility often went to convent schools, where they learned more courtly skills including how to read, both for their own spiritual enlightenment and for the entertainment of their companions. There are references to books in many noble women's wills in the late fourteenth and early fifteenth centuries; for example, in 1395 Alice, Lady West left her daughter-in-law all her books in Latin, English and French. Moreover, the Virgin Mary is commonly shown reading a religious text in contemporary paintings of the annunciation. Not only did women read widely, and in several languages, but they were also tacitly praised for doing so if the text was a devotional one, like that belonging to the Virgin. Less common was the notion of a woman writing for herself; this would have carried overtones of individual expression perhaps not utterly condonable in such an overtly patriarchal society. Still Chaucer's character Criseyde writes love letters to Troilus (*Troilus and Criseyde* II.1212–25 and V.1590–631), and a few women, such as Christine de Pisan, did write and publish their own books.

Most of a woman's education was, however, directed towards her main employment in life, that is wedlock. The anti-marriage texts of the medieval Church have already been discussed and matrimony was only condoned as a poor remedy for the sin of lust; as St Paul advised, 'it is better to marry than to burn' (1. Cor. 7.9). Chaucer himself repeats this doctrine in 'Lenvoy de Chaucer a Bukton' where he advocates marriage – 'bet ys to wedde than brenne in worse wise' – but points to his own creation, the Wife of Bath, to illustrate the woes that may be expected for men in the wedded state. The Church itself was generally antagonistic towards women, since it perceived them as the inspiration to lust, encapsulated in the image of Eve whose sexuality was seen as the origin of all sin. Women were therefore preordained as inferior to men and their submission to their husbands was seen to be founded unassailably in God's law not man's. Women were not without hope of redemption, however, for the Church offered, as the opposite to Eve, the Virgin Mary, who was docile, humble and chaste. Thus a moral dualism prevailed in the medieval Church's image of women: the cult of the Virgin Mary ran parallel with a powerful attack on female sexuality. Celibacy was judged to be the most blessed state, while physical love was seen as a destructive and sinful influence emanating from women. Chaucer may be seen to draw on this dialectic in the figures of the overtly sexual Wife and the meek Griselda.

Official ecclesiastical doctrine, however, hardly explains the utter dominance of marriage as a form of familial bonding. Instead, what we perceive is the practical efforts of a patrilineal society to bequeath sole possession of property to a legitimate and direct heir. Marriage was an economic contract mostly forged between families rather than individuals, and took into account commercial and landowning interests rather than personal preference. As such, little independent choice existed and very often the couple were children, like the Wife of Bath when she first marries, 'sith that I twelf yeer was of age' (4), and Griselda's daughter (736). Although legally condoned, marriages of unequal ages like these were beginning to be condemned by the end of the fourteenth century, for example by Langland (*Piers Plowman* A text X.180–7) and Wycliffe ('Of Weddid Men and Wifis').

Whatever the ages, marriage was primarily for the procreation of heirs; as such a woman's chastity was of immense importance and carried a commensurate economic value. Both the Wife and Griselda subscribe to this view: the former when she interprets the marriage vow in terms of the ownership of bodies (131–2 and 152–3), and the latter when she bargains for a smock in return for her virginity,

> Wherfore, in gerdoun of my maydenhede,
> Which that I broghte, and noght agayn I bere,
> As voucheth sauf to yeve me, to my mede,
> But swich a smok as I was wont to were.

> (883–6)

The assertive and independent voices of Chaucer's female characters hardly reflect what we have customarily accepted to be the more valid picture of a medieval wife. Yet if Patient Griselda, the archetype of humility, is able to assert her rights in contractual terms, then the totally submissive and dominated female type we have posited must be inadequate.

Similar ambiguities may be found in medieval law and its relationship to women, for although they often appear to have no rights whatsoever, there were a considerable number of loopholes which accessed small, but nevertheless legally inviolable, claims to an independent female subject position. In the late fourteenth century women had no representation on any ruling body, they could not serve as judges or lawyers and had no individual rights in public law, with the exception of paying taxes. Their identity as far as the law was concerned was subsumed into that of their husbands, and as with marriage, the law treated a woman as the property of her familial group, rather than protecting her personal interests. This is particularly true of rape, which was seen as the crime of theft against another man's material rights, and not a case of physical assault on the woman. If proven guilty the attacker faced an array of deterring punishments: blinding, castrating and death. But in practice there was a virtually nil conviction rate. Anyway, if the rapist offered to marry his victim all charges were dropped, and if she was a peasant then he was merely fined.

Attitudes to rape are particularly important for an understanding of the Wife's tale, which commences with the sexual assault, by a knight, on a young maiden. The people clamour for the accepted punishment, 'That dampned was this knyght for to be deed' (891), and the knight's life is saved, as was legally acceptable, through a marriage at the end of the narrative. The text conforms with contemporary expectations of rape. Moreover, it is interesting to note that none of the analogues to 'The Wife of Bath's Tale' includes a sexual assault. Chaucer's introduction of rape into the tale might originate in his personal experience, for in 1380 he was cleared of the charge of *raptus* against Cecilia Chaumpaigne. There has been vigorous critical dispute over whether Chaucer had been accused of physical rape or of abduction, which *raptus* may equally mean. There was a series of complex monetary exchanges which lead us to infer the latter, and this interpretation would comply with the contemporary evaluation of female bodies as primarily economic, rather than sexual. It would also align neatly, as we have seen, with the Wife's and Griselda's notions of their own worth. But Chaucer manifestly complicates the issue with the hag's speech on the importance of inner personal worth, which results in the knight responding to her sexually, regardless of her physical or material self. Rape, then, may act as a metaphor for absolute male domination over women, which Chaucer uses to question tacitly the more pervasive power structures between the genders.

The Wife is an important focus for challenging patriarchal ideologies for, apart from the rape in her tale, she belongs to a specifically privileged group in medieval English law: the *femme sole*, the unmarried or widowed, but financially independent, woman. The Plantagenet public laws, which were resoundingly feudal in design, treated women as the property of men, but the common law carried traces of the Anglo-Saxon legal system with its more equal treatment of gender and class groupings. Through the tenets of common law women were able to retain their property and be dealt with in the same way as men. Chaucer was clearly aware of the benefits for a woman of being a *femme sole*, for Criseyde is given the frequently discussed 'liberation speech' in which she affirms her independence: 'I am myn owene womman' (*Troilus and Criseyde*, II.750; 750–73).

Most of the women involved in business in the fourteenth century were widows; their husbands had died leaving them in possession of their property and with full representational powers in the guilds. They were mainly involved in cloth production and the preparation of food and drink, but during the fourteenth century, out of five hundred guilds, only five did *not* contain women. At the time Chaucer was writing the Marriage Group, the Holy Trinity Guild in London contained 274 women and 530 men. Moreover, because of the labour shortage in the 1370s and 1380s women could demand relatively equal pay and their wages did rise from 68 per cent of men's in 1326–50 to 75 per cent in 1376–1400. It is important to realise that the Wife's commercial expertise and economic independence does not make her an oddity, but aligns her to a substantial female group.

Aristocratic women similarly benefited from being left without male support. The violent life of a medieval knight often resulted in premature death on the battlefield, leaving his wife either to inherit the fief or in charge of it until their young sons came of age. Even when alive the knight was mostly away from his lands, either at war, on a crusade, or at court, and noble women had, necessarily, to accept the responsibilities of running the estates. In 'The Clerk's Tale' Griselda acts as a judge in local disputes when Walter is away (435–41) and Christine de Pisan, a woman writing at the turn of the century, offered women advice on how to manage their domains when alone. In her book *The Treasure of the City of Ladies* (1405), Christine writes,

> Because barons and still more commonly knights and squires and gentlemen travel and go off to wars, their wives should be wise and sound administrators and manage their affairs well, because most of the time they stay at home without their husbands, who are at court or abroad. (de Pisan, 1985, p. 130)

Although schooled to submissiveness in marriage, noble and bourgeois women had to accept the managerial duties attributed by common expectation to their husbands. Similarly, although women had no ecclesiastical power in the Church's hierarchy, the abbesses asserted almost feudal control within their own territories.

Significantly, it is a woman writer who offers us this different view of women's lives, and in her own textual productivity clearly proves that medieval women could and did write, and that their works were both popular and influential. Christine de Pisan (1363–c.1429) was a French noble woman who became a widow at the age of twenty-five, and resorted to writing in order to support her mother and three children. Apart from advice on female conduct, she also wrote in defence of women in *The Book of the City of Ladies* (1404) which specifically refutes the misogynist attacks by Jean de Meun in the *Roman de la Rose*. As such her work became part of a literary debate about the virtues and vices of women, the *querelle des femmes*, which commenced in the medieval period and did not cease to produce virulent attacks and defences until the mid seventeenth century. Although Chaucer does not use Christine, he certainly drew upon the idea of the *querelle*, for the Wife and Griselda feature as archetypes on either side of the debate. The Wife, in that she is drawn from Jean de Meun's La Vielle, functions as a misogynist personification of women's failings. In contrast, the entrenched masculine ideal of feminine virtue was often illustrated by the tale of Patient Griselda. Yet, as we have seen, Chaucer's characters only superficially draw upon these stereotypes, before revealing more complex and liberating views of women.

In 1418 Christine de Pisan entered a convent and continued to write with the increased economic security this institution provided. Two other women writers worthy of mention also recorded their experiences within the, sometimes begrudging, auspices of the Church; they are the women mystics, Julian of Norwich (1343–1413) and Margery Kempe (1373–1439). Julian was a recluse who wrote down her visions (c.1373), while Margery was a pilgrim who had visionary experiences, which were put into literary form by a priest listening to her dictation (1436 and 1438). It is Margery's confessional autobiography with its quasi-Lollard sympathies which provides the nearest analogue for the Wife of Bath's prologue, but what is important to note is the existence of powerful female vocalisations of their own experiences in the same period as Chaucer was writing *The Canterbury Tales*.

Whatever the formal, ideological consensus on women's absolute submission to men in the medieval period, the documentary evidence recently uncovered reveals a very different practical situation. Women were educated, and did exercise self-expression and control in their homes, businesses and writing. Far from taking Griselda as the archetype of medieval women, we must turn to the Wife to provide a viable alternative to pervasive submission. Indeed, rather than privilege one over the other, we can see the two female characters as enacting a perpetual dialogue between textual paradigm and lively individualism. As the Wife says, we must confront clerical authority with the evidence of women's actual experiences, Patient Griselda with the Wife of Bath.

LANGUAGE AND FORM

Chaucer's language is recognisable as the antecedent of our own modern English. However, there are a number of differences which often make it difficult for us to understand the text completely without the use of a glossary and notes. This edition uses both of these devices to facilitate a more accurate interpretation of the text, but there are some general comments and rules which apply throughout and are better understood before reading is begun. Firstly, it is essential to remember that Chaucer's poetry was written to be spoken aloud and that if we wish to follow this example we must know how late fourteenth-century pronunciation and stress patterns differ from our own. Moreover, the language of that time, known to us as Middle English, was not standardised; indeed Chaucer's English was a London dialect and very different from contemporary regional variations.

Perhaps the most interesting change in pronunciation has occurred in stress patterns. To a great extent, Chaucer's English is stressed in the same way as our own: the emphasis being placed on the first syllable of a noun, although words deriving from French were still in a period of transition, and for these the stress must be on the second syllable. But the real problem for critics until the late eighteenth century was the final 'e' of a word, which in Chaucerian English is pronounced like the 'a' in sofa. Since this 'e' often acts as the final unstressed syllable of a line, earlier readers imagined Chaucer's rhythms to be crude, and this resulted in a general dismissal of his poetic achievement.

Most vowel sounds have changed considerably since Chaucer's day, when there was a much more pronounced difference between long and short, as well as open and closed vowels. Diphthongs, that is sounds composed of two vowels spoken quickly together, were also more prevalent.

Vowel	Spelling	Middle English example	Pronunciation in Modern English
Short			
a	a	what	what
e	e	hem	set
i	i/y	thyng	pit
o	o	for	top
u	u/o	ful	put
Long			
a	a/aa	caas	father
e (open)	e/ee	mete	there
e (closed)	e/ee	swete	as 'a' in mate
i	i/y	whit	machine
o (open)	o/oo	lore	as 'oa' in broad
o (closed)	o/oo	roote	note
u	ou/ow	aboute	as 'oo' in root
u	u/eu/ew	vertu	rude
Diphthong			
au	au/aw	lawe	as 'ou' in house
ei	ay/ai/ey/ei	feith	as 'ay' in day
eu (open)	eu/ew	lewed	ME short 'e' and 'u'
eu (closed)	eu/ew	newe	as 'ew' in few
oi	oi/oy	joye	as 'oy' in boy
ou	o/ou/ow	thoght	as 'aw' in law

Consonants were more similar to those in Modern English, with a few variations: most consonants are pronounced so that there are no silent letters in words containing 'kn', 'gn', 'lk', 'rd' or 'wr'; however, an initial 'h' is often silent, especially in words of French origin. 'Gh' is pronounced like 'ch' in the Scottish 'loch'.

Another difference in Chaucer's English is the preservation of the inflectual system of Old English, although this was to cease after the fifteenth century. Inflection means varying endings in order to express information such as gender, number and tense. Nouns add 'e' and/or 's' in order to indicate the genitive or possessive case and/or a plural number. Adjectives and adverbs occasionally end in 'e'. Other grammatical differences to note are: the retention of 'thou' and 'thee' for the second person singular and to distinguish it from the more formal 'ye' or 'you' of the second person plural; and the use of 'hir(e)' and 'hem' for 'their' and 'them'. Verb endings signifying tense were as follows:

Present Tense

	Singular	*Plural*
i(ch)	went – e	we went – e(n)
thou	went – (e)st	ye went – e(n)
s/he	went – (e)th	they went – e(n)

The past participle often keeps the Old English preface of 'y', such as in 'yhad', and double negatives indicate emphasis, rather than the positive as in Modern English. This edition retains some of the Middle English spellings; 'i/y', 'y/g' and 'ou/ow' are unchanged, but I have modernised '3' to 'y' or 'gh' , as well as regularising 'u/v' and 'i/j'. In the case of proper names, I have sometimes added capitals as in God and Christ, and I have also joined up words which are more commonly linked today such as 'therby' and 'withouten' (in the manuscript these are 'ther by' and 'with outen').

While Chaucer's language may be unfamiliar to us, his verse forms would often have been unknown to his contemporaries, for Chaucer was a major stylistic innovator. He often uses the long line of five stresses which was quite rare in the late fourteenth century; this may be seen in 'The Clerk's Tale' where it is linked to a seven-line stanza rhymed ABABBCC. This particular form of metre is called rhyme royal. However, Chaucer's own contribution to English versification is the five-stressed line arranged in rhyming couplets. Most of *The Canterbury Tales* is written in this metre, including the Wife of Bath's prologue and tale.

Although Chaucer's poetic technique was innovative in many ways the stylistic devices he employs are more conventional. In the medieval period there were set rules of expression which came under the heading 'rhetoric', that is the elegant and orderly use of language. Originally rhetoric was one part of the academic curriculum, the *trivium*, the other two components being grammar and logic. It developed into more specific guidelines for poetic composition, which concentrated upon the processes of organisation (*dispositio*), cutting back unwanted material (*abbreviatio*) and adding new lines (*amplificatio*). The most famous text outlining these rules was Geoffrey de Vinsauf's *Poetria nova* (c.1210), which Chaucer most certainly knew since he parodies it in 'The Nun's Priest's Tale' (3347–52). A similar freedom with these well known poetic conventions may be found in 'The Wife of Bath's Prologue' where Chaucer subtly combines several types of *amplificatio* with the Wife's naturally garrulous style. As the author he is thus able to comment simultaneously on the linguistic excesses of both rhetorical device and narratorial character. Chaucer makes his criticism more clear by allowing the Clerk to speak simply, unaided by formal rhetoric. At the same time, it is as fitting for the humble Clerk to talk plainly as for the dramatic Wife to employ every possible means to catch her audience's attention. Chaucer remains the skilful manipulator behind these narrative voices, balancing form, style and character in an imaginative exploration of contrasts.

NOTE ON THE TEXT

Any edition of Chaucer's poetry has to contend with a vast array of manuscript and editorial material. For example, there are eighty surviving manuscripts of *The Canterbury Tales* and no two are exactly alike. Moreover, there can be no final authoritative text since all the extant scribal copies were made after Chaucer's death. Still, there are two manuscripts which are used more often than the others: the sumptuous and beautiful Ellesmere Manuscript, and the plainer, but earlier, Hengwrt Manuscript. The Ellesmere, which is at the Huntington Library in California (Ms Ellesmere 26 C 9), is a neat and clean manuscript with fine illustrations of the different pilgrims. As such, it proved attractive to early editors of Chaucer and it was used by F.N. Robinson in his edition, *The Works of Geoffrey Chaucer* (1933). Robinson was the preferred edition for student use until it was updated and emended by Larry D. Benson as *The Riverside Chaucer* (1988), but although this later work provides contemporary critical annotation its text remains within the confines of Robinson's almost slavish adherence to the Ellesmere.

It is now accepted that the Hengwrt, which is at the National Library of Wales in Aberystwyth (Ms Peniarth 392 D), is the earliest extant manuscript of *The Canterbury Tales*. This dirty and disorganised copy is inferior to the Ellesmere in terms of page size, design, coherence and decoration. Indeed, one part of the manuscript has been gnawed through by rats. But it was copied close to the time of Chaucer's death (1400–10) and it is probably nearest to his own final version. Its haphazard compilation suggests that the scribe made his transcriptions as the material was received, and this lack of formal ordering, in addition to the plainness of the manuscript in general, lead us to believe that no editorial changes have been made. The same scribe probably copied the Ellesmere not long after he had completed the Hengwrt, but this time he was able to impose more order on the tales, trying to make sense of the narrative. The Ellesmere clearly has more editorial interference and, as such, we must consider it an inferior manuscript source to the Hengwrt. The arguments for using the Hengwrt may be found in the 'Paleographical Introduction' to *The Variorum Chaucer*'s facsimile reproduction of *The Canterbury Tales* (1979) and in N.F. Blake's *The Textual Tradition of the Canterbury Tales* (1985). It is also worth looking at J.M. Manly's and E. Rickert's eight-volume *The Text of The Canterbury Tales* (1940), which does not overtly recommend the Hengwrt, but which shows that, of all the possible manuscripts, it most nearly approximates to their ideal source text. Although older editions have used the Ellesmere, it is the Hengwrt that is the most important manuscript source for *The Canterbury Tales*, and it has been chosen as the base text for *The Variorum Chaucer*. Unfortunately, since the Wife's and the Clerk's tales have not yet been published in variorum form, I was unable to make use of them.

When compiling an edition there can be no substitute for returning to manuscript sources. Therefore, although I consulted several editions of *The Canterbury Tales* (these are listed at the beginning of the Bibliography), my text is based on the Hengwrt manuscript. I also occasionally refer to the Ellesmere and other manuscripts in the notes, and have sometimes followed Ellesmere, especially for indentation in long and complicated passages, such as may be found in the Wife's prologue. There are also four passages in Ellesmere which, while they do not occur in Hengwrt, are probably authorial revisions and therefore must be included in the text. These passages are in 'The Wife of Bath's Prologue' at lines 575–84, 609–12, 619–26 and 717–20; they are indicated in the text with square brackets. Although I made one visit to Aberystwyth to see the Hengwrt itself, I used the facsimile version of this and other manuscript material for the final editing process. Finally, what is important to remember is that the choices made here and in other texts are *editorial* ones and not *authorial*. As such we must keep an open mind about how far we can accept claims to an absolute authority on the text, and instead enjoy the experience of Chaucer's poetry. As the Wife of Bath says,

Experience thogh noon auctoritee
Were in this world is right ynogh for me.

THE WIFE OF BATH'S PROLOGUE AND TALE

and

THE CLERK'S PROLOGUE AND TALE

Here bigynneth the prologe of the tale of the Wyf of Bathe

'Experience thogh noon auctoritee   1
Were in this world is right ynogh for me
To speke of wo that is in mariage;
For, lordynges, sith that I twelf yeer was of age,
Thonked be God that is eterne on lyve,   5
Housbondes atte chirche dore I have had fyve –
If I so ofte myghte han wedded be –
And alle were worthy men in hir degree.
But me was told, certeyn, noght longe agon is,
That sith that Crist ne wente nevere but onys   10
To weddyng in the Cane of Galilee,
That by the same ensample taughte he me
That I ne sholde wedded be but ones.
   Herke eek, lo, which a sharp word for the nones:
Bisyde a welle, Jesus, God and man,   15
Spak in repreeve of the Samaritan,
   "Thow hast yhad fyve housbondes," quod he,
"And that ilke man which that now hath thee
Is nat thyn housbonde", thus he seyde certeyn.
What that he mente therby, I kan nat seyn,   20
But that I axe, why that the fifthe man
Was noon housbonde to the Samaritan?
How manye myghte she han in mariage?
Yet herde I nevere tellen in myn age
Upon this nombre diffynycioun.   25
Men may dyvyne and glosen up and doun,
But wel I woot, expres, withouten lye,

1 *auctoritee* textual authority
5 *eterne on lyve* immortal
10 *onys* once
14 *for the nones* to the purpose
16 *repreeve* reproof
21 *axe* ask
26 *dyvyne* conjecture; *glosen* interpret
27 *expres* clearly
★ Numbers in square brackets refer to pages on which notes may be found.

God bad us for to wexe and multiplye;
That gentil text kan I wel understonde.

 Eek wel I woot, he seyde that myn housbonde   30
Sholde lete fader and moder, and take to me.
But of no nombre mencioun made he,
Of bigamye or of octogamye;
Why sholde men thanne speke of it vileynye?

 Lo, here the wise kyng, daun Salomon,   35
I trowe he hadde wyves many oon.
As wolde God it leveful were to me
To be refresshed half so ofte as he!
Which yifte of God hadde he for alle hise wyvys!
No man hath swich that in this world alyve is.   40
God woot, this noble kyng, as to my wit,
The firste nyght hadde many a murye fit
With ech of hem, so wel was hym on lyve.
Blessed be god that I have wedded fyve!
Wel come the sixte, whan that evere he shal.   45
For sith, I wol nat kepe me chaast in al.
Whan myn housbonde is fro the world agon,
Som Cristen man shal wedde me anon,
For thanne, th'apostle seith that I am free
To wedde, a Goddes half, where it liketh me.   50
He seith that to be wedded is no synne;
Bet is to be wedded than to brynne.
What rekketh me, theigh folk seye vileynye

28 *wexe* increase
31 *lete* leave
34 *speke vileynye* reproach
35 *here* hear; *daun* master
37 *leveful* allowed
39 *Which yifte* what a gift
41 *wit* understanding
42 *fit* bout
45 *shal* shall (come)
50 *a Goddes half* by God
52 *brynne* burn
53 *rekketh me* do I care; *vileynye* scandal

Of shrewed Lameth and his bigamye?
I woot wel Abraham was an holy man,   55
And Jacob eek, as fer as evere I kan,
And ech of hem hadde wyves mo than two,
And many another holy man also.
　　Where kan ye seye in any maner age,
That heighe God defended mariage   60
By expres word? I pray yow, telleth me.
Or where comanded he virgynytee?
I woot as wel as ye, it is no drede,
Th'apostle, whan he speketh of maydenhede,
He seyde that precept therof hadde he noon.   65
Men may conseille a womman to be oon,
But conseillyng nys no comandement.
He put it in oure owene juggement;
For hadde God comanded maydenhede,
Thanne hadde he dampned weddyng with the dede.   70
And certes, if ther were no seed ysowe,
Virgynytee thanne wherof sholde it growe?
Poul dorste nat comanden, at the leeste,
A thyng of which his mayster yaf noon heeste.
The dart is set up for virgynytee: 75
Cacche who so may, who renneth best lat se.
　　But this word is noght take of every wight,
But ther as God list yeve it of his myght.
I woot wel that th'apostle was a mayde,

54 *shrewed* wicked
56 *kan* know
60 *defended* forbade
61 *expres* explicit
63 *drede* doubt
66 *oon* single
70 *with the dede* by so doing
73 *at the leeste* at least
74 *yaf* gave; *heeste* commandment
76 *Cacche* catch it
77 *take* accepted
78 *list* wishes
79 *mayde* virgin

But nathelees, thogh that he wroot or sayde 80
He wolde that every wight were swich as he,
Al nys but conseil to virgynytee.
And for to been a wyf he yaf me leve
Of indulgence; so nys it no represe
To wedde me, if that my make dye, 85
Withouten excepcioun of bigamye.
Al were it good no womman for to touche –
He mente as in his bed or in his couche –
For peril is bothe fyr and tow t'assemble –
Ye knowe what this ensample may resemble. 90
This al and som, he heeld virgynytee
Moore parfit than weddyng in freletee.
Freletee clepe I, but if that he and she
Wolde leden al hir lyf in chastitee.

I graunte it wel, I have noon envye, 95
Thogh maydenhede preferre bigamye.
It liketh hem to be clene in body and goost.
Of myn estat ne wol I make no boost,
For wel ye knowe, a lord in his houshold
Ne hath nat every vessel al of gold; 100
Somme been of tree, and doon hir lord servyse.
God clepeth folk to hym in sondry wyse,
And everich hath of God a propre yifte,
Som this, som that, as hym liketh shifte.

Virgynytee is greet perfeccioun, 105
And continence eek with devocioun,
But Crist, that of perfeccioun is welle,

82 *but* only; *conseil* advice
84 *represe* shame
85 *make* mate
86 *excepcioun* objection
89 *tow* flax
91 *al and som* the whole matter
92 *freletee* frailty
96 *preferre* is preferable to
101 *tree* wood
104 *shifte* to provide
107 *welle* source

Bad nat every wight he sholde go selle
Al that he hadde and yeve it to the poore
And in swich wise folwe hym and his foore.   110
He spak to hem that wol lyve parfitly;
And lordynges, by youre leve, that am nat I.
I wol bistowe the flour of al myn age
In th'actes and in fruyt of mariage.

Telle me also, to what conclusioun   115
Were membres maad of generacioun,
And of so parfit wys a wight ywroght?
Trusteth right wel they were nat maad for noght.
Glose whoso wole, and seye bothe up and doun,
That they were maad for purgacioun   120
Of uryne, and oure bothe thynges smale
Was eek to knowe a femelle from a male,
And for noon oother cause – sey ye no?
Th'experience woot wel it is noght so.
So that the Clerkes be nat with me wrothe,   125
I sey this, that they maked been for bothe,
That is to seyn, for office and for ese
Of engendrure, ther we nat God displese.
Why sholde men ellis in hir bokes sette
That man shal yelde to his wyf hir dette?   130
Now wherwith sholde he make his paiement
If he ne used his sely instrument?
Thanne were they maad upon a creature
To purge uryne and eek for engendrure.

But I seye noght that every wight is holde,   135
That hath swich harneys as I to yow tolde,
To goon and usen hem in engendrure.
Thanne sholde men take of chastitee no cure.
Crist was a mayde, and shapen as a man,
And many a seynt, sith that the world bigan;   140

110 *foore* footsteps
119 *Glose* interpret
127 *office* urinating
128 *engendrure* procreation
135 *holde* obligated

31

Yet lyved they evere in parfit chastitee.
I nyl envie no virgynytee.
Lat hem be breed of pured whete seed,
And lat us wyves hote barly breed;
And yet with barly breed, Mark telle kan,   145
Oure lord Jesu refresshed many a man.
In swich estat as God hath clepyd us
I wol persevere; I nam nat precius.
In wifhode wol I use myn instrument
As frely as my makere hath it sent.   150
If I be daungerous, God yeve me sorwe.
Myn housbonde shal it han bothe eve and morwe,
Whan that hym list com forth and paye his dette.
And housbonde wol I have, I wol nat lette,
Which shal be bothe my dettour and my thral,   155
And have his tribulacion withal
Upon his flessh, whil that I am his wyf.
I have the power duryng al my lyf
Upon his propre body, and nat he.
Right thus th'apostle tolde it unto me,   160
And bad oure housbondes for to love us wel.
Al this sentence me liketh every del.'–

   Up stirte the Pardoner, and that anon:
'Now dame,' quod he, 'by God and by Seint John!
Ye been a noble prechour in this cas.   165
I was aboute to wedde a wyf, allas:
What sholde I bye it on my flessh so deere?
Yet hadde I levere wedde no wyf to-yeere.'

   'Abyd,' quod she, 'my tale is nat bigonne.
Nay, thow shalt drynken of another tonne,   170
Er that I go, shal savoure wors than ale.

144 *hote* be called
148 *precius* fussy
151 *daungerous* reluctant
154 *lette* stop
155 *thral* slave
167 *What* why; *bye* pay for
168 *to-yeere* this year
170 *tonne* barrel

And whan that I have toold thee forth my tale
Of tribulacion in maryage.
Of which I am expert in al myn age,
This is to seye, my self have been the whippe, –   175
Thanne maystow, chese wheither that thou wolt sippe
Of thilke tonne that I shal abroche.
Be war of it, er thow to neigh approche;
For I shal telle ensamples mo than ten.
"Whoso that nyle be war by othere men,   180
By hym shal othere men corrected be."
Thise same wordes writeth Protholome;
Rede in his Almageste, and take it there.'
    'Dame, I wolde pray yow, if youre wyl it were,'
Seyde this Pardoner, 'as ye bigan   185
Telle forth youre tale, spareth for no man,
And techeth us yonge men of youre praktyke.'
    'Gladly,' quod she, 'syn it may yow lyke;
But that I praye to al this compaignye,
If that I speke after my fantasye,   190
As taketh nat agrief of that I seye,
For myn entente nys but for to pleye.
    Now sire, thanne wol I telle yow forth my tale. –
As evere moot I drynke wyn or ale
I shal seye sooth, tho housbondes that I hadde,   195
As three of hem were goode and two were badde.
The thre men were goode, and ryche, and olde;
Unnethe myghte they the statut holde
In which that they were bounden unto me.
Ye woot wel what I mene of this pardee!   200
As help me God, I laughe whan I thynke
How pitously a-nyght I made hem swynke!
And, by my fey, I tolde of it no stoor.
They hadde me yeven hir land and hir tresoor;

177 *abroche* open
187 *praktyke* practice
190 *after* following; *fantasye* desire
198 *Unnethe* hardly; *statut* law
203 *tolde* took; *stoor* account

Me neded nat do lenger diligence   205
To wynne hir love, or doon hem reverence.
They loved me so wel, by God above,
That I ne tolde no deyntee of hir love.
A wys womman wol bisye hire evere in oon
To gete hire love, ye ther as she hath noon.   210
But sith I hadde hem hoolly in myn hond,
And sith that they hadde yeven me al hir lond,
What sholde I take kepe hem for to plese,
But it were for my profit and myn ese.
I sette hem a-werk, by my fey,   215
That many a nyght they songen "weylawey!"
The bacon was nat fet for hem, I trowe,
That som men han in Essexe at Donmowe.
I governed hem so wel after my lawe,
That ech of hem ful blisful was and fawe   220
To brynge me gaye thynges fro the feyre.
They were ful glad when I spak to hem feyre;
For God it woot, I chidde hem spitously.
    Now herkneth how I bar me proprely,
Ye wise wyves that konne understonde.   225
Thus sholde ye speke and bere hem wrong on honde;
For half so boldely kan ther no man
Swere and lye as a womman kan.
I sey nat this by wyves that ben wyse,
But if it be whan they hem mysavyse.   230
A wys wyf, if that she kan hir good,
Shal bere hym an hond the cow is wood,
And take witnesse of hir owene mayde
Of hire assent; but herkneth how I sayde:

208 *tolde* set; *deyntee* value
209 *evere in oon* constantly
213 *kepe* care
220 *fawe* eager
223 *spitously* cruelly
226 *bere hem wrong* accuse falsely
229 *by* about
230 *mysavyse* behave inadvisedly
232 *cow* chough

"Sire olde kaynard, is this thyn array?   235
Why is my neghebores wyf so gay?
She is honoured overal ther she goth;
I sitte at hoom, I have no thrifty cloth.
What dostow at my neghebores hous?
Is she so fair? artow so amorous?   240
What rowne ye with oure mayde? Benedicite!
Sire olde lechour, lat thy japes be.
And if I have a gossib or a freend,
Withouten gilt, ye chiden as a feend,
If that I walke or pleye unto his hous.   245
Thou comest hoom as dronken as a mous,
And prechest on thy bench, with yvel preef!
Thou seyst to me, it is a greet mescheef
To wedde a povre womman, for costage;
And if that she be ryche, of heigh parage,   250
Thanne seistow that it is a tormentrye
To suffre hir pryde and hir malencolye.
And if that she be fair, thow verray knave,
Thow seist that every holour wol hire have;
She may no while in chastitee abyde,   255
That is assayled upon ech a syde.

    Thow seyst som folk desiren us for richesse,
Somme for oure shape, and somme for our fairnesse,
And somme for she kan outher synge or daunce,
And somme for gentillesse and dalyaunce,   260
Somme for hir handes and hir armes smale:
Thus goth al to the devel, by thy tale.
Thow seyst men may nat kepe a castel wal,
It may so longe assaylled been over al.

235 *kaynard* dotard
237 *overal ther* wherever
238 *thrifty* serviceable
241 *rowne* whisper
247 *yvel preef* bad luck to you
249 *costage* expense
250 *parage* birth
254 *holour* lecher
256 *ech a* every

And if that she be foul, thow seyst that she   265
Coveiteth every man that she may se,
For as a spaynel she wol on hym lepe,
Til that she fynde som man hir to chepe.
Ne noon so grey goos goth ther in the lake
As, seistow, wol be withoute make.   270
And seyst it is an hard thyng for to wolde
A thyng that no man wol, his thankes, holde.
Thus seistow, lorel, whan thow goost to bedde;
And that no wys man nedeth for to wedde,
Ne no man that entendeth unto hevene.   275
With wilde thonder-dynt and firy levene
Moote thy welked nekke be tobroke!
    Thow seyst that droppyng houses, and eke smoke,
And chidyng wyves maken men to flee
Out of hir owene houses; a, benedictee!   280
What eyleth swich an old man for to chide?
    Thow seyst we wyves wil oure vices hyde
Til we be fast and thanne we wol hem shewe –
Wel may that be a proverbe of a shrewe!
    Thow seist that oxen, asses, hors, and houndes,   285
They been assayed at dyverse stoundes;
Bacynes, lavours, er that men hem bye,
Spoones, stooles, and al swich housbondrye,
And so been pottes, clothes, and array
But folk of wyves maken noon assay,   290

268 *chepe* do business with
270 *make* mate
271 *wolde* control
272 *his thankes* willingly
273 *lorel* scoundrel
275 *entendeth* hopes to go
276 *dynt* blow; *levene* lightning
277 *welked* withered
278 *droppyng* leaking
283 *fast* secure
286 *stoundes* times
287 *lavours* washing bowls
288 *housbondrye* household goods

36

Til they be wedded; olde dotard shrewe.
And thanne, seistow, we wil oure vices shewe.
    Thow seist also that it displeseth me
But if that thow wolt preise my beautee,
And but thow powre alwey upon my face,   295
And clepe me 'faire dame' in every place.
And but thow make a feeste on thilke day
That I was born, and make me fressh and gay;
And but thow do to my norice honour,
And to my chambrere withinne my bour,   300
And to my fadres folk and his allyes, –
Thus seistow, olde barelful of lyes!
    And yet of oure apprentice Jankyn
For his crispe heer, shynyng as gold so fyn,
And for he squyereth me bothe up and doun,   305
Yet hastow caught a fals suspecioun.
I wil hym nat, thogh thow were deed tomorwe.
    But tel me this: why hidestow, with sorwe,
The keyes of thy cheste awey fro me?
It is my good as wel as thyn, pardee!   310
What, wenestow make an ydiote of oure dame?
Now by that lord that called is Seint Jame,
Thow shalt noght bothe, thogh that thow were wood,
Be maister of my body and my good;
That oon thow shalt forgo, maugree thyne eyen!   315
What helpeth it of me enquere or spyen?
I trowe thow woldest lok me in thy chiste!
Thow sholdest seye, 'Wyf, go wher thee liste;
Taak youre disport, I nyl leve no talis.

291 *dotard* foolish
295 *powre* gaze
299 *norice* nurse
300 *chambrere* chamber maid; *bour* bedroom
301 *folk* family
304 *crispe* curly
305 *squyereth* escorts
311 *wenestow* do you think
317 *chiste* chest
319 *leve* believe

I knowe yow for a trewe wyf, Dame Alis.'   320
We love no man that taketh kepe or charge
Wher that we goon, we wol been at oure large.
　　Of alle men yblessed moote he be,
The wise astrologen, Daun Protholome,
That seith this proverbe in his Almageste: 325
'Of alle men his wisdom is the hyeste
That rekketh nat who hath the world in honde.'
By this proverbe thow shalt understonde,
Have thow ynogh, what thar thee rekke or care
How myrily that othere folkes fare?   330
For certes, olde dotard, by youre leve,
Ye shal han queynte right ynogh at eve.
He is to greet a nygard that wil werne
A man to lighte a candle at his lanterne;
He shal han never the lasse light pardee!   335
Have thow ynogh thee thar nat pleyne thee.
　　Thow seist also, that if we make us gay
With clothyng, and with precious array,
That it is peril of oure chastitee;
And yet, with sorwe, thow most enforce thee,   340
And seye thise wordes in th'apostles name:
'In habit maad with chastitee and shame
Ye wommen shal apparaille yow,' quod he,
'And nat in tressed heer and gay perree,
As perlys, ne with gold, ne clothes ryche.'   345
After thy text, ne after thy rubryche,
I wol nat werke as muche as is a gnat.

322 *been at oure large* act as we wish
327 *in honde* in his control
331 *dotard* senile fool
332 *queynte* sex
333 *werne* refuse
336 *pleyne* complain
342 *habit* clothes
343 *apparaille* dress
344 *perree* precious stones
346 *rubryche* quoted authority

Thow seydest this, that I was lyk a cat;
For who so wolde senge a cattes skyn,
Thanne wolde the cat wel dwellen in his in;   350
And if the cattes skyn be slyk and gay,
She wol nat dwelle in house half a day,
But forth she wole, er any day be dawed,
To shewe hir skyn and goon a caterwawed.
This is to seye, if I be gay sire shrewe,   355
I wol renne out, my borel for to shewe.
   Sire, olde fool, what helpeth thee t'espyen?
Thogh thow preye Argus with his hundred eyen
To be my warde corps as he kan best,
In feith he shal nat kepe me but me lest;   360
Yet koude I make his berd, as mote I thee!
   Thow seydest eek that ther ben thynges three,
The whiche thynges troublen al this erthe,
And that no wight may endure the ferthe.
O leeve sire shrewe, Jesu shorte thy lyf!   365
Yet prechestow and seist an hateful wyf
Yrekened is, for oon of thise myschaunces.
Been ther noone othere resemblaunces
That ye may likne youre parables to,
But if a sely wyf be oon of tho?   370
   Thow liknest eek wommanes love to helle,
To bareyne lond ther water may nat dwelle.
Thow liknest it also to wilde fyr;
The moore it brenneth, the moore it hath desyr
To consumen every thyng that brent wol be.   375
Thow seist right, as wormes shende a tree,
Right so a wyf destroyeth hir housbonde;

349 *senge* singe
350 *in* dwelling place
353 *dawed* dawned
354 *caterwawed* caterwauling
356 *borel* poor cloth
359 *warde corps* bodyguard
360 *me lest* pleases me
367 *Yrekened* counted
376 *shende* destroy

This knowen they that been to wyves bonde."

Lordynges, right thus, as ye han understonde,
Bar I stifly myne olde housbondes on honde   380
That thus they seyden in hir dronkenesse;
And al was fals, but that I took witnesse,
On Jankyn, and on my nece also.
O Lord, the pyne I dide hem and the wo,
Ful giltlees, by Goddes sweete pyne!   385
For as an hors I koude byte and whyne.
I koude pleyne, and I was in the gilt,
Or ellis often tyme I hadde been spilt.
Whoso that first to mille comth, first grynt;
I pleyned first, so was oure werre stynt.   390
They were ful glad to excusen hem ful blyve
Of thyng of which they nevere agilte hir lyve.

Of wenches wolde I bern hem on honde,
Whan that for syk they myghte unnethe stonde.
Yet tikled I his herte, for that he   395
Wende that I hadde had of hym so greet chiertee!
I swoor that my walkyng out by nyghte
Was for to espye wenches that he dight;
Under that colour hadde I many a myrthe.
For al swich wit is yeven us in oure birthe;   400
Deceite, wepyng, spynnyng, God hath yeve
To wommen kyndely, whil they may lyve.

380 *Bar I stifly . . . on honde* bear down with arguments
382 *but* except
387 *gilt* wrong
388 *split* found out
389 *grynt* grind
390 *stynt* prevented
391 *blyve* quickly
392 *agilte* being guilty in
393 *bern hem* accuse them
394 *unnethe* hardly
396 *chiertee* affection
398 *dight* had sex with
399 *colour* pretence
402 *kyndely* by nature

And thus of o thyng I avaunte me,
At ende I hadde the bet in ech degree,
By sleighte, or force, or by som maner thyng,   405
As by continuel murmur or grucchyng.
Namely abedde hadden they meschaunce:
Ther wolde I chide, and do hem no plesaunce;
I wolde no lenger in the bed abyde,
If that I felte his arm over my syde,   410
Til he hadde maad his raunceon unto me;
Thanne wolde I suffre hym do his nycetee.
And therfore every man this tale I telle,
Wynne who so may, for al is for to selle;
With empty hond men may none haukes lure.   415
For wynnyng wolde I al his lust endure,
And make me a feyned appetit;
And yet in bacoun hadde I nevere delit;
That made me that evere I wolde hem chyde.
For thogh the pope hadde seten hem bisyde,   420
I wolde noght spare hem at hir owene bord;
For, by my trouthe, I quytte hem word for word.
As help me verray God omnipotent,
Togh I right now sholde make my testament,
I ne owe hem nat a word that it nys quyt.   425
I broghte it so aboute by my wit
That they moste yeve it up, as for the beste,
Or ellis hadde we nevere been in reste.
For thogh he looked as a wood leoun,
Yet sholde he faille of his conclusioun.   430

403 *avaunte* boast
404 *degree* respect
406 *murmur* grumbling; *grucchyng* complaining
411 *maad* paid; *raunceon* penalty
412 *nycetee* sexual act
414 *Wynne* profit; *is for to selle* has its price
416 *wynnyng* profit
421 *bord* table
422 *quytte* paid back
424 *testament* will
430 *faille of his conclusioun* not get his way

Thanne wolde I seye, "Good lief, taak keepe
How mekely looketh Wilkyn, oure sheepe!
Com neer, my spouse, lat me ba thy cheke!
Ye sholden be al pacient and meke,
And han a swete spyced conscience,   435
Sith ye so preche of Jobes pacience.
Suffreth alwey, syn ye so wel kan preche;
And but ye do, certeyn we shal yow teche
That it is fair to han a wyf in pees.
Oon of us two moste bowen, doutelees;   440
And sith a man is moore resonable
Than womman is, ye mosten been suffrable.
What eyleth yow to grucche thus and grone?
Is it for ye wolde have my queynte allone?
Wy, taak it al. Lo, have it every del!   445
Peter! I shrewe yow, but ye love it wel.
For if I wolde selle my bele chose,
I koude walke as fressh as is a rose;
But I wol kepe it for youre owene tooth.
Ye be to blame, by God! I sey yow sooth."   450
    Swiche manere wordes hadde we on honde.
Now wol I speke of my ferthe housbonde.
My ferthe housbonde was a revelour;
This is to seyn he hadde a paramour;
And I was yong and ful of ragerye,   455

431 *Good lief* dear heart
433 *ba* kiss
435 *spyced* scrupulous
442 *suffrable* patient
444 *queynte* pudendum
445 *del* bit of it
446 *shrewe* curse; *but* unless
447 *bele chose* beautiful thing
449 *tooth* taste
453 *revelour* profligate
454 *paramour* mistress
455 *ragerye* wantonness

Stibourne and strong, and joly as a pye.
How koude I daunce to an harpe smale,
And synge, ywys, as any nyghtyngale,
Whan I hadde dronke a draghte of swete wyn.
Metellyus, the foule cherl, the swyn,   460
That with a staf birafte his wyf hir lyf,
For she drank wyn, though I hadde been his wyf,
He sholde nat han daunted me fro drynke!
And after wyn on Venus moste I thynke,
For also siker as coold engendreth hayl,   465
A likerous mouth moste han a likerous tayl.
In womman vynolent is no defence, –
This knowen lechours by experience.
   But, Lord Crist! whan that it remembreth me
Upon my youthe, and on my jolytee,   470
It tikeleth me aboute myn herte roote.
Unto this day it dooth myn herte boote
That I have had my world as in my tyme.
But age, allas, that al wole envenyme,
Hath me biraft my beautee and my pith.   475
Lat go, farwel, the devel go therwith!
The flour is goon, ther is namoore to telle;
The bren, as I best kan, now moste I selle;
But yet to be right murye wol I fonde.
Now wol I tellen of my ferthe housbonde.   480
   I seye, I hadde in herte gret despit

456 *pye* magpie
460 *cherl* villain
461 *birafte* took away
462 *though* although if
465 *siker* surely
466 *likerous* gluttonous, lecherous
467 *vynolent* drunk
471 *roote* bottom
472 *boote* good
473 *had my world* enjoyed myself
474 *envenyme* poison
475 *biraft* taken away; *pith* energy
478 *bren* bran
479 *fonde* try

That he of any oother had delit.
But he was quyt, by God and by Seint Joce!
I made hym of the same wode a croce;
Nat of my body, in no foul manere,   485
But certeynly, I made folk swich chiere
That in his owene grece I made hym frye,
For angre and for verray jalousye.
By God! in erthe I was his purgatorie,
For which I hope his soule be in glorie.   490
For, God it woot, he sat ful ofte and soong,
Whan that his shoo ful bitterly hym wroong.
Ther was no wight, save God and he, that wiste,
I many wise, how soore I hym twiste.
He deyde whan I cam fro Jerusalem,   495
And lyth ygrave under the roode beem,
Al is his toumbe noght so curyus
As was the sepulcre of hym Daryus,
Which that Appellus wroghte subtilly,
It nys but wast to burye hym preciously.   500
Lat hym fare wel, God gyve his soule reste!
He is now in his grave and in his cheste.
    Now of my fifhe housbonde wol I telle
God lat his soule nevere come in helle!
And yet was he to me the mooste shrewe;   505
That feele I on my rybbes al by rewe,
And evere shal unto myn endyng day.
But in oure bed he was so fressh and gay,
And ther withal so wel koude he me glose,

482 *delit* sexual enjoyment
484 *croce* cross
490 *hope* suppose
492 *wroong* pinched
494 *twiste* tortured
496 *ygrave* buried
500 *preciously* expensively
502 *cheste* coffin
505 *mooste shrewe* cruellest
506 *by rewe* in a row
509 *glose* flatter

44

Whan that he wolde han my bele chose,   510
That thogh he hadde me bet on every bon,
He koude wynne agayn my love anon.
I trowe I loved hym best, for that he
Was of his love daungerous to me.
We wommen han, if that I shal nat lye,   515
In this matere a queynte fantasye;
Wayte what thyng we may nat lightly have,
Therafter wol we crye al day and crave.
Forbede us thyng, and that desiren we;
Preesse on us faste, and thanne wol we fle.   520
With daunger oute we al oure chaffare;
Greet prees at market maketh deere ware,
And to greet cheepe is holden at litel prys;
This knoweth every womman that is wys.
    My fifthe housbonde, God his soule blesse.   525
Which that I took for love, and no rychesse,
He som tyme was a clerk of Oxenford,
And hadde laft scole, and wente at hom to bord
With my gossyb, dwellynge in oure town;
God have hir soule! hir name was Alisoun.   530
She knew myn herte, and eek my pryvetee,
Bet than oure parysshe preest, as mote I thee.
To hire biwreyed I my conseil al;
For hadde myn housbonde pissed on a wal,
Or doon a thyng that sholde have cost his lyf,   535
To hire and to another worthy wyf,
And to my nece, which that I loved wel,
I wolde han toold his conseil every del.
And so I dide ful often, God it woot,

510 *bele chose* beautiful thing
514 *daungerous* disdainful
516 *queynte fantasye* strange desire
517 *What* whatever
522 *prees* crowd
523 *to greet cheepe* too good a bargain
527 *som tyme* formerly
528 *scole* university
533 *biwreyed* confessed

That made his face often reed and hoot   540
For verray shame, and blamed hymself for he
Hadde toold to me so greet a pryvetee.
        And so bifel that ones in a Lente –
So often tymes I to my gossyb wente,
For evere yet I lovede to be gay,   545
And for to walke in March, Averyll, and May,
From hous to hous, to here sondry tales –
That Jankyn clerk, and my gossyb dame Alys,
And I myself, into the feeldes wente.
Myn housbonde was at Londoun al that Lente;   550
I hadde the bettre leyser for to pleye,
And for to se, and eek for to be seye
Of lusty folk. What wiste I wher my grace
Was shapen for to be, or in what place?
Therfore I made my visitacions   555
To vigilies and to processions,
To prechyng eek, and to thise pilgrymages,
To pleyes of myracles, and to mariages,
And wered upon my gaye scarlet gytes –
Thise wormes, ne thise motthes, ne thise mytes,   560
Upon my peril frete hem never a del;
And wostow why? for they were used wel!
        Now wol I tellen forth what happed me.
I seye that in the feeldes walked we,
Til trewely we hadde swich daliaunce,   565
This clerk and I, that of my purveiaunce
I spak to hym and seyde hym how that he,
If I were wydewe, sholde wedde me.
For certeynly, I seye for no bobaunce,
Yet was I nevere withouten purveiaunce   570
Of mariage, n'of othere thynges eek.

542 *pryvetee* secret
554 *shapen* destined
559 *gytes* long robes
560 *motthes* moths; *mytes* insects
561 *frete* consumed
566 *purveiaunce* foresight
569 *bobaunce* boast

I holde a mouses herte noght worth a leek
That hath but oon hole for to sterte to,
And if that faille, thanne is al ydo.

[I bar hym on honde he hadde enchanted me,   575
My dame taughte me that soutiltee.
And eek I seyde I mette of hym al nyght,
He wolde han slayn me as I lay upright,
And al my bed was ful of verray blood;
But yet I hope that he shal do me good,   580
For blood bitokeneth gold, as me was taught.
And al was fals; I dremed of it right naught,
But I folwed ay my dammes loore,
As wel of this as othere thynges moore.]

But now, sire, lat me se, what shal I seyn?   585
A ha! by God I have my tale ageyn.

Whan that my fourthe housbonde was a beere,
I weep algate, and made sory cheere,
As wyves mooten, for it is usage,
And with my coverchief covered my visage,   590
But for that I was purveyed of a make,
I wepte but smal, and that I undertake.

To chirche was myn housbonde born a morwe
With neghebores, that for hym maden sorwe;
And Jankyn, oure clerk, was oon of tho.   595
As help me God, whan that I saw hym go
After the beere, me thoughte he hadde a payre
Of legges and of feet so clene and fayre
That al myn herte I yaf unto his hoold.

574 *al ydo* all over
575 *bar hym on honde* led him to believe
577 *mette* dreamed
578 *upright* face up
582 *right naught* not at all
587 *a beere* on his bier
588 *algate* always
591 *purveyed of* provided with
592 *undertake* affirm
593 *a morwe* next morning
598 *clene* shapely

He was, I trowe, twenty wynter oold,   600
And I was fourty, if I shal seye sooth;
But yet I hadde alwey a coltes tooth.
Gat tothed I was, and that bicam me weel;
I hadde the preente of Seynt Venus seel.
As help me God, I was a lusty oon,   605
And fayr, and ryche, and yong, and wel bigoon;
And trewely, as myne housbondes tolde me,
I hadde the beste quonyam myghte be.
[For certes, I am al Venerien
In feelynge, and myn herte is Marcien.   610
Venus me yaf my lust, my likerousnesse,
And Mars yaf me my sturdy hardynesse;]
Myn ascendent was Taur, and Mars therinne.
Allas! allas! that evere love was synne!
I folwed ay myn inclinacioun   615
By vertu of my constellacioun;
That made me I koude noght withdrawe
My chambre of Venus from a good felawe.
[Yet have I Martes mark upon my face,
And also in another privee place.   620
For God so wys be my savacioun,
I ne loved nevere by no discrecioun,
But evere folwed myn appetit,
Al were he short, or long, or blak, or whit,
I took no kepe, so that he liked me,   625
How poore he was, ne eek of what degree.]
    What sholde I seye? but, at the monthes ende,
This joly clerk, Jankyn, that was so hende,
Hath wedded me with greet solempnytee;

602 *coltes tooth* taste for young men
604 *preente* imprint; *seel* mark
606 *bigoon* situated
608 *quonyam* thing (pudendum)
612 *hardynesse* boldness
616 *constellacioun* horoscope
621 *so wys be* will surely; *savacioun* salvation
625 *so that* providing
628 *hende* courteous

And to hym yaf I al the lond and fee   630
That evere was me yeven ther bifore.
But afterward repented me ful sore;
He nolde suffre no thyng of my list.
By God! he smoot me ones on the lyst,
For that I rente out of his book a leef,   635
That of the strook myn ere weex al deef.
Stibourne I was as is a leonesse,
And of my tonge a verray jangleresse,
And walke I wolde, as I hadde doon biforn,
From hous to hous, althogh he hadde it sworn;   640
For which he often tymes wolde preche,
And me of olde Romayn gestes teche:
How he Symplicius Gallus lafte his wif,
And hire forsook for terme of al his lif,
Noght but for open heveded he hir say   645
Lokynge out at his dore upon a day.
   Another Romayn tolde he me by name,
That, for his wyf was at a someres game
Withouten his wityng, he forsook hire eke.
And thanne wolde he upon his Bible seke   650
That ilke proverbe of Ecclesiaste
Where he comandeth, and forbedeth faste,
Man shal nat suffre his wyf go roule aboute.
Thanne wolde he seye right thus, withouten doute:
   "Who so that buyldeth his hous al of salwes,   655
And priketh his blynde hors over the falwes,

630 *fee* property
633 *list* desire
634 *lyst* ear
635 *rente* tore
638 *jangleresse* chatterbox
640 *it* it
642 *gestes* tales
645 *open heveded* bareheaded; *say* saw
648 *someres game* midsummer festival
653 *roule* wander
655 *salwes* willow branches
656 *priketh* spurs; *falwes* open fields

    And suffreth his wyf to go seken halwes,
Is worthy to ben hanged on the galwes!"
But al for noght. I sette noght an hawe
Of his proverbe n'of his olde sawe,   660
N'Y wolde nat of hym corrected be.
I hate hym that my vices telleth me,
And so doon mo, God woot, of us than I.
This made hym with me wood al-outrely;
I nolde noght forbere hym in no cas.   665
    Now wol I sey yow sooth, by seint Thomas,
Why that I rente out of his book a leef,
For which he smoot me so that I was deef.
    He hadde a book that gladly, nyght and day,
For his disport he wolde rede alway;   670
He clepyd it Valerie and Theofraste,
At which book he logh alwey ful faste.
And eek ther was somtyme a clerk at Rome,
A cardynal, that highte Seint Jerome,
That made a book agayn Jovinian;   675
In which book eek ther was Tertulan,
Crisippus, Trotula, and Helowys,
That was abbesse nat fer fro Parys;
And eek the Parables of Salomon,
Ovydes Art, and bokes many on,   680
And alle thise were bounden in o volume.
And every nyght and day was his custume,
When he hadde leyser and vacacioun
From oother worldly ocupacioun,
To reden in this book of wikked wyves.   685
He knew of hem mo legendes and lyves
Than been of goode wyves in the Bible.

657 *go seken halwes* go on pilgrimages
659 *hawe* hawthorn berry
664 *al-outrely* completely
670 *disport* amusement
672 *logh* laughed; *faste* hard
680 *on* a one
683 *vacacioun* spare time

For trusteth wel, it is an inpossible
That any clerk wol speke good of wyves,
But if it be of holy seintes lyves,   690
N'of noon oother womman never the mo.
Who peynted the leoun, tel me who?
By God! if wommen hadden writen stories,
As clerkes han withinne hir oratories,
They wolde han writen of men moore wikkednesse   695
Than al the mark of Adam may redresse.
The children of Mercurie and Venus
Been in hir wirkyng ful contrarius;
Mercurie loveth wysdam and science.
And Venus loveth riot and dispence.   700
And, for hir diverse disposicioun,
Ech faileth in ootheres exaltacioun.
And thus, God woot, Mercurie is desolat
In Pisces, wher Venus is exaltat;
And Venus faileth ther Mercurie is reysed.   705
Therfore no womman of no clerk is preysed.
The clerk, whan he is old, and may noght do
Of Venus werkes worth his olde sho,
Thanne sit he doun, and writ in his dotage
That wommen kan nat kepe hir mariage!   710
    But now to purpos, why I tolde thee
That I was beten for a book, pardee!
Upon a nyght Jankyn, that was oure sire,
Redde on his book, as he sat by the fire,

688 *inpossible* impossibility
690 *But if* unless
694 *oratories* rooms for private meditation
696 *mark of* image of; *Adam* male sex
698 *wirkyng* actions
699 *science* knowledge
700 *riot* wanton revelry; *dispence* extravagance
701 *disposicioun* position
703 *desolat* powerless
706 *of* by
709 *writ* writes

Of Eva first, that for hir wikkednesse   715
Was al mankynde broght to wrecchednesse,
[For which Crist hymself was slayn,
That boghte us with his herte blood agayn.
Lo, heere expres of womman may ye fynde,
That womman was the los of al mankynde.]   720
    Tho redde he me how Sampson loste his herys:
Slepynge, his lemman kitte it with hir sherys;
Thurgh which tresoun loste he bothe hise eyen.
    Tho redde he me, if that I shal nat lyen,
Of Hercules and of his Dianyre,   725
That caused hym to sette hymself afyre.
    No thyng forgat he the sorwe and wo
That Socrates hadde with hise wyves two;
How Xantippa caste pisse upon his heed.
This sely man sat stille as he were deed;   730
He wipte his heed, namoore dorste he seyn,
But "Er that thonder stynte, comth a reyn!"
    Of Phasifpha, that was the queene of Crete,
For shrewednesse, hym thoughte the tale swete;
Fy! spek namoore – it is a grisly thyng –   735
Of hire horrible lust and hir likyng.
    Of Clitermystra, for hir lecherye,
That falsly made hir housbonde for to dye,
He redde it with ful good devocioun.
    He tolde me eek for what occasioun   740
Amphiorax at Thebes loste his lyf.
Myn housbonde hadde a legende of his wyf,
Eriphilem, that for an ouch of gold
Hath prively unto the Greky told

718 *boghte agayn* redeemed
719 *expres* recorded
720 *los of al mankynde* cause of perdition
721 *herys* hair
722 *lemman* mistress; *kitte* cut
730 *deed* dead
734 *shrewednesse* malice
735 *grisly* horrible
743 *ouch* brooch

Wher that hir housbonde hidde hym in a place,   745
For which he hadde at Thebes sory grace.
    Of Lyvia tolde he me, and of Lucie:
They bothe made hir housbondes for to dye;
That oon for love, that oother was for hate.
Lyvia hir housbonde, on an even late,   750
Empoysoned hath, for that she was his fo;
Lucya, likerous, loved hir housbonde so
That, for he sholde alwey upon hir thynke,
She yaf hym swich a manere love-drynke
That he was deed er it were by the morwe;   755
And thus algates housbondes han sorwe.
    Thanne tolde he me how that oon Latumyus
Compleyned unto his felawe Arrius
That in his gardyn growed swich a tree
On which he seyde how that his wyves thre   760
Honged hemself for hertes despitus.
"O leeve brother," quod this Arrius,
"Yif me a plante of thilke blessed tree,
And in my gardyn planted shal it be."
    Of latter date, of wyves hath he red   765
That somme han slayn hir housbondes in hir bed,
And lete hir lechour dighte hire al the nyght,
Whan that the corps lay in the floor upryght.
And somme han dryven nayles in hir brayn,
Whil that they sleepe, and thus they han hem slayn.   770
    Somme han hem yeven poysoun in hir drynke.
He spak moore harm than herte may bithynke;

746 *sory grace* misfortune
751 *even* evening
755 *er . . . morwe* just before dawn
756 *algates* always
761 *Honged* hanged; *despitus* spiteful
762 *leeve* permit
763 *plante* cutting
765 *Of latter date* recently
767 *dighte* copulate with
768 *upryght* face up
772 *bithynke* imagine

And therwithal he knew of mo proverbes
Than in this world ther growen gras or herbes.
"Bet is", quod he, "thyn habitacioun   775
Be with a leoun or a foul dragoun,
Than with a womman usyng for to chide."
"Bet is", quod he, "hye in the roof abyde,
Than with an angry wyf down in the hous;
They been so wikked and contrarious,   780
They haten that hir housbondes loveth ay."
He seyde, "a womman cast hir shame away,
Whan she cast of hir smok"; and forthermo,
"A fair womman, but she be chaast also,
Is lyk a gold ryng in a sowes nose."   785
Who wolde wene, or who wolde suppose,
The wo that in myn herte was, and pyne?
    And whan I say he wolde nevere fyne
To reden on this cursed book al nyght,
Al sodeynly thre leves have I plyght   790
Out of his book, right as he radde, and eke
I with my fist so took on the cheke
That in oure fyr he fil bakward adown.
And he up stirte as dooth a wood leoun,
And with his fest he smoot me on the heed,   795
That in the floor I lay as I were deed.
And whan he say how stille that I lay,
He was agast, and wolde have fled his way,
Til atte laste out of my swowgh I brayde.
"O! hastow slayn me, false theef?" I sayde,   800
"And for my land thus hastow mordred me?
Er I be deed, yet wol I kisse thee."

777 *usyng for* accustomed
783 *of* off; *smok* shift
787 *pyne* pain
788 *fyne* cease
790 *plyght* plucked
791 *radde* read
794 *wood* mad
799 *swowgh* swoon; *brayde* woke up
800 *theef* villain

And neer he cam, and kneled faire adown,
And seyde, "Deere suster Alisoun,
As help me God! I shal thee nevere smyte.   805
That I have doon, it is thyself to wyte.
Foryeve it me, and that I thee biseke!"
And yet eftsoones I hitte hym on the cheke,
And seyde, "Theef, thus muchel am I wreke;
Now wol I dye, I may no lenger speke."   810
    But at the laste, with muchel care and wo,
We fille acorded by us selven two.
He yaf me al the brydel in myn hond,
To han the governance of hous and lond,
And of his tonge, and of his hond also;   815
And made hym brenne his book anon right tho.
And whan that I hadde geten unto me,
By maistrye, al the soveraynetee,
And that he seyde, "Myn owene trewe wyf,
Do as thee lust the terme of al thy lyf;   820
Keepe thyn honour, and keepe eek myn estaat" –
After that day we hadden never debaat.
God help me so, I was to hym as kynde
As any wyf from Denmark unto Inde,
And also trewe, and so was he to me.   825
I pray to God, that sit in magestee,
So blesse his soule for his mercy deere.
Now wol I seye my tale, if ye wol heere.'

[Biholde the wordes bitwene the Somonour and the Frere.]

The Frere logh whan he hadde herd al this;
'Now Dame,' quod he, 'so have I joye or blys,   830

806 *that* what; *wyte* blame
808 *eftsoones* immediately
809 *wreke* avenged
820 *as thee lust* as you please
822 *debaat* dispute
824 *Inde* India

This is a long preamble of a tale!'
And whan the Somnour herde the Frere gale,
   'Lo,' quod the Somnour, 'Goddes armes two!
A frere wol entremette hym everemo.
Loo, goode men, a flye and eek a frere   835
Wol falle in every dyssh and matere.
What spekestow of preambulacioun?
What! amble, or trotte, or pees, or go sit doun!
Thow lettest oure disport in this manere.'
   'Ye, woltow so, sir Somnour,' quod the Frere;   840
'Now, by my feith, I shal er that I go,
Telle of a somnour swich a tale or two
That al the folk shal laughen in this place.'
   'Now ellis, Frere, I wol bishrewe thy face,'
Quod this Somnour, 'and I bishrewe me,   845
But if I telle tales two or thre
Of freres er I come to Sydyngborne,
That I shal make thyn herte for to morne,
For wel I woot thy pacience is gon.'
Oure Hoost cryde 'Pees! And that anon!'   850
And seyde, 'lat the womman telle hire tale.
Ye fare as folk that dronken ben of ale.
Do, Dame, tel forth youre tale and that is best.'
   'Al reddy, sire,' quod she, 'right as yow lest,
If I have licence of this worthy Frere.'   855
   'Yis, Dame', quod he, 'tel forth and I wol heere.'

Here endeth the prologe of the Wyf of Bathe

832 *gale* cry out
834 *entremette* interfere
837 *preambulacioun* preambling
838 *pees* shut up
839 *lettest* hinder
844 *beshrewe* curse
848 *morne* mourn
856 *yis* yes indeed

Here bigynneth the tale of the Wyf of Bathe

In th'olde dayes of the kyng Arthour,
Of which that Britons speken greet honour,
Al was this land fulfild of fairye.
The elf-queene, with hir joly compaignye,   860
Daunced ful ofte in many a grene mede.
This was the olde opynyoun, as I rede;
I speke of many hundred yerys ago.
But now can no man se none elves mo,
For now the grete charitee and prayeres   865
Of lymytours and othere holy freres,
That serchen every lond and every streem,
As thikke as motes in the sonne-beem,
Blessynge halles, chambres, kichenes, boures,
Citees, burghes, castels, hye toures,   870
Thropes, bernes, shipnes, dayeryes –
This maketh that ther been no fairyes.
For ther as wont to walken was an elf,
Ther walketh now the lymytour hymself,
In undermelys and in morwenynges,   875
And seith his matyns and his holy thynges
As he gooth in his lymytacioun.
Wommen may go saufly up and down.
In every bussh or under every tree
Ther is noon oother incubus but he,   880
And he ne wol doon hem but dishonour.

859 *fulfild* filled
860 *elf-queene* fairy queen
866 *lymytours* friars
867 *serchen* haunt
868 *motes* specks of dust
869 *boures* bedrooms
870 *burghes* boroughs
871 *Thropes* villages; *bernes* barns; *shipnes* stables
875 *undermelys* late mornings; *morwenynges* early mornings
876 *matyns* morning prayers
877 *lymytacioun* district
880 *incubus* evil spirit

And so bifel that this kyng Arthour
Hadde in his hous a lusty bachiler,
That on a day cam ridyng fro ryver;
And happed that, allone as he was born,   885
He say a mayde walkynge hym biforn,
Of which mayde anoon, maugree hir hed,
By verray force, he rafte hir maydenhed;
For which oppressioun was swich clamour
And swich pursuyte unto the king Arthour,   890
That dampned was this knyght for to be deed,
By cours of lawe and sholde han lost his heed –
Paraventure swich was the statut tho –
But that the queene and othere ladyes mo
So longe preyden the kyng of grace,   895
Til he his lyf hym graunted in the place,
And yaf hym to the queene, al at hir wille,
To chese wheither she wolde hym save or spille.
[The queene thanketh the kyng with al hir myght,]
And after this thus spak she to the knyght,   · 900
Whan that she saw hir tyme, upon a day:
'Thow standest yet', quod she, 'in swich array
That of thy lyf yet hastow no suretee.
I graunte thee lyf, if thow kanst tellen me
What thyng is it that wommen moost desiren.   905
Be war, and keepe thy nekke-boon from iren!
And if thow kanst nat tellen me anon,
Yet wol I yeve thee leve for to gon
A twelf-monthe and a day, to seche and lere

883 *bachiler* young knight
884 *ridyng fro ryver* hawking for waterfowl
890 *pursuyte* demand for justice
893 *Paraventure* by chance
896 *in the place* on the spot
898 *hym spille* execute him
903 *suretee* security
906 *iren* iron
909 *seche* seek; *lere* learn

An answere suffisant in this matere;   910
And seuretee wol I han, er that thow pace,
Thy body for to yelden in this place.'
   Wo was this knyght, and sorwefully he siketh;
But what, he may nat doon al as hym liketh.
And atte laste he chees hym for to wende,   915
And come agayn, right at the yeres ende,
With swich answere as God wolde hym purveye;
And taketh his leve, and wendeth forth his weye.
   He seketh every hous and every place
Where as he hopeth for to fynde grace,   920
To lerne what thyng wommen love moost;
But he ne koude arryven in no coost
Where as he myghte fynde in this matere
Two creatures acordyng in-feere.
   Somme seyden wommen loven best richesse,   925
Somme seyde honour, somme seyde jolinesse,
Somme riche array, somme lust abedde,
And ofte tyme to be widwe and wedde.
Somme seyde that oure herte is moost esed
Whan that we been yflatered and yplesed.   930
He gooth ful ny the sothe, I wol nat lye.
A man shal wynne us best with flaterye;
And with attendaunce, and with bisynesse,
Been we ylymed, bothe moore and lesse.
   And somme seyn that we loven best   935
For to be free, and do right as us lest,

911 *seuretee* security
912 *yelden* yield
913 *siketh* sighs
915 *chees* chose
917 *purveye* provide
922 *coost* coast
924 *acordyng* in agreement
926 *jolinesse* pleasure
931 *ful ny* very close
933 *attendaunce* attention
934 *ylymed* trapped
936 *us lest* we wish

And that no man repreve us of oure vice,
But seye that we be wise, and no thyng nyce.
For trewely ther is noon of us alle,
If any wight wolde clawe us on the galle,   940
That we nyl kike, for he seith us sooth.
Assay, and he shal fynde it that so dooth;
For, be we never so vicious withinne,
We wol be holden wise and clene of synne.

   And somme seyn that greet delit han we   945
For to be holden stable, and eek secree,
And in o purpos stedefastly to dwelle,
And nat biwreye thyng that men us telle.
But that tale is nat worth a rake-stele.
Pardee, we wommen konne no thyng hele;   950
Witnesse on Mida, - wol ye heere the tale?

   Ovyde, amonges othere thynges smale,
Seyde Mida hadde, under his longe herys,
Growynge upon his heed two asses erys,
The which vice he hidde, as he best myghte,   955
Ful sotilly from every mannes sighte,
That, save his wyf, ther wiste of it namo.
He loved hire moost, and trusted hire also;
He preyed hire that to no creature
She sholde tellen of his disfigure.   960

   She swoor hym, 'Nay,' for al this world to wynne,
She nolde do that vileynye or syn,
To make hir housbonde han so foul a name.
She nolde nat telle it for hir owene shame.
But nathelees, hir thoughte that she dyde,   965

937 *repreve* reprove
941 *nyl kike* will not kick
944 *holden* considered
946 *secree* discreet
948 *biwreye* betray
949 *stele* handle
950 *hele* keep secret
951 *Mida* Midas
952 *Ovyde* Ovid
956 *sotilly* subtly

That she so longe sholde a conseil hyde;
Hir thoughte it swal so soore aboute hir herte
That nedely som word hir moste asterte;
And sith she dorste nat telle it to no man,
Doun to a marys faste by she ran –   970
Til she cam there, hir herte was a-fyre –
And as a bitore bombleth in the myre,
She leyde hir mouth unto the water down:
'Biwrey me nat, thow water, with thy sown,'
Quod she, 'to thee I telle it and namo;   975
Myn housbonde hath longe asses erys two!
Now is myn herte al hool, now it is oute.
I myghte ne lenger kepe it, out of doute.'
Heere may ye see, thogh we a tyme abyde,
Yet out it moot; we kan no conseil hyde.   980
The remenant of the tale if ye wol heere,
Redeth Ovyde, and ther ye may it leere.

     This knyght, of which my tale is specially,
Whan that he say he myghte nat come therby,
This is to seye, what wommen loven moost,   985
Withinne his brest ful sorweful was the goost.
But hom he gooth, he myghte nat sojorne;
The day was com that homward moste he torne.
And in his wey it happed hym to ryde,
In al this care, under a forest syde,   990
Wher as he say upon a daunce go
Of ladyes foure and twenty, and yet mo;
Toward the whiche daunce he drow ful yerne,

966 *conseil* secret
967 *swal* swelled
968 *nedely* necessarily; *asterte* escape
970 *marys* marsh
974 *Biwrey* betray
982 *leere* learn
986 *goost* spirit
987 *sojorne* remain
989 *it happed hym* he chanced
990 *under* near
993 *yerne* eagerly

In hope that som wisdom sholde he lerne.
But certeynly, er he cam fully there,   995
Vanysshed was this daunce, he nyste where.
No creature say he that bar lyf,
Save on the grene he say sittynge a wyf –
A fouler wight ther may no man devyse.
Agayn the knyght this olde wyf gan ryse,   1000
And seyde, 'Sire knyght, heer forth ne lyth no wey.
Tel me what that ye seken, by youre fey.
Paraventure it may the bettre be;
Thise olde folk konne muchel thyng', quod she.
   'My leeve moder,' quod this knyght, 'certeyn   1005
I nam but deed, but if that I kan seyn
What thyng it is that wommen moost desire.
Koude ye me wisse, I wolde wel quyte youre hyre.'
   'Plight me thy trouthe here in myn hand,' quod she,
'The nexte thyng that I requere thee,   1010
Thow shalt it do, if it lye in thy myght,
And I wol telle it yow er it be nyght.
   'Have here my trouthe,' quod the knyght, 'I graunte.'
   'Thanne', quod she, 'I dar me wel avaunte
Thy lyf is sauf; for I wole stonde therby,   1015
Upon my lyf, the queene wol seye as I.
Lat see which is the prouddeste of hem alle,
That wereth on a coverchief or a calle,
That dar seye nay of that I shal thee teche.
Lat us go forth, withouten lenger speche.'   1020
Tho rowned she a pistel in his ere,
And bad hym to be glad, and have no fere.
   Whan they be comen to the court, this knyght

996 *nyste* knew not
999 *devyse* imagine
1000 *Agayn* towards
1008 *wisse* instruct; *quyte* reward; *hyre* efforts
1014 *avaunte* boast
1016 *seye as* agree with
1018 *calle* hair net
1021 *rowned* whispered; *pistel* message

Seyde he hadde holde his day, as he had hight,
And redy was his answere, as he sayde. 1025
Ful many a noble wyf, and many a mayde,
And many a widwe, for that they ben wise,
The queene hirself sittyng as justise,
Assembled been, this answere for to here;
And afterward this knyght was bode appere. 1030
    To every wight comanded was silence,
And that the knyght sholde telle in audience
What thyng that worldly wommen loven best.
This knyght ne stood nat stille as dooth a best,
But to his question anon answerde 1035
With manly voys, that al the court it herde:
    'My lige lady, generally,' quod he,
'Wommen desire to have sovereyntee
As wel over hir housbonde as hir love,
And for to been in maistrie hym above. 1040
This is youre mooste desir, thogh ye me kille.
Dooth as yow list; I am here at youre wille.'
    In al the court ne was ther wyf, ne mayde,
Ne wydwe, that contraryed that he sayde,
But seyden he was worthy han his lyf. 1045
    And with that word up stirte that olde wyf,
Which that the knyght say sittyng on the grene:
'Mercy,' quod she, 'my sovereyn lady queene!
Er that youre court departe, do me right.
I taughte this answere unto the knyght; 1050
For which he plighte me his trouthe there,
The firste thyng I wolde hym requere,
He wolde it do, if it laye in his myght.
Bifore the court thanne preye I thee, sire knyght,'
Quod she, 'that thow me take unto thy wyf; 1055
For wel thow woost that I have kept thy lyf.

1024 *hight* promised
1030 *bode* commanded
1034 *stille* silent
1042 *wille* wish
1044 *contraryed* contradicted

If I seye fals, sey nay, upon thy fey!'
   This knyght answerde, 'Allas! and weilawey!
I woot right wel that swich was my biheste.
For Goddes love, as chees a newe requeste.   1060
Taak al my good, and lat my body go.'
   'Nay, thanne,' quod she, 'I shrewe us bothe two!
For thogh that I be foul, old, and poore,
I nolde for al the metal, ne for oore,
That under erthe is grave, or lith above,   1065
But if thy wyf I were, and eek thy love.'
   'My love?' quod he, 'nay, my dampnacioun!
Allas! that any of my nacioun
Sholde evere so foule disparaged be!'
But al for noght; th'ende is this, that he   1070
Constreyned was, he nedes moste hir wedde;
And taketh his olde wyf, and goth to bedde.
   Now wolden som men seye, paraventure,
That for my necligence I do no cure
To tellen yow the joye and al th'array   1075
That at the feste was that ilke day.
To which thyng shortly answere I shal:
I seye ther nas no joye ne feste at al;
Ther nas but hevynesse and muche sorwe.
For prively he wedded hire on a morwe,   1080
And al day after hidde hym as an owle,
So wo was hym, his wyf looked so foule.
   Greet was the wo the knyght hadde in his thoght,
Whan he was with his wyf abedde ybroght;
He walweth and he turneth to and fro.   1085
His olde wyf lay smylyng evere mo,
And seyde, 'O deere housbonde, benedicite!

1059 *biheste* promise
1060 *chees* choose
1061 *good* property
1064 *oore* ore
1065 *grave* buried
1068 *nacioun* family
1075 *array* rich display
1085 *walweth* tosses

Fareth every knyght thus with his wyf as ye?
Is this the lawe of kyng Arthures hous?
Is every knyght of his thus daungerous?   1090
I am youre owene love and youre wyf;
I am she which that saved hath youre lyf,
And, certes, yet ne dide I yow nevere unright;
Why fare ye thus with me this firste nyght?
Ye faren lyk a man hadde lost his wit.   1095
What is my gilt? For Goddes love, tel it,
And it shal ben amended, if I may.'
    'Amended?' quod this knyght, 'allas! nay, nay!
It wol nat ben amended nevere mo.
Thow art so loothly, and so old also,   1100
And ther to comen of so lowe a kynde,
That litel wonder is thogh I walwe and wynde.
So wolde God myn herte wolde breste!'
    'Is this', quod she, 'the cause of youre unreste?'
'Ye, certeynly,' quod he, 'no wonder is.'   1105
'Now, sire,' quod she, 'I koude amende al this,
If that me liste, er it were dayes thre,
So wel ye myghte bere yow unto me.
    But, for ye speken of swich gentillesse
As is descended out of old richesse,   1110
That therfore sholden ye be gentil men,
Swich arrogance is nat worth an hen,
Looke who that is moost vertuous alway,
Pryvee and apert, and moost entendeth ay
To do the gentil dedes that he kan;   1115
Taak hym for the gentileste man.
Crist wol we clayme of hym oure gentilesse,
Nat of oure eldres for hir old richesse.

1090 *daungerous* distant
1100 *loothly* ugly
1102 *walwe and wynde* twist and turn
1104 *unreste* distress
1108 *bere yow unto* behave towards
1110 *old richesse* inherited wealth
1114 *Pryvee* private; *apert* public; *entendeth* strives
1117 *wol* wishes

For thogh they yeve us al hir heritage,
For which we clame to been of heigh parage,   1120
Yet may they nat biquethe, for no thyng,
To noon of us hir vertuous lyvyng,
That made hem gentil men ycalled be,
And bad us folwen hem in swich degree.
    Wel kan the wise poete of Florence,   1125
That highte Dant, speken in this sentence.
Lo, in swich maner rym is Dantes tale:
"Ful selde up riseth by his braunches smale
Prowesse of man, for God of his prowesse,
Wole that of hym we clayme oure gentilesse";   1130
For of oure eldres may we no thyng clayme
But temporel thyng, that man may hurte and mayme.
    Eek every wight woot this as wel I,
If gentilesse were planted naturelly
Unto a certeyn lynage doun the lyne,   1135
Pryvee and apert, thanne wolde they nevere fyne
To doon of gentilesse the faire office;
They myghte do no vileynye or vice.
    Taak fyr, and bere it in the derkeste hous
Bitwix this and the mount of Kaukasous,   1140
And lat men shette the dores and go thenne;
Yet wol the fyr as faire lye and brenne
As twenty thousand men myghte it biholde;
His office naturel ay wol it holde,
Up peril of my lyf, til that it dye.   1145
    Here may ye se wel how that genterye
Is nat annexed to possessioun,
Sith folk ne doon hir operacioun

1120 *parage* lineage
1126 *Dant* Dante
1130 *Wole* desires
1136 *fyne* end
1137 *office* duties
1140 *Kaukasous* Caucasus
1141 *thenne* thence
1142 *lye and brenne* blaze and burn
1146 *genterye* gentility

Alwey, as dooth the fyr, lo, in his kynde.
For, God it woot, men may wel often fynde   1150
A lordes sone do shame and vileynye;
And he that wol han prys of his gentrye,
For he was born of a gentil hous,
And hadde hise eldres noble and vertuous,
And nyl hymselven do no gentil dedis,   1155
Ne folwen his gentil auncestre that deed is,
He nys nat gentil, be he duc or erl;
For vileynes synful dedes maken a cherl.
For gentilesse nys but renomee
Of thyne auncestres, for hir hye bountee,   1160
Which is a straunge thyng for thy persone.
Thy gentilesse cometh fro God allone.
Thanne comth oure verray gentilesse of grace;
It was no thyng biquethe us with oure place.

    Thenketh how noble, as seith Valerius,   1165
Was thilke Tullius Hostillius,
That oute of poverte roos to heigh noblesse.
Redeth Senek, and redeth eek Boece;
Ther shul ye seen expres that no drede is
That he is gentil that dooth gentil dedis.   1170
And therfore, leve housbonde, I thus conclude:
Al were it that myne auncestres weren rude,
Yet may the hye God, and so hope I,
Graunte me grace to lyven vertuously.
Thanne am I gentil, whan that I bigynne   1175
To lyven vertuously and weyve synne.
    And ther as ye of poverte me repreve,
The hye God, on whom that we bileve,

1152 *prys* praise; *gentrye* nobility
1155 *nyl* will not
1159 *renomee* renown
1161 *a straunge thyng for* not natural to
1164 *place* rank
1168 *Senek* Seneca; *Boece* Boethius
1172 *Al were it that* even if; *rude* humble
1176 *weyve* abandon

In wilful poverte chees to lyve his lyf.
And certes every man, mayden, or wyf,   1180
May understonde that Jesus, hevene king,
Ne wolde nat chees a vicious lyvyng.
Glad poverte is an honeste thyng, certeyn;
This wol Senek and othere clerkes seyn.
Whoso that halt hym payd of his poverte,   1185
I holde hym riche, al hadde he nat a sherte.
He that coveiteth is a povre wight,
For he wolde han that is nat in his myght;
But he that noght hath, ne coveiteth have,
Is riche, althogh ye holde hym but a knave.   1190
Verray poverte, it syngeth proprely;
Juvenal seith of poverte myrily:
    "The povre man, whan he gooth by the weye,
Biforn the theves he may synge and pleye."
Poverte is hateful good and as I gesse,   1195
A ful greet bryngere out of bisynesse;
A greet amendere eek of sapience
To hym that taketh it in pacience.
Poverte is thyng, althogh it seme elenge,
Possessioun that no wight wol chalenge.   1200
Poverte ful often, whan a man is lowe,
Maketh hymself and eek his God to knowe.
Poverte a spectacle is, as thynketh me,
Thurgh which he may his verray freendes se.
And therfore, sire, syn that I noght yow greve,   1205
Of my poverte namoore ye me repreve.
    Now, sire, of elde ye repreve me;
And certes, sire, thogh noon auctoritee
Were in no book, ye gentils of honour

1179 *wilful* willing
1185 *halt hym payd* is satisfied
1190 *knave* peasant
1196 *bryngere out* encourager; *bisynesse* industry
1197 *amendere* improver; *sapience* wisdom
1199 *elenge* wearisome
1203 *spectacle* eyeglass
1209 *gentils* nobles

Seyn that men an old wight sholde doon favour,   1210
And clepe hym fader, for youre gentilesse;
And auctours shal I fynden, as I gesse.
  Now ther ye seye that I am foul and old,
Thanne drede yow noght to been a cokewold;
For filthe and elde, also mote I thee,   1215
Been grete wardeyns upon chastitee.
But nathelees, syn I knowe youre delit,
I shal fulfille youre worldly appetit.
  Chese now', quod she, 'oon of this thynges tweye:
To han me foul and old til that I deye,   1220
And be to yow a trewe, humble wyf,
And nevere yow displese in al my lyf;
Or ellis ye wol han me yong and fair,
And take youre aventure of the repair
That shal be to youre hous by cause of me,   1225
Or in som oother place may wel be.
Now chese yourselven, wheither that yow liketh.'
  This knyght avyseth hym and soore siketh,
But atte laste he seyde in this manere:
'My lady and my love, and wyf so deere,   1230
I putte me in youre wise governaunce;
Cheseth youreself which that may be moost plesaunce,
And moost honour to yow and me also.
I do no fors the wheither of the two;
For as yow liketh it suffiseth me.'   1235
  'Thanne have I gete of yow maistrye,' quod she,
'Syn I may chese and governe as me lest?'
  'Ye, certes, wyf,' quod he, 'I holde it best.'
  'Kys me,' quod she, 'we be no lenger wrothe;
For by my trouthe, I wol be to yow bothe,   1240

1212 *auctours* authorities
1214 *cokewold* cuckold
1215 *mote I thee* as I thrive
1218 *delit* desire
1224 *aventure* chance; *repair* return
1227 *wheither that* which
1228 *siketh* sighs
1234 *I do no fors* I don't mind

This is to seyn, ye, bothe fair and good.
I pray to God that I mote sterven wood,
But I to yow be also good and trewe
As evere was wyf, syn that the world was newe.
And but I be to-morn as fair to sene   1245
As any lady, emperice, or queene,
That is bitwix the est and eek the west,
Do with my lyf and deth right as yow lest.
Cast up the curtyn, looke how that it is.'
   And whan the knyght say verraily al this,   1250
That she so fair was, and so yong therto,
For joye he hente hire in his armes two,
His herte bathed in a bath of blisse.
A thousand tyme a-rewe he gan hir kisse,
And she obeyed hym in every thyng   1255
That myght do hym plesance or likyng.
   And thus they lyve unto hir lyves ende
In parfit joye; and Jesu Crist us sende
Housbondes meke, yonge, and fressh abedde,
And grace t'overbyde hem that we wedde;   1260
And eek I praye Jesu shorte hir lyves
That noght wol be governed by hir wyves;
And olde and angry nygardes of dispence,
God sende hem soone verray pestilence!

Here endeth the Wyves tale of Bathe

1242 *sterven wood* die mad
1245 *to-morn* in the morning
1252 *hente* took
1254 *a-rewe* in succession
1260 *overbyde* outlive
1263 *nygardes* misers; *dispence* spending

The prohemie of the Clerkys tale of Oxenford

'Sire clerk of Oxenford,' oure Hoost sayde,   1
'Ye ride as coy and stille as dooth a mayde
Were newe spoused, sittyng at the bord;
This day ne herde I of youre tonge a word.
I trowe ye studie aboute som sophyme;   5
But Saloman seith "every thyng hath tyme."
    For Goddes sake, as beth of bettre cheere!
It is no tyme for to studien heere.
Tel us som murie tale, by youre fey!
For what man that is entred in a pley,   10
He nedes moot unto the pley assente.
But precheth nat, as freres doon in Lente,
To maken us for oure olde synnes wepe,
Ne that thy tale make us nat to slepe.
    Tel us som murye thyng of aventures.   15
Youre termes, youre colours, and youre figures,
Kepe hem in stoor til so be ye endite
Heighe style, as whan that men to kynges write.
Speketh so pleyn at this tyme, we yow preye,
That we may understonde what ye seye.'   20
    This worthy clerk benygnely answerde:
'Hoost,' quod he, 'I am under youre yerde;
Ye han of us as now the governaunce,
And therfore wol I do yow obeisaunce,
As fer as reson asketh, hardily.   25

2 *coy* demure
3 *bord* table
5 *sophyme* sophism
7 *beth* be
10 *pley* game
11 *pley* rules
17 *stoor* reserve
18 *Heighe* elaborate
22 *yerde* authority
24 *do yow obseisaunce* obey

I wol yow telle a tale which that I
Lerned at Padwe of a worthy clerk,
As proved by his wordes and his werk.
He is now deed and nayled in his cheste,
I pray to God so yeve his soule reste! 30

    Frauncys Petrak, the laureyat poete,
Highte this clerk, whos rethoryk swete
Enlumyned al Ytaille of poetrie,
As Lynyan dide of philosophie,
Or lawe, or oother art particuler; 35
But deth, that wol nat suffre us dwellen her,
But as it were a twynklyng of an eye,
Hem bothe hath slayn, and alle shul we dye.

    But forth to tellen of this worthy man
That taughte me this tale, as I bigan, 40
I seye that first with heigh stile he enditeth,
Er he the body of his tale writeth,
A prohemie, in which discryveth he
Pemond, and of Saluces the contree,
And speketh of Appenyn, the hilles hye, 45
That been the boundes of West Lumbardye,
And of Mount Vesulus in special,
Wher as the Poo out of a welle smal
Taketh his first spryngyng and his cours,
That estward ay encresseth in his cours 50
To Emele-ward, to Ferare and Venyse;
The which a long thyng were to devyse.
And trewely, as to my juggement,
Me thynketh it a thyng inpertinent,

27 *Padwe* Padua
29 *cheste* coffin
33 *Enlumyned* gave lustre to; *Ytaille* Italy
35 *art* study
43 *prohemie* introduction; *discryveth* describes
44 *Pemond* Piedmont; *Saluces* Saluzzo
47 *Vesulus* Visio
48 *Poo* River Po; *welle* spring
51 *Emele-ward* Emilia; *Ferare* Ferrara; *Venyse* Venice
54 *inpertinent* irrelevant

Save that he wole convoien his matere;   55
But this his tale, which that ye shal heere.'

Here bigynneth the tale

Ther is, at the west syde of Ytaille,
Doun at the roote of Vesulus the colde,
A lusty playne, habundant of vitaille,
Wher many a tour and town thow mayst biholde,   60
That founded were in tyme of fadres olde,
And many another delitable sighte,
And Saluces this noble contree highte.

A markys whilom lord was of that lond,
As were his worthy eldres hym bifore;   65
And obeysant, and redy to his hond,
Were alle his liges, bothe lasse and moore.
Thus in delit he lyveth, and hath doon yoore,
Biloved and drad, thurgh favour of Fortune,
Bothe of his lordes and of his commune.   70

Therwith he was, to speke as of lynage,
The gentileste yborn of Lumbardye,
A fair persone, and strong, and yong of age,
And ful of honour and of curteisye;
Discret ynogh his contree for to gye,   75
Save in some thynges that he was to blame;
And Walter was this yonge lordes name.

55 *convoien* introduce
58 *roote* foot
59 *vitaille* agriculture
60 *tour* castle
64 *markys* marquis
69 *drad* feared
75 *gye* govern

I blame hym thus, that he considered noght
In tyme comynge what myghte hym bityde.
But on his lust present was al his thoght,   80
As for to hauke and hunte on every syde.
Wel neigh alle oothere cures leet he slyde,
And eek he nolde - and that was worst of alle -
Wedde no wyf, for noght that may bifalle.

Oonly that point his peple bar so soore   85
That flokmele on a day they to hym wente,
And oon of hem, that wisest was of loore -
Or ellis that the lord best wolde assente
That he sholde telle hym what his peple mente,
Or ellis koude he shewe wel swich mateere -   90
He to the markys seyde as ye shal heere:

'O noble markys, youre humanitee
Assureth us and yeveth us hardynesse,
As ofte as tyme is of necessitee,
That we to yow mowe telle oure hevynesse.   95
Accepteth, lord, now of youre gentillesse
That we with pitous herte unto yow pleyne,
And lat youre erys noght my voys disdeyne.

'Al have I noght to doone in this matere
Moore than another man hath in this place.   100
Yet for as muche as ye, my lord so deere,
Han alwey shewed me favour and grace
I dar the bettre aske of yow a space
Of audience, to shewen oure requeste,

80 *lust present* immediate pleasure
82 *cures. . . slyde* neglected cares
85 *bar so soore* took badly
86 *flokmele* in a flock
88 *Or ellis* either because
90 *shewe* present
92 *humanitee* benevolence
93 *hardynesse* boldness
103–4 *space Of audience* a hearing

And ye, my lord, to doon right as yow leste. 105

'For certes, lord, so wel us liketh yow
And al youre werk, and evere han doon, that we
Ne kouden nat us self devysen how
We myghte lyven in moore felicitee,
Save o thyng, lord, if it youre wille be, 110
That for to ben a wedded man yow leste;
Thanne were youre peple in sovereyn hertes reste.

'Boweth youre nekke under that blisful yok
Of sovereyntee, noght of servyse,
Which that men clepe spousaille or wedlok; 115
And thenketh, lord, among youre thoghtes wyse
How that oure dayes passe in sondry wyse;
For thogh we slepe, or wake, or renne, or ryde,
Ay fleeth the tyme; it ne no man abyde.

'And thogh youre grene youthe floure as yit, 120
In crepeth age alwey, as stille as stoon,
And deth manaceth every age, and smyt
In ech estat, for ther escapeth noon;
And also certeyn as we knowe echon
That we shal dye, as uncerteyn we alle 125
Been of that day whan deth shal on us falle.

'Accepteth thanne of us the trewe entente,
That nevere yet refuseden thyn heste,
And we wol, lord, if that ye wol assente,
Chese yow a wyf, in short tyme at the leeste, 130
Born of the gentileste and of the meeste

105 *leste* wish
107 *han doon* have done so
108 *us self* ourselves
115 *spousaille* marriage
122 *smyt* smites
123 *estat* rank
131 *meeste* greatest

Of al this lond, so that it oghte seme
Honour to God and yow, as we kan deme.

'Delyvere us out of al this bisy drede,
And tak a wyf, for heighe Goddes sake! 135
For if so bifelle, as God forbede,
That thurgh youre deeth youre ligne sholde slake,
And that a straunge successour sholde take
Youre heritage, O wo were us alyve!
Wherfore we pray yow hastily to wyve. 140

Hir meke prayere and hir pitous cheere
Made the markys herte han pitee.
'Ye wol,' quod he, 'myn owene peple deere,
To that I nevere erst thoghte streyne me.
I me rejoysed of my libertee, 145
That selde tyme is founde in mariage;
Ther I was free, I moot ben in servage.

'But nathelees I se youre trewe entente,
And truste upon youre wit, and have doon ay;
Wherfore of my free wyl I wol assente 150
To wedde me, as soone as evere I may.
But ther as ye han profred me to-day
To chese me a wyf I yow relesse
That choys, and pray yow of that profre cesse.

'For God it woot, that children ofte ben 155
Unlyk hir worthy eldres hem bifore;
Bountee comth al of God, nat of the stren

134 *bisy drede* constant fear
137 *slake* fail
143 *wol* want
144 *streyne me* constrained myself
146 *selde* seldom
149 *wit* judgement
152 *profred* offered
153 *relesse* release
154 *pray* request; *cesse* desist
157 *Bountee* goodness; *stren* family

Of which they been engendred and ybore.
I triste in Goddes bountee, and therfore
My mariage and myn estat and reste   160
I hym bitake; he may doon as hym leste.

    'Lat me allone in chesyng of my wyf, –
That charge upon my bak I wol endure.
But I pray yow, and charge upon youre lyf,
That what wyf that I take, ye me assure   165
To worshipe hire, whil that hir lyf may dure,
In word and werk, bothe here and everywhere,
As she an emperours doghter were,

    'And ferthermoore, this shal ye swere, that ye
Agayn my choys shal neither grucche ne stryve;   170
For sith I shal forgoon my libertee
At your requeste, as evere mote I thryve,
Ther as myn herte is set, ther wol I wyve;
And but ye wol assente in swich manere,
I pray yow, speketh namoore of this matere.'   175

    With hertly wyl they sworen and assenten
To al this thyng, ther seyde no wight nay;
Bisekynge hym of grace, er that they wenten,
That he wolde graunten hem a certein day
Of his spousaille, as soone as evere he may;   180
For yet alwey the peple somwhat dredde,
Lest that the markys no wyf wolde wedde.

    He graunted hem a day, swich as hym leste,
On which he wolde be wedded sikerly,
And seyde he dide al this at hir requeste.   185
And they, with humble entente, buxomly,

161 *hym bitake* trust to him
163 *charge* responsibility
173 *as myn herte is set* for love
174 *but* unless
180 *spousaille* wedding
186 *buxomly* obediently

Knelynge upon hir knees ful reverently,
Hym thanken alle; and thus they han an ende
Of hir entente, and hom agayn they wende.

And herupon he to his officers   190
Comaundeth for the feste to purveye,
And to his pryvee knyghtes and squyers
Swich charge yaf as hym liste on hem leye;
And they to his comandement obeye,
And ech of hem dooth al his diligence   195
To doon unto the feste reverence.

Explicit prima pars

Incipit pars secunda

Noght fer fro thilke paleys honurable,
Wher as this markys shoope his mariage,
Ther stood a throope, of site delitable,
In which that povre folk of that village   200
Hadden hir bestes and hir herberage,
And of hir labour token hir sustenance,
After that the erthe yaf hem habundance.

Among thise povre folk ther dwelte a man
Which that was holden povrest of hem alle;   205
But heighe God som tyme senden kan
His grace into a litel oxes stalle;
Janicula men of that throope hym calle.
A doghter hadde he, fair ynogh to sighte,

188 *ende* conclusion
189 *entente* liking
191 *purveye* prepare
192 *pryvee* personal
198 *shoope* planned
199 *throope* village
201 *herberage* lodging

78

And Grisildis this yonge mayden highte.　　　　210

But for to speke of vertuous beautee,
Thanne was she oon the faireste under the sonne;
For povreliche yfostred up was she,
No likerous lust was thurgh hir herte yronne.
Wel ofter of the welle than of the tonne　　　　215
She drank, and for she wolde vertu plese,
She knew wel labour, but noon ydel ese.

But thogh this mayde tendre were of age,
Yet in the brest of hir virginitee
Ther was enclosed rype and sad corage;　　　　220
And in gret reverence and charitee
Hir olde povre fader fostred she.
A fewe sheepe, spynnynge, on feld she kepte;
She wolde noght been ydel til she slepte.

And whan she homward cam, she wolde brynge　　225
Wortes or othere herbes tymes ofte,
The whiche she shredde and seeth for hir lyvynge,
And made hir bed ful harde and nothyng softe;
And ay she kepte hir fadres lyf on-lofte
With every obeysance and diligence　　　　230
That child may doon to fadres reverence.

Upon Grisilde, this povre creature,
Ful ofte sithe this markys sette his eye

212 *faireste under the sonne* fairest of all
213 *povreliche* in poverty
214 *likerous lust* sensual desire
215 *tonne* wine barrel
216 *plese* satisfy the demands of
220 *rype* mature; *sad* steadfast
222 *fostred* supported
226 *Wortes* cabbages
227 *shredde* sliced; *seeth* boiled
229 *kepte. . . on-lofte* sustained

As he on huntyng rood paraventure;
And whan it fil that he myghte hire espie,   235
He noght with wantowne lookyng of folye
Hise eyen caste on hire, but in sad wyse
Upon hir cheere he wolde hym ofte avyse,

Commendynge in his herte hir wommanhede,
And eek hir vertu, passyng any wight   240
Of so yong age, as wel in cheere as dede.
For thogh the peple hath no greet insight
In vertue, he considered ful right
Hir bountee, and disposed that he wolde
Wedde hire oonly, if evere he wedden sholde.   245

The day of the weddyng cam, but no wight kan
Telle what womman that it sholde be;
For which merveille wondred many a man,
And seyden, whan they were in privetee,
'Wol nat oure lord yet leve his vanytee?   250
Wol he nat wedde? allas, the while!
Why wol he thus hymself and us bigyle?'

But nathelees this markys hath doon make
Of gemmes, set in gold and in asure,
Broches and rynges, for Grisildis sake;   255
And of hir clothyng took he the mesure
Of a mayde lyk to hir stature,
And eek of othere aournementes alle
That unto swich a weddyng sholde falle.

The tyme of undren of the same day   260

234 *paraventure* by chance
236 *wantowne* wanton; *folye* lust
237 *in sad wyse* seriously
239 *wommanhede* femininity
244 *disposed* decided
258 *aournements* ornaments
260 *undren* mid morning

Approcheth, that this weddyng sholde be;
And al the palays put was in array,
Bothe halle and chambres, ech in his degree;
Houses of office stuffed with plentee
Ther maystow seen, of deynteuous vitaille   265
That may be founde as fer as last Ytaille.

This roial markys, richeliche arrayed,
Lordes and ladys in his compaignye,
The whiche that to the feste were yprayed,
And of his retenue the bachilrye,   270
With many a sown of sondry melodye,
Unto the village of the which I tolde,
In this array the righte wey han holde.

Grisilde of this, God woot, ful innocent,
That for hire shapen was al this array,   275
To fecchen water at a welle is went,
And cometh hom as soone as ever she may;
For wel she hadde herd seyd that thilke day
The markys sholde wedde, and if she myghte,
She wolde fayn han seyn som of that sighte.   280

She thoghte, 'I wole with othere maydens stonde,
That been my felawes, in oure dore and se
The markisesse, and therfore wol I fonde
To doon at hom, as soone as it may be,
The labour which that longeth unto me;   285
And thanne I may at leyser hir biholde,
Yf she this wey unto the castel holde.'

264 *Houses of office* service buildings
265 *deynteuous* delicious
266 *last Ytaille* farthest Italy
269 *yprayed* invited
270 *retenue* retinue; *bachilrye* knights
273 *righte* direct
283 *markisesse* marchioness; *fonde* strive
285 *longeth* belongs

And as she wolde over the thresshfold gon,
The markys cam, and gan hire for to calle;
And she sette doun hir water pot anon,   290
Bisyde the thresshfold, in an oxes stalle,
And doun upon hir knees she gan to falle,
And with sad contenance kneleth stille,
Til she hadde herd what was the lordes wille.

This thoghtful markys spak unto this mayde   295
Ful sobrely, and seyde in this manere:
'Where is youre fader, O Grisildis?' he sayde.
And she with reverence, in humble cheere,
Answerde, 'Lord, he is al redy heere.' *delay*
And in she goth withouten lenger lette,   300
And to the markys she hir fader fette.

He by the hand than took this olde man,
And seyde thus, whan he hym hadde asyde:
'Janicula, I neither may ne kan
Lenger the plesance of myn herte hyde.   305
If that thow vouche sauf, what so bityde,
Thy doghter wol I take, er that I wende,
As for my wyf, unto my lyves ende.

'Thow lovest me, I woot it wel certeyn,
And art my feithful lige man ybore;   310
And al that liketh me, I dar wel seyn
It liketh thee, and specially therfore
Tel me that point that I have seyd bifore,
If that thow wolt unto that purpos drawe,
To take me as for thy sone-in-lawe.'   315

sodden change of affair   astonished
The sodeyn cas this man astoneyd so

288 *thresshfold* theshold
300 *lette* delay
306 *vouche sauf* permit
310 *ybore* born
314 *unto that purpos drawe* make an arrangement

That reed he weex; abayst and al quakyng
He stood; unnethe seyde he wordes mo,
But oonly this: 'Lord,' quod he, 'my willyng
Is as ye wole, ne ayeins youre likyng   320
I wol no thyng, ye be my lord so deere;
Right as yow list, governeth this matere.'

'Yet wol I', quod this markys softely,
'That in thy chambre I and thow and she
Have a collacioun and wostow why?   325
For I wol aske if it hir wille be
To be my wyf, and rule hire after me.
And al this shal be doon in thy presence;
I wol noght speke out of thyn audience.'

And in the chambre, whil they were aboute   330
Hir tretys, which as ye shal after heere,
The peple cam unto the hous withoute,
And wondred hem in how honeste manere
And tentifly she kepte hir fader deere.
But outrely Grisildis wondre myghte,   335
For nevere erst ne saw she swich a sighte.

No wonder is thogh that she were astoned
To seen so greet a gest come into place;
She nevere was to swiche gestes woned,
For which she looked with ful pale face.   340
But shortly forth this matere for to chace,
Thise arn the wordes that this markys sayde
To this benygne, verray, feithful mayde.

'Grisilde,' he seyde, 'ye shal wel understonde

317 *abayst* embarrassed
325 *collacioun* discussion
329 *audience* hearing
331 *tretys* marriage contract
334 *tentifly* attentively
336 *erst* before
339 *woned* accustomed
341 *chace* pursue

It liketh to youre fader and to me   345
That I yow wedde, and eek it may so stonde,
As I suppose, ye wol that it so be.
But thise demandes aske I first,' quod he,
'That, sith it shal be doon in hastif wyse,
Wol ye assente, or ellis yow avyse?   350

'I sey this, be ye redy with good herte
To al my lust, and that I frely may,
As me best thynketh, do yow laughe or smerte,
And nevere ye to grucche it, nyght ne day?
And eek whan I sey "ye" ne sey nat "nay",   355
Neither by word ne frownyng contenance?
Swere this, and heere I swere oure alliance.'

Wondrynge upon this word, quakyng for drede,
She seyde, 'Lord, undigne or unworthy
I am to thilke honour that ye me bede,   360
But as ye wol yourself, right so wol I.
And heere I swere that nevere willyngly,
In werk ne thoght, I nel yow disobeye,
For to be deed, thogh me were looth to deye.'

'This is ynough, Grisilde myn', quod he.   365
And forth he goth, with a ful sobre cheere,
Out at the dore, and after that cam she,
And to the peple he seyde in this manere:
'This is my wyf', quod he, 'that standeth heere.
Honureth hire and loveth hire, I preye,   370
Whoso me loveth; ther is namoore to seye.'

And for that no thyng of hir olde gere
She sholde brynge into his hous, he bad
That wommen sholde dispoylen hir right there;
Of which thise ladys were noght right glad   375

350 *avyse* consider further
354 *grucche* begrudge
359 *undigne* unsuitable
360 *bede* offer
374 *dispoylen* undress

84

To handle hir clothes, wherinne she was clad.
But nathelees, this mayde bright of hewe
Fro foot to heed they clothed han al newe.

  Hir herys han they kembd, that laye untressed
Ful rudely, and with hir fyngres smale   380
A coroune on hir heed they han ydressed,
And sette hire ful nowches grete and smale.
Of hir array what sholde I make a tale?
Unnethe the peple hir knew for hir fairnesse,
Whan she translated was in swich richesse.   385

  This markys hath hire spoused with a ryng
Broght for the same cause, and thanne hir sette
Upon an hors, snow-whyt and wel amblyng,
And to his palays, er he lenger lette,
With joyful peple that hir ledde and mette,   390
Convoied hire, and thus the day they spende
In revel, til the sonne gan descende.

  And shortly forth this tale for to chace,
I seye that to this newe markysesse
God hath swich favour sent hire of his grace,   395
That it ne semed nat by liklynesse
That she was born and fed in rudenesse,
As in a cote or in an oxes stalle,
But norissed in an emperours halle.

  To every wight she woxen is so deere   400

379 *untressed* unkempt
380 *rudely* roughly
381 *coroune* wedding garland
382 *ful nowches grete and smale* all sorts of jewellery
385 *translated* transformed
388 *amblyng* gently walking
396 *by liklynesse* credible
397 *rudenesse* humble conditions
398 *cote* hut
400 *woxen* became

And worshipful that folk ther she was bore,
That from hir burthe knewe hire yeer by yeere,
Unnethe trowed they – but dorste han swore –
That to Janicle, of which I spak bifore,
She doghter were, for, as by conjecture,   405
Hem thoughte she was another creature.

   For thogh that evere vertuous was she,
She was encressed in swich excellence
Of thewes goode, yset in heigh bountee,
And so discreet and fair of eloquence,   410
So benygne and so digne of reverence,
And koude so the peples herte embrace,
That ech hir lovede that looked on hir face.

   Noght oonly of Saluce in the town
Publissed was the bountee of hir name,   415
But eek bisyde in many a regioun,
If oon seyde wel, another seyde the same;
So spradde of hir heighe bountee the fame
That men and wommen, as wel yonge as olde,
Goon to Saluce, on hire to biholde.   420

   Thus Walter lowely – nay, but roially –
Wedded with fortunat honestetee,
In Goddes pees lyveth ful esily
At hom, and outward grace ynow hath he;
And for he saugh that under lowe degree   425
Was ofte vertu hyd, the peple hym helde
A prudent man, and that is seyn ful selde.

   Noght oonly this Grisildis thurgh hir wit
Koude al the feet of wifly humblenesse, _domestic skills_

403 *dorste han swore* dare have sworn
409 *thewes* morals
422 *honestetee* honour
427 *selde* seldom
429 *feet of wifly humblenesse* domestic skills

But eek, whan that the cas required it,   430
The commune profit koude she redresse.
Ther nas discord, rancour, ne hevynesse
In al that land, that she ne koude apese,
And wisly brynge hem alle in reste and ese.

Thogh that hir housbond absent were anon,   435
If gentil men or othere of hir contree
Were wrothe, she wolde bryngen hem aton;
So wise and rype wordes hadde she,
And juggementz of so greet equytee,
That she from hevene sent was, as men wende,   440
Peple to save and every wrong t'amende.

  Nat longe tyme after that this Grisild
Was ywedded, she a doghter hath ybore.
Al hadde hir levere have had a knave child,
Glad was the markys and the folk therfore;   445
For thogh a mayde child coome al bifore,
She may unto a knave child atteyne
By liklyhede, syn she nys nat bareyne.

Explicit secunda pars

Incipit pars tercia

  Ther fil, as it bifalleth tymes mo,
Whan that this child hath souked but a throwe,   450
This markys in his herte longeth so
To tempte his wyf, hir sadnesse for to knowe,

431 *commune profit* common good; *redresse* promote
437 *aton* to agreement
444 *levere* rather; *knave* boy
449 *tymes mo* often
450 *souked* breastfed; *throwe* short while
452 *tempte* test; *sadnesse* constancy

That he ne myghte out of his herte throwe
This mervellous desir his wyf t'assaye;
Nedelees, God woot, he thoghte hire for t'afraye.   455

He hadde assayed hire ynow bifore,
And fond hir evere good; what neded it
Hir for to tempte, and alwey moore and moore,
Thogh som men preyse it for a subtil wit?
But as for me, I seye that yvele it sit   460
T'assaye a wyf whan that it is no nede,
And putten hire in angwyssh and in drede.

For which this markys wroghte in this manere:
He cam allone a-nyght, ther as she lay,
With steerne face and with ful trouble cheere,   465
And seyde thus, 'Grisilde,' quod he, 'that day
That I yow took out of youre povre array,
And putte yow in estat of heighe noblesse, –
Ye have nat that forgeten, as I gesse?

'I seye, Grisilde, this present dignitee,   470
In which that I have put yow, as I trowe,
Maketh yow nat foryetful for to be
That I yow took in povre estat ful lowe,
For any wele ye mote yourselven knowe.
Tak hede of every word that I yow seye;   475
Ther is no wight that hereth it but we tweye.

'Ye woot yourself wel how that ye cam heere
Into this hous, it is nat longe ago;
And thogh to me that ye be lief and deere,

454 *t'assaye* to test
455 *t'afraye* to frighten
459 *subtil wit* clever plan
460 *yvele it sit* it ill befits one
465 *trouble* disturbed
470 *dignitee* high social rank
474 *wele* wealth

88

Unto my gentils ye be no thyng so.   480
They seyn, to hem it is greet shame and wo
For to be subgitz and been in servage
To thee, that born art of a smal village.

   'And namely sith thy doghter was ybore
Thise wordes han they spoken, doutelees.   485
But I desire, as I have doon bifore,
To lyve my lyf with hem in reste and pees.
I may nat in this cas be recchelees;
I moot doon with thy doghter for the beste,
Nat as I wolde, but as my peple leste.   490

   'And yet, God woot, this is ful looth to me;
But nathelees withouten youre wityng
I wol nat doon but this wol I,' quod he,
'That ye to me assente as in this thyng,
Shewe now youre pacience in youre wirkyng,   495
That ye me highte and swore in youre village
That day that maked was oure mariage.'

   Whan she hadde herd al this, she noght ameved
Neither in word, or cheere, or contenance;
For, as it semed, she was nat agreved.   500
She seyde, 'Lord, al lith in youre plesance.
My child and I, with hertly obeisance,
Been youres al, and ye mowe save or spille
Youre owene thyng; werketh after youre wille.

   'Ther may no thyng, God so my soule save,   505

480 *gentils* nobles
483 *smal* humble
488 *recchelees* careless
495 *wirkyng* behaviour
496 *highte* promised
498 *ameved* changed
502 *hertly obeisance* sincere obedience
503 *spille* destroy

Liken to yow that may displesen me;
Ne I ne desire no thyng for to have,
Ne drede for to lese, save oonly thee.
This wyl is in myn herte, and ay shal be;
No lengthe of tyme or deth may this deface,   510
Ne chaunge my corage to oother place.'

Glad was this markys of hir answeryng,
But yet he feyned as he were nat so;
Al drery was his cheere and his lookyng,
Whan that he sholde out of the chambre go.   515
Soone after this, a furlang wey or two,
He pryvely hath told al his entente
Unto a man, and to his wyf hym sente.

A maner sergeant was this privee man,
The which that feithful ofte he founden hadde   520
In thynges grete, and eek swich folk wel kan
Doon execucioun in thynges badde.
The lord knew wel that he hym loved and dradde;
And whan this sergeant wiste his lordes wille,
Into the chambre he stalked hym ful stille.   525

'Madame,' he seyde, 'ye mote foryeve it me,
Thogh I do thyng to which I am constreyned.
Ye ben so wys that ful wel knowe ye
That lordes hestes mowe nat ben yfeyned;
They mowe wel been biwailled or compleyned   530
But men mote nede unto hir lust obeye,
And so wol I; ther is namoore to seye.

'This child I am comaunded for to take –'

514 *drery* gloomy; *lookyng* expression
519 *maner* kind of
521 *thynges* affairs
525 *stalked hym full stille* went quietly
529 *hestes* commands; *yfeyned* avoided
530 *biwailled* regretted

And spak namoore, but out the child he hente
Despitously, and gan a cheere make   535
As thogh he wolde han slayn it er he wente.
Grisildis moot al suffre and al consente;
And as a lamb she sitteth meke and stille,
And leet this crewel sergeant doon his wille.

    Suspecious was the diffame of this man,   540
Suspect his face, suspect his word also;
Suspect the tyme in which he this bigan.
Allas! hir doghter that she loved so,
She wende he wolde han slayn it right tho.
But nathelees she neither weepe ne syked,   545
Conformynge hire to that the markys liked.

    But at the laste speken she bigan,
And mekely she to the sergeant preyde,
So as he was a worthy gentil man,
That she moste kisse hir child er that it deyde.   550
And in her barm this litel child she leyde
With ful sad face, and gan the child to blesse,
And lulled it, and after gan it kesse.

    And thus she seyde in hir benygne voys,
'Farewel my child! I shal thee nevere see.   555
But sith I thee have marked with the croys
Of thilke Fader, blessed mote he be,
That for us deyde upon a croys of tree,
Thy soule, litel child, I hym bitake,
For this nyght shaltow dyen for my sake.   560

534 *hente* seized
535 *cheere* expression
540 *diffame* bad reputation
544 *right tho* at once
545 *syked* sighed
551 *barm* lap
558 *tree* wood
559 *bitake* entrust

I trowe that to a norice in this cas
It hadde been hard this routhe for to se;
Wel myghte a moder have cryd 'allas!'
But nathelees so sad stedefast was she
That she endured al adversitee,   565
And to the sergeant mekely she sayde,
'Have here agayn youre litel yonge mayde.

'Goth now,' quod she, 'and doth my lordes heste;
But o thyng wol I pray yow of youre grace,
That, but my lord forbad yow, atte leeste   570
Burieth this litel body in som place
That bestes ne no bryddes it to race.'
But he no word wol to that purpos seye,
But took the child and wente upon his weye.

This sergeant cam unto his lord agayn,   575
And of Grisildis wordes and hir cheere
He tolde hym poynt for poynt, in short and playn,
And hym presenteth with his doghter deere.
Somwhat this lord hadde routhe in his manere,
But nathelees his purpos held he stille,   580
As lordes doon whan they wol han hir wille;

And bad this sergeant that he pryvely
Sholde this child softe wynde and wrappe,
With alle circumstances tendrely,
And carie it in a cofre or in a lappe;   585
But, upon peyne his heed of for to swappe,
That no man sholde knowe of this entente,

561 *norice* nurse
562 *routhe* pitiful situation
564 *sad stedefast* firm and steadfast
570 *but* unless
572 *bryddes* birds; *to race* tear to pieces
577 *in short* directly
579 *routhe* pity
584 *alle circumstances* every care
585 *cofre* basket; *lappe* fold of cloth
586 *swappe* strike off

Ne whennes he cam, ne whider that he wente;

But at Boloigne he to his suster deere,
That thilke tyme of Panyk was countesse, 590
He sholde it take, and shewe hire this matere,
Bisekynge hire to doon hir bisynesse
This child to fostre in alle gentilesse;
And whos child that it was he bad hire hyde
From every wight, for aught that may bityde. 595

The sergeant goth, and hath fulfild this thyng;
But to this markys now retourne we.
For now goth he ful faste ymagynyng
If by his wyves cheere he myghte se,
Or by hir word aperceyve, that she 600
Were chaunged, but he nevere hir koude fynde
But evere in oon ylike sad and kynde.

As glad, as humble, as busy in servyse,
And eek in love, as she was wont to be,
Was she to hym in every maner wise; 605
Ne of hir doghter noght a word spak she.
Noon accident for noon adversitee,
Was seyn in hire ne nevere hir doghter name
Ne nempned she in ernest ne in game.

Explicit tercia pars

Incipit pars quarta

In this estat ther passed ben four yeer 610

588 *whennes* whence
592 *bisynesse* special care
598 *ymagynyng* wondering
602 *evere in oon ylike* consistently
607 *accident for* outward sign of
609 *nempned* mentioned

93

Er she with childe was, but, as God wolde,
A knave child she bar by this Walter,
Ful gracious and fair for to biholde.
And whan that folk it to his fader tolde,
Nat oonly he, but al his contree merye   615
Was for this child, and God they thanke and herye.

    Whan it was two yeer old, and fro the brest
Departed of his norice, on a day
This markys caughte yet another lest
To tempte his wyf yet ofter, if he may.   620
O nedelees was she tempted in assay!
But wedded men ne knowe no mesure,
Whan that they fynde a pacient creature.

    'Wyf,' quod this markys, 'ye han herd er this,
My peple sikly berth this mariage;   625
And namely sith my sone yborn is,
Now is it worse than evere in al oure age.
The murmur sleeth myn herte and my corage,
For to myne erys comth the voys so smerte
That it wel neigh destroyed hath myn herte.   630

    'Now sey they thus: "Whan Walter is agon,
Thanne shal the blood of Janycle succede
And been oure lord, for oother have we noon."
Swiche wordes seith my peple out of drede.
Wel oghte I of swich murmur taken hede;   635
For certeinly I drede swich sentence,

615 *herye* praise
617 *fro the brest* weaned
619 *lest* desire
620 *yet ofter* once again
622 *mesure* moderation
625 *sikly berth* disapprove of
627 *age* lifetime
628 *murmur* grumbling
629 *smerte* sharply
636 *sentence* opinion

Though they nat pleyn speke in myn audience.

'I wolde lyve in pees, if that I myghte;
Wherfore I am disposed outrely,
As I his suster served by nyghte,   640
Right so thenke I to serve hym prively.
This warne I yow, that ye nat sodeynly
Out of yourself for no wo sholde outraye;
Beth pacient, and therof I yow praye.'

'I have', quod she, 'seyde thus, and evere shal: 645
I wol no thyng, ne nyl no thyng, certeyn,
But as yow list. Noght greveth me at al,
Thogh that my doghter and my sone be slayn,
At youre comandement, this is to seyn.
I have nat had no part of children tweyne   650
But first siknesse, and after, wo and peyne.

'Ye ben oure lord, dooth with youre owene thyng
Right as yow list; axeth no reed of me.
For as I lefte at hom al my clothyng,
Whan I first cam to yow, right so', quod she,   655
'Lefte I my wyl and al my libertee,
And took youre clothyng; wherfore I yow preye,
Dooth youre plesance, I wol youre lust obeye.

'And certes, if I hadde prescience
Youre wyl to knowe, er ye youre lust me tolde,   660
I wolde it doon withouten necligence;
But now I woot youre lust, and what ye wolde,
Al youre plesance ferm and stable I holde;

637 *audience* hearing
639 *disposed outrely* firmly decided
640 *served* treated
643 *outraye* passionately break out
653 *axeth no reed* consult
659 *prescience* foreknowledge
663 *stable I holde* constantly obey

For wiste I that my deeth wolde doon yow ese,
Right gladly wolde I dyen, yow to plese.   665

   'Deeth may nat make no comparisoun
Unto youre love.' And whan this markys say
The constance of his wyf, he caste adoun
Hise eyen two, and wondreth that she may
In pacience suffre al this array;   670
And forth he goth with drery contenance,
But to his herte it was ful gret plesance.

   This uggly sergeant, in the same wyse
That he hir doghter caughte, right so he,
Or worse, if men worse kan devyse,   675
Hath hent hir sone, that ful was of beautee.
And evere in oon so pacient was she
That she no cheere made of hevynesse,
But kiste hir sone, and after gan it blesse;

   Save this, she prayde hym that, if he myghte,   680
Hir litel sone he wolde in erthe grave,
His tendre lymes, delicat to sighte,
Fro foweles and fro bestes hem to save.
But she noon answere of hym myghte have.
He wente his wey, as hym no thyng roghte;   685
But to Boloigne he tendrely it broghte.

   This markys wondreth, ever lenger the moore,
Upon hir pacience, and if that he
Ne hadde soothly knowen ther bifoore

667 *say* saw
670 *array* arrangement
677 *evere in oon* just the same
678 *hevynesse* grief
681 *grave* bury
682 *delicat* pleasing
685 *roghte* cared
687 *ever lenger the moore* increasingly

That parfitly hir children loved she,   690
He wolde have wend that of som subtiltee,
And of malice, or of cruel corage,
That she hadde suffred this with sad visage.

    But wel he knew that next hymself, certayn,
She loved hir children best in every wise.   695
But now of wommen wolde I asken fayn
If thise assayes myghte nat suffise?
What koude a sturdy housbond moore devyse
To prove hir wifhod and hir stedfastnesse,
And he contynuynge evere in sturdynesse? *cruelty*   700

    But ther ben folk of swich condicioun
That whan they have a certeyn purpos take,
They kan nat stynte of hir entencioun,
But, right as they were bounden to that stake,
They wol nat of that firste purpos slake.   705
Right so this markys fulliche hath purposed
To tempte his wyf as he was first disposed.

    He wayteth if by word or contenance
That she to hym was chaunged of corage;
But nevere koude he fynde variance.   710
She was ay oon in herte and in visage;
And ay the ferther that she was of age,
The moore trewe, if that it were possible,
She was to hym in love, and moore penyble.

For which it semed thus, that of hem two   715

691 *subtiltee* guile
692 *corage* heart
698 *sturdy* cruel
700 *sturdynesse* cruelty
705 *slake* desist
706 *purposed* decided
711 *ay oon* unchanged
714 *penyble* attentive

Ther nas but o wyl; for, as Walter leste,
The same lust was hir plesance also.
And, God be thanked, al fyl for the beste.
She shewed wel, for no worldly unreste
A wyf, as of hirself, no thyng ne sholde   720
Wille in effect, but as hir housbond wolde.

   The sclaundre of Walter ofte and wyde spradde,
That of a cruel herte he wikkedly,
For he a povre womman wedded hadde,
Hath mordred bothe his children pryvely.   725
Swich murmur was among hem comunly.
No wonder is, for to the peples ere
Ther cam no word, but that they mordred were.

   For which, wher as his peple ther bifore
Hadde loved hym wel, the sclaundre of his diffame   730
Made hem that they hym hated therfore.
To ben a mordrere is an hateful name;
But natheles, for ernest ne for game,
He of his cruel purpos nolde stente;
To tempte his wyf was set al his entente.   735

   Whan that this doghter twelve yer was of age,
He to the court of Rome, in subtil wise
Enformed of his wil, sente his message,
Comaundynge hem swiche bulles to devyse
As to his cruel purpos may suffise,   740
How that the pope, as for his peples reste,

718 *fyl* happened
719 *worldly unreste* human distress
721 *Wille in effect* desire in fact
722 *sclaundre* slander
730 *diffame* bad reputation
734 *stente* cease
737 *in subtil wise* craftily
738 *message* messenger
739 *bulles* papal edicts

Bad hym to wedde another, if hym leste.

    I seye, he bad they sholde contrefete
The popes bulles, makyng mencioun
That he hath leve his firste wyf to lete,   745
As by the popes dispensacioun,
To stynte rancour and dissencioun
Bitwix his peple and hym; thus seyde the bulle,
The which they han publissed at the fulle.

    The rude peple, as it no wonder is,   750
Wenden ful wel that it hadde ben right so;
But whan thise tidynges cam to Grisildis,
I deme that hir herte was ful wo.
But she, ylike sad for evere mo,
Disposed was, this humble creature,   755
Th'adversitee of Fortune al t'endure,

    Abidynge evere his lust and his plesance,
To whom that she was yeven herte and al,
As to hire verray worldly suffisance.
But shortly if this storie I tellen shal,   760
This markys writen hath in special
A lettre in which he sheweth his entente,
And secrely he to Boloigne it sente.

    To the Erl of Panyk, which that hadde tho
Wedded his suster, prayde he specially   765
To bryngen hom agayn his children two
In honurable estat al openly.
But o thyng he hym prayde outrely,

745 *lete* leave
749 *publissed* made public
750 *rude* ignorant
754 *ylike sad* remaining constant
759 *suffisance* happiness
763 *secrely* secretly
768 *outrely* emphatically

That he to no wight, thogh men wolde enquere,
Sholde nat tellen whos children that they were,   770

  But seye, the mayden sholde ywedded be
Unto the Markys of Saluce anon.
And as this erl was prayd so dide he;
For at day set he on his wey is gon
Toward Saluce, and lordes many oon   775
In riche array, this mayden for to gyde,
Hir yonge brother ridyng hir bisyde.

  Arrayed was toward hir mariage
This fresshe mayde ful of gemmes clere;
Hir brother, which that seven yeer was of age,   780
Arrayed eek ful fressh in his manere.
And thus in gret noblesse and with glad cheere,
Toward Saluces shapyng hir journey,
Fro day to day they ryden in hir wey.

Explicit quarta pars

Incipit pars quinta

  Among al this, after his wikke usage,   785
This markys, yet his wif to tempte moore
To the outreste preve of hir corage,
Fully to han experience and loore
If that she were as stedefast as bifore,
He on a day, in open audience,   790
Ful boystously hath seyd hire this sentence:

778 *toward* in readiness for
779 *clere* sparkling
785 *Among al this* meanwhile
787 *outreste preve* uttermost proof
788 *loore* knowledge
791 *boystously* roughly

'Certes, Grisilde, I hadde ynogh plesance
To han yow to my wyf for youre goodnesse,
As for your trouthe and for youre obeysance,
Noght for youre lynage, ne for youre richesse;   795
But now knowe I in verray sothfastnesse
That in gret lordshipe, if I wel avyse,
Ther is gret servitute in sondry wyse.

'I may nat do as every plowman may.
My peple me constreyneth for to take   800
Another wyf, and cryen day by day;
And eek the pope, rancour for to slake,
Consenteth it, that dar I undertake;
And trewely thus muche I wol yow seye,
My newe wif is comynge by the weye.   805

'Be strong of herte, and voyde anon hir place,
And thilke dowere that ye broghten me,
Tak it agayn, I graunte it of my grace.
Retourneth to youre fadres hous', quod he;
No man may alwey han prosperitee.   810
With evene herte I rede yow t'endure
The strook of Fortune or of aventure.'

And she agayn answerde in pacience,
'My lord,' quod she, 'I woot, and wiste alway,
How that bitwixen youre magnificence   815
And my poverte no wight kan ne may
Maken comparisoun; it is no nay.
I ne heeld me nevere digne in no manere
To be youre wyf, no ne youre chambrere.

792 *ynogh* sufficient
794 *obeysance* faithfulness
797 *avyse* judge correctly
806 *voyde* vacate
811 *evene* tranquil; *rede* advise
817 *is no nay* cannot be denied
818 *digne* worthy
819 *chambrere* chambermaid

And in this hous, ther ye me lady made –   820
The heighe God take I for my witnesse,
And also wisly he my soule glade –
I nevere heeld me lady ne maistresse,
But humble servant to youre worthynesse,
And evere shal, whil that my lyf may dure,   825
Aboven every worldly creature.

'That ye so longe of youre benygnyte
Han holden me in honour and nobleye,
Where as I was noght worthy for to be,
That thonke I God and yow, to whom I preye   830
Foryelde it yow; ther is namoore to seye.
Unto my fader gladly wol I wende,
And with hym dwelle unto my lyves ende.

'Ther I was fostred of a child ful smal,
Til I be deed my lyf ther wol I lede,   835
A wydewe clene in body, herte, and al.
For sith I yaf to you my maydenhede,
And am youre trewe wyf, it is no drede,
God shilde swich a lordes wyf to take
Another man to housbond or to make!   840

'And of youre newe wyf God of his grace
So graunte yow wele and prosperitee!
For I wol gladly yelden hire my place,
In which that I was blisful wont to be.
For sith it liketh yow, my lord,' quod she,   845
'That whilom weren al myn hertes reste,
That I shal goon, I wol goon whan yow leste.

822 *wisly* surely
825 *dure* endure
831 *Foryelde it yow* may he reward you
836 *clene* chaste
839 *shilde* forbid
840 *make* mate
842 *wele* happiness

'But ther as ye me profre swich dowaire
As I first broghte, it is wel in my mynde
It were my wrecched clothes, no thyng faire,
The whiche to me were hard now for to fynde.
O goode God! how gentil and how kynde
Ye semed by youre speche and youre visage
The day that maked was oure mariage!

'But sooth is seyd – algate I fynde it trewe,   855
For in effect it proved is on me –
Love is noght old as whan that it is newe.
But certes, lord, for noon adversitee,
To dyen in this cas, it shal nat be
That evere in word or werk I shal repente   860
That I yow yaf myn herte in hool entente.

'My lord, ye woot that in my fadres place
Ye dide me strepe out of my povre wede,
And richely me cladden, of youre grace.
To yow broghte I noght ellis, out of drede,   865
But feith, and nakednesse, and maydenhede;
And here agayn my clothyng I restore,
And eek my weddyng ryng, for evere moore.

'The remenant of youre jewels redy be
Inwith youre chambre, dar I saufly sayn.   870
Naked out of my fadres hous', quod she,
'I cam, and naked moot I turne agayn.
Al youre plesance wol I folwen fayn;
But yet I hope it be nat youre entente
That I smoklees out of youre palays wente.   875

848 *dowaire* dowry
858 *for noon adversitee* whatever happens
859 *To dyen in this cas* even to die
861 *in hool entente* completely
863 *strepe* strip; *wede* clothing
870 *Inwith* within
875 *smoklees* without a smock

'Ye koude nat doon so dishoneste a thyng,
That thilke wombe in which youre children leye
Sholde biforn the peple, in my walkyng,
Be seyn al bare; wherfore I yow preye,
Lat me nat lyk a worm go by the weye.   880
Remembre yow, myn owene lord so deere,
I was youre wyf, thogh I unworthy weere.

'Wherfore, in gerdoun of my maydenhede,
Which that I broghte, and noght agayn I bere,
As voucheth sauf to yeve me, to my mede,   885
But swich a smok as I was wont to were
That I therwith may wrye the wombe of here
That was youre wyf. And here I take my leeve
Of yow, myn owene lord, lest I yow greeve.'

'The smok', quod he, 'that thow hast on thy bak,   890
Lat it be stille, and bere it forth with thee.'
But wel unnethes thilke word he spak,
But wente his wey, for routhe and for pitee.
Biforn the folk hirselven strepeth shee,
And in hir smok, with heved and feet al bare,   895
Toward hir fader hous forth is she fare.

The folk hir folwen, wepynge in hir weye,
And Fortune ay they cursen as they goon;
But she fro wepyng kepte hir eyen dreye,
Ne in this tyme word ne spak she noon.   900
Hir fader, that this tidynge herde anon,
Curseth the day and tyme that nature
Shoope hym to been a lyves creature.

876 *dishoneste* shameful
883 *gerdoun of* return for
885 *mede* reward
886 *smok* smock
887 *wrye* cover
891 *be stille* remain
892 *wel unnethes* with great difficulty
903 *Shoope* made; *lyves* living

104

For out of doute this olde povre man
Was evere in suspect of hir mariage: 905
For evere he demed, sith that it bigan,
That whan the lord fulfild hadde his corage,
Hym wolde thynke it were a disparage
To his estat so lowe for t'alighte,
And voyden hire as soone as evere he myghte.   910

Agayns his doghter hastiliche goth he,
For he by noyse of folk knew hir comynge,
And with hir olde cote, as it myghte be
He covered hire, ful sorwefully wepynge.
But on hir body myghte he it nat brynge,   915
For rude was the clooth, and she moore of age
By dayes fele than at hir mariage.

Thus with hir fader, for a certein space,
Dwelleth this flour of wifly pacience,
That neyther by hir wordes ne hir face,   920
Biforn the folk, ne eek in hir absence,
Ne shewed she that hir was doon offence;
Ne of hir heighe estat no remembrance
Ne hadde she, as by hir contenance.

No wonder is, for in hir grete estat   925
Hir goost was evere in pleyn humylitee;
No tendre mouth, noon herte delicat,
No pompe, no semblent of realtee,
But ful of pacient benygnytee,

907 *corage* desire
908 *disparage* dishonour
909 *alighte* descend
910 *voyden* get rid of
911 *Agayns* towards
917 *fele* many
921 *in hir absence* by avoiding company
927 *tendre* pampered; *delicat* self-indulgent
928 *semblent* appearance; *realtee* royalty

Discreet and pridelees, ay honurable,   930
And to hir housbonde evere meke and stable.

   Men speke of Job, and moost for his humblenesse,
As clerkes, whan hem lest, konne wel endite,
Namely of men, but as in soothfastnesse,
Thogh clerkes preyse wommen but alite,   935
Ther kan no man in humblesse hym acquite
As wommen kan, ne kan be half so trewe
As wommen been, but it be falle of newe.

   Fro Boloigne is this Erl of Panyk come,
Of which the fame up sprong to moore and lesse,   940
And to the peples erys, alle and some,
Was kouth eek that a newe markisesse
He with hym broghte, in swich pompe and richesse
That nevere was ther seyn with mannes eye
So noble array in al West Lumbardye.   945

   The markys, which that shoope and knew al this,
Er that this erl was come, sente his message
For thilke sely povre Grisildis;
And she with humble herte and glad visage,
Nat with no swollen thoght in hir corage,   950
Cam at his heste, and on hir knees hir sette,
And reverently and wysly she hym grette.

   'Grisilde,' quod he, 'my wyl is outrely,
This mayden, that shal wedded been to me,
Receyved be tomorwe as really   955

930 *prideless* humble
938 *but* unless; *falle of newe* recently happened
940 *moore* great; *lesse* humble
941 *alle and some* one and all
942 *kouth* known
946 *shoope* planned
950 *swollen thoght* haughtiness
955 *really* royally

As it possible is in myn hous to be
And eek that every wight in his degree
Have his estat, in sittyng and servyse
And heigh plesance, as I kan best devyse.

'I have no wommen suffisant, certayn,   960
The chambres for t'araye in ordynance
After my lust, and therfore wolde I fayn
That thyn were al swich manere governance.
Thow knowest eek of old al my plesance;
Though thyn array be badde and yvel biseye,   965
Do thow thy devoir at the leeste weye.'

'Nat oonly, lord, that I am glad', quod she,
'To doon youre lust, but I desire also
Yow for to serve and plese in my degree
Withouten feyntyng, and shal everemo;   970
Ne nevere, for no wele ne no wo,
Ne shal the goost withinne myn herte stente
To love yow best with al my trewe entente.'

And with that word she gan the hous to dighte,
And tables for to sette, and beddes make;   975
And peyned hire to doon al that she myghte,
Preyynge the chambreres, for Goddes sake,
To hasten hem, and faste swepe and shake;
And she, the mooste servysable of alle,
Hath every chambre arrayed and his halle.   980

Abouten undren gan this erl alighte,

960 *suffisant* capable
961 *t'araye in ordynance* put in order
965 *yvel biseye* ill looking
966 *devoir* duty
970 *feyntyng* weakening
974 *dighte* prepare
976 *peyned hire* took pains
977 *chambreres* chambermaids
979 *servysable* hard working

That with hym broghte thise noble children tweye,
For which the peple ran to seen the sighte
Of hire array, so richely biseye;
And thanne at erst amonges hem they seye   985
That Walter was no fool, thogh that hym leste
To chaunge his wyf, for it was for the beste.

For she is fairer, as they demen alle,
Than is Grisilde, and moore tendre of age,
And fairer fruyt bitwene hem sholde falle,   990
And moore plesant, for hire heigh lynage.
Hir brother eek so fair was of visage
That hem to seen the peple hath caught plesance,
Commendynge now the markys goverance. –

'O stormy peple! unsad and evere untrewe!   995
Ay undiscreet and chaungynge as a vane!
Delitynge evere in rumbel that is newe,
For lyk the moone ay wexe ye and wane!
Ay ful of clappyng, deere ynow a jane!
Youre doom is fals, youre constance yvele preveth;   1000
A ful greet fool is he that on yow leveth.'

Thus seyden sadde folk in that citee,
Whan that the peple gazed up and doun;
For they were glad, right for the noveltee,
To han a newe lady of hir town.   1005
Namoore of this make I now mencioun,

984 *richely biseye* rich looking
985 *at erst* first time
995 *unsad* inconstant
996 *undiscreet* undiscerning; *vane* weathervane
997 *rumbel* rumour
998 *wexe* wax
999 *clappyng* chattering
1000 *doom* judgement
1001 *leveth* believes
1002 *sadde* constant

But to Grisilde agayn wol I me dresse,
And telle hir constance and hir bisynesse. –

  Ful bisy was Grisilde in every thyng
That to the feste was apertinent.   1010
Right noght was she abayst of hir clothyng,
Thogh it were rude and somdel eek to rent;
But with glad cheere to the yate is she wente
With oother folk, to greete the markysesse,
And after that dooth forth hir bisynesse.   1015

  With so glad cheere his gestes she receyveth,
And so konnyngly, everich in his degree,
That no defaute no man aperceyveth,
But ay wondren what she myghte be
That in so povre array was for to se,   1020
And koude swich honour and reverence
And worthily they preysen hir prudence.

  In al this menewhile she ne stente
This mayde and eek hir brother to commende
With al hir herte, in ful benygne entente,   1025
So wel that no man koude hir prys amende.
But at the laste, whan that thise lordes wende
To sitten doun to mete, he gan to calle
Grisilde, as she was bisy in his halle.

  'Grisilde,' quod he, as it were in his pley,   1030
'How liketh thee my wyf and hir beautee?'
'Right wel,' quod she, 'my lord, for in good fey,
A fairer saw I nevere noon than she.

1007 *dresse* address
1010 *apertinent* suitable
1011 *abayst* embarrassed
1012 *to rent* ragged
1017 *konnyngly* skilfully
1018 *defaute* fault
1026 *prys* praise; *amende* improve

I prey to God yeve hire prosperitee;
And so hope I that he wol to yow sende   1035
Plesance ynogh unto youre lyves ende.

'O thyng biseke I yow, and warne also,
That ye ne prike with no tormentynge
This tendre mayden, as ye han do mo;
For she is fostred in hir norissynge   1040
Moore tendrely, and, to my supposynge,
She koude nat adversitee endure
As koude a povre fostred creature.'

And whan this Walter saw hir pacience,
Hir glad cheere, and no malice at al,   1045
And he so ofte had doon to hire offence,
And she ay sad and constant as a wal,
Continuynge evere hir innocence over al,
This sturdy markys gan his herte dresse
To rewen upon hir wifly stedfastnesse.   1050

'This is ynogh, Grisilde myn,' quod he;
'Be now namoore agast ne yvele apayed.
I have thy feith and thy benygnytee,
As wel as evere womman was, assayed,
In greet estat, and povreliche arrayed.   1055
Now knowe I, deere wyf, thy stedfastnesse' –
And hire in armes took and gan hir kesse.

And she for wonder took of it no keepe;

1038 *prike* afflict
1039 *mo* others
1040 *norissynge* upbringing
1041 *supposynge* belief
1047 *sad* steadfast
1048 *over al* in every way
1049 *sturdy* harsh; *dresse* prepare
1050 *rewen* pity
1052 *yvele apayed* displeased
1055 *povreliche* poorly

She herde nat what thyng he to hir seyde;
She ferde as she hadde stirt out of a sleepe, 1060
Til she out of hir mazednesse abreyde.
'Grisilde,' quod he, 'by God, that for us deyde,
Thow art my wyf, noon oother I have,
Ne nevere hadde, as God my soule save!

'This is thy doghter, which thow hast supposed 1065
To be my wyf; that oother feithfully
Shal be myn heir, as I have ay supposed;
Thow bare hym in thy body trewely.
At Boloigne have I kept hem prively;
Tak hem agayn, for now maistow nat seye 1070
That thow hast lorn noon of thy children tweye.

'And folk that oother weys han seyd of me,
I warne hem wel that I have doon this dede
For no malice, ne for no crueltee,
But for t'assaye in thee thy wommanhede, 1075
And nat to sleen my children – God forbede! –
But for to kepe hem pryvely and stille,
Til I thy purpos knewe and al thy wille.'

Whan she this herde, aswowne doun she falleth
For pitous joye, and after hir swownynge 1080
She bothe hir yonge children unto hire calleth,
And in hir armes, pitously wepynge,
Embraceth hem, and tendrely kissynge
Ful lyk a moder, with hir salte terys
She batheth bothe hir visage and hir herys. 1085

O which a pitous thyng it was to se
Hir swownyng, and hir humble voys to heere!
'Grant mercy, lord, God thanke it yow', quod she,

1060 *ferde* behaved
1061 *mazednesse* swoon; *abreyde* awakened
1071 *lorn* lost
1079 *aswowne* in a faint

111

'That ye han saved me my children deere!
Now rekke I nevere to been ded right heere;   1090
Sith I stonde in youre love and in youre grace,
No fors of deeth, ne whan my spirit pace!

   'O tendre, o deere, o yonge children myne!
Youre woful moder wende stedefastly
That cruel houndes or som foul vermyne   1095
Hadde eten yow; but God, of his mercy,
And youre benygne fader tendrely
Hath doon yow kept' – and in that same stounde
Al sodeynly she swapte adoun to grounde.

   And in hir swogh so sadly holdeth she   1100
Hir children two, whan she gan hem t'embrace,
That with greet sleghte and greet difficultee
The children from hir arm they gonne arace.
O many a teer O many a pitous face
Doun ran of hem that stoden hir bisyde;   1105
Unnethe aboute hire myghte they abyde.

   Walter hir gladeth, and hir sorwe slaketh;
She riseth up, abaysed, from hir traunce,
And every wight hir joye and feste maketh
Til she hath caught agayn hir contenaunce.   1110
Walter hir dooth so feithfully plesaunce
That it was deyntee for to seen the cheere
Bitwix hem two, now they ben met yfeere.

1090 *rekke* care
1092 *pace* depart
1094 *wende* believed
1098 *doon. . . kept* protected; *stounde* moment
1099 *swapte* dropped
1102 *sleghte* ingenuity
1103 *gonne arace* freed
1108 *abaysed* disconcerted
1109 *feste maketh* does her honour
1110 *caught agayn* composed
1113 *yfeere* together

Thise ladies, whan that they hir tyme say,
Han taken hire and in to chambre goon,   1115
And strepen hire out of hir rude aray,
And in a clooth of gold that brighte shoon,
With a coroune of many a riche stoon
Upon hir hed, they in to halle hir broghte,
And ther she was honured as hir oghte.   1120

Thus hath this pitous day a blisful ende,
For every man and womman dooth his myght
This day in murthe and revel to dispende
Til on the welkne shoon the sterres lyght.
For moore solempne in every mannes syght   1125
This feste was, and gretter of costage.
Than was the revel of hir mariage.

Ful many a yeer in heigh prosperitee
Lyven thise two in concord and in reste,
And richely his doghter maried he   1130
Unto a lord, oon of the worthyeste
Of al Ytaille; and thanne in pees and reste
His wyves fader and his court he kepeth,
Til that the soule out of his body crepeth.

His sone succedeth in his heritage   1135
In reste and pees, after his fader day,
And fortunat was eek his mariage,
Al putte he nat his wyf in gret assay.
This world is nat so strong it is no nay,
As it hath been in olde tymes yore,   1140
And herkneth what this auctour seith therfore.

This storie is seyd, nat for that wyves sholde

1114 *tyme* suitable moment
1124 *welkne* sky
1126 *gretter of costage* more costly
1139 *it is no nay* it cannot be denied
1141 *therfore* concerning this

113

Folwen Grisilde as in humylitee,
For it were inportable, thogh they wolde;
But for that every wight, in his degree,   1145
Sholde be constant in adversitee
As was Grisilde, therfore Petrak writeth
This storie, which he with heigh stile enditeth.

For, sith a womman was so pacient
Unto a mortal man, wel moore us oghte   1150
Receyven al in gree that God us sent;
For gret skile is, he preve that he wroghte.
But he ne tempteth no man that he boghte,
As seith Seint Jame, if ye his pistel rede;
He preveth folk al day, it is no drede,   1155

And suffreth us, as for oure exercise,
With sharpe scourges of adversitee
Ful ofte to be bete in sondry wise;
Nat for to knowe oure wyl, for certes he,
Er we were born, knew al oure freletee;   1160
And for oure beste is al his governance.
Lat us thanne lyve in vertuous suffrance.

But O word, lordynges, herkneth er I go:
It were ful hard to fynde now-a-dayes
In al a town Grisildis thre or two;   1165
For if that they were put to swiche assayes,
The gold of hem hath now so badde alayes

1144 *inportable* intolerable
1151 *gree* good spirit
1153 *boghte* redeemed
1154 *pistel* epistle
1155 *drede* doubt
1156 *exercise* discipline
1160 *freletee* weakness
1162 *suffrance* patience
1167 *allays* alloys

With bras, that thogh the coigne be fair at eye,
It wolde rather breste a-two than plye.

For which heere, for the Wyves love of Bathe – 1170
Whos lyf and al hir secte God mayntene
In heighe maistrie, or ellis were it scathe –
I wol with lusty herte, fressh and grene,
Seye yow a song to glade yow, I wene;
And lat us stynte of ernestful matere. 1175
Herkneth my song that seith in this manere:

Here is ended the tale of the Clerk of Oxenford

L'envoy de Chaucer

Grisilde is deed, and eek hir pacience,
And bothe atones buryed in Ytaille;
For which I crye in open audience,
No wedded man so hardy be t'assaille 1180
His wyves pacience in trust to fynde
Grisildis, for in certein he shal faille.

O noble wyves, ful of heigh prudence,
Lat noon humilitee youre tonge nayle,
Ne lat no clerk have cause or diligence 1185
To write of yow a storie of swich mervaile
As of Grisildis pacient and kynde,
Lest chichyvache yow swelwe in hir entrayle!

Folweth Ekko, that holdeth no silence,

1168 *at eye* to look at
1169 *breste* burst; *plye* bend
1172 *scathe* pity
1181 *trust* hope
1184 *nayle* restrain
1188 *swelwe* swallow
1189 *Ekko* Echo

But evere answereth at the countretaile.   1190
Beth nat bidaffed for youre innocence,
But sharply tak on yow the governaile.
Emprinteth wel this lessoun in youre mynde,
For commune profit sith it may availe.

Ye archewyves, stondeth at defense,   1195
Syn ye be strong as is a gret camaile;
Ne suffreth nat that men yow doon offense.
And sklendre wyves, fieble as in bataile,
Beth egre as is a tigre yond in Ynde;
Ay clappeth as a mille, I yow consaile.   1200

Ne dreed hem nat, dooth hem no reverence,
For thogh thyn housbond armed be in maile,
The arwes of thy crabbed eloquence
Shal perce his brest, and eek his aventaile.
In jalousie I rede eek thow hym bynde,   1205
And thow shalt make hym couche as dooth a quaile.

If thow be fair, ther folk ben in presence,
Shewe thow thy visage and thyn aparaile;
If thow be foul, be fre of thy dispence;
To gete thee freendes ay do thy travaile;   1210
Be ay of cheere as light as leef on lynde,
And lat hym care, and wepe, and wrynge, and wayle!

1190 *at the countretaile* in reply
1192 *governaile* control
1194 *commune profit* common good
1196 *camaile* camel
1198 *sklendre* slender
1199 *egre* fierce
1200 *Ay clappeth* always nag
1202 *maile* armour
1203 *crabbed* spiteful
1205 *rede* advise
1206 *couche* cower
1209 *dispence* spending
1211 *lynde* linden tree
1212 *care* grieve; *wrynge* wring his hands

116

Explicit

[*Bihoold the murye wordes of the Hoost*]

   This worthy Clerk, whan ended was his tale,
Oure Hooste seyde, and swoor, 'By Goddes bones,
Me were levere than a barel ale   1215
My wyf at hom had herd this legende ones!
This is a gentil tale for the nones,
As to my purpos, wiste ye my wille;
But thyng that wol nat be, lat it be stille.'

Critical commentary

I

By day she woos me, soft, exceeding fair:
   But all night as the moon so changeth she;
   Loathsome and foul with hideous leprosy
And subtle serpents gliding in her hair.
By day she woos me to the outer air,
   Ripe fruit, sweet flowers, and full satiety:
   But through the night, a beast she grins at me,
A very monster void of love and prayer.
By day she stands a lie: by night she stands
   In all the naked horror of the truth
With pushing horns and clawed and clutching hands.
Is this a friend indeed; that I should sell
   My soul to her, give her my life and youth,
Till my feet, cloven too, take hold on hell?
                              (Rossetti, 1970, p. 62)

The above sonnet, entitled 'The World', was written by Christina
Rossetti in the nineteenth century; it personifies the earth as a woman
who is fair and good by day, but foul and evil at night. This split image
of women is part of a long-standing tradition, to which Rossetti's
World and Chaucer's Wife of Bath and Patient Griselda belong. It is an
idea which emerges from the canon of classical literature, which is
outlined in the Introduction, and perpetuates itself in contemporary
popular culture. For example, the sexually rapacious and homicidal
female protagonist in the film *Fatal Attraction* is a polarised feminine

119

opposite to the demure and acquiescent role formulated for Princess Diana by the tabloid press. What is interesting about Rossetti's poem is that it offers a female perspective on this doubleness, suggesting that the two images are part of the same identity, and that the poet herself, even though conscious of the dialectic, runs the risk of becoming similarly 'cloven'.

If Rossetti is right, then any gendered subject's attempt at self-description will invariably continue the ideological assumptions made by society about their sex. Hence, Chaucer through the narratorial voice of the Wife of Bath may be seen to sustain the same complexity: while defending women, the Wife at the same time encodes misogynist attacks. But, instead of settling for this self-contained dualism, Chaucer offers us a pervasive dialogue on gender and sexuality, setting the flawed humanity of the Wife against the idealised Griselda, and the female voice of personal experience against the male voice of textual authority. What this commentary intends is an exploration of how and where these parallel issues have developed, both in the cultural and social background of the medieval period, and in the subsequent critical readings of Chaucer's texts. Above all, I hope to demonstrate the necessity for a self-conscious approach to any theoretical and historical interpretations undertaken. The reader too must be 'cloven': determined both to understand the period in which Chaucer wrote, and to be aware that full and exclusive access to medieval value systems can never be attained by those from later centuries. We perforce bring our own ideological baggage with us. For example, a feminist critic – like myself – must realise that, although feminine roles are central to the tales of the Wife and Clerk, it is only our contemporary literary and historical emphases on women's experiences that have enabled us to examine the poems afresh in this light. Whatever our critical allegiances, it is essential to recognise that they are social, cultural, political and personal constructions, rather than immovable and unassailable certainties. Indeed, as Rossetti suggests, we cannot help but be altered by our constantly changing experience of the world, and literature is, by its very nature, an element in that power of mutability.

II

And as of men, loke ye which tirannye
They doon alday; assay hem whoso lyste,

The trewest ys ful brotel for to triste.
The Legend of Good Women 1883–4

To begin, let us take one theme already mentioned and focus upon the *experience* of women in the medieval period, asking: 'what actually happens to the women in the Wife's and Clerk's prologues and tales?' The Wife was married at the age of twelve, she has been beaten by one of her husbands so severely that she became deaf, and her tale commences with the rape of a young girl. Griselda has had her children taken away from her, believing that they have been murdered. She is rejected by her husband who, supposedly, supplants her with a younger, more beautiful and wealthier woman. The new wife is really Griselda's twelve-year-old daughter, but her fate is little better than that of her mother. She has been taken away from her home as a child, is to be married to a man she has never seen, who is old enough to be her father, and who has cruelly put aside his first wife.

Any narrative content expressed in this manner must entail a distortion of the tales. There are omissions in this version that are essential to the understanding of the texts; for example, that Alison retaliates physically against Jankyn, and that the whole point of the Patient Griselda story is how much Griselda must suffer. But it is equally important to realise that the events recorded in the tales evolve from the realities of medieval life. Both the Wife and Griselda's daughter are marriageable at the age of twelve, as the Wife points out at the beginning of her prologue,

> For, lordynges, sith that I twelf yeer was of age,
> Thonked be God that is eterne on lyve,
> Housbondes atte chirche dore I have had fyve.
>
> 'WBP' 4–6

Walter in 'The Clerk's Tale' decides to test Griselda further by pretending to marry their daughter, 'Whan that this doghter twelve yer was of age' (736). Certainly, twelve years was the legal age for girls to be married in canon law, and the inequality of age which is proposed in the matches for both girls was common. One of the manuals of instruction discussed in the Introduction, *The Goodman of Paris* (c.1393), was written by a sixty-year-old husband for his fifteen-year-old wife.

That the Wife is severely beaten is hardly surprising, for the courts accepted the right of a man to beat his wife, and physical violence,

121

irrespective of gender, was common in most medieval households. She says of her fifth husband, Jankyn,

> By God! he smoot me ones on the lyst,
> For that I rente out of his book a leef,
> That of the strook myn ere weex al deef.
>
> 'WBP' 634–6

The Wife repeats these accusations six times (505–7; 509–10; 668; 712; 795; and 805–7) ensuring our own familiarity with the affront, but also, intriguingly, suggesting her own outrage and surprise at the blow. However, physical violence against women should not be seen as something instigated, in isolation, by the shrew-like character of the Wife. Another of the instruction books discussed in the Introduction, *The Book of the Knight of La Tour-Landry* (c.1371), recounts how, because a woman has used bad language to her husband in public, he beat her so badly that he broke her nose. The moral the Knight draws from this incident was: 'And therfor the wiff aught to suffre and lete the husbonde have the wordes, and to be maister, for that is her worshippe' (*La Tour-Landry*, 1906, p. 25). Unlike the Knight, I would like to direct attention towards the parallels that exist not only between the Wife of Bath's infringement of masculine written authority and the cursing wife's breaching of masculine linguistic codes, but also between both husbands' use of physical force to silence their womenfolk. The control of language is a recurring theme in *The Canterbury Tales* and one which Chaucer evokes repeatedly in the Marriage Group; this interplay between gender, power and language is dealt with fully in Section VI.

'The Wife of Bath's Tale' pursues the theme of physical assault by commencing with the rape of a young girl:

> And so bifel that this kyng Arthour
> Hadde in his hous a lusty bachiler,
> That on a day cam ridyng fro ryver;
> And happed that, allone as he was born,
> He say a mayde walkynge hym biforn,
> Of which mayde anoon, maugree hir hed,
> By verray force, he rafte hir maydenhed;
> For which oppressioun was swich clamour
> And swich pursuyte unto the king Arthour,
> That dampned was this knyght for to be deed,

By cours of lawe and sholde han lost his heed –
Paraventure swich was the statut tho –
But that the queene and othere ladyes mo
So longe preyden the kyng of grace,
Til he his lyf hym graunted in the place,
And yaf hym to the queene, al at hir wille,
To chese wheither she wolde hym save or spille.

'WBT' 882–98

This description of the consequences of rape is not entirely fictional since,
as we have noted in the Introduction, the redemption of the knight was
validated by English fourteenth-century criminal law. By allowing the
knight a chance to save himself, the queen in the Wife's tale does no more
than adopt the usual laws of the day, and the knight is eventually granted a
pardon in conjunction with a marriage. The Wife's condemnation of rape
in her tale may be read as a proto-feminist response, as was written by
Christine de Pisan a decade later; Christine devotes three chapters of *The
Book of the City of Ladies* (1404) to rape. However, given that none of
Chaucer's analogues includes such an incident and that in 'The Clerk's
Tale' he engenders sympathy for Griselda's sufferings, it seems more
likely that the author himself was interested in depicting extremes of
female travail. Rape demonstrates the absolute power of one person over
another and, as such, it may act as a metaphor for men's control over
women – this time focusing upon sexuality rather than language. What the
Wife's tale allows us to see is the continuing thematic display of gender and
control, the 'sovereyntee' in marriage, but it simultaneously foregrounds
the horrors of such domination when taken to extremes.

The Wife of Bath depicts forms of female suffering, but not ones we
would consider surprising. The experiences of Patient Griselda cannot
be analysed in the same way: Griselda is a Christian exemplar, not a
realistically portrayed woman, and the experiences of medieval women
have little material connection with her exaggerated trials. What then is
the purpose of the Clerk's concluding implication that contemporary
women are 'alayes / With bras' in comparison with Griselda's 'gold'
('CIT' 1167–8)? Why does Chaucer ironically encourage women to
reject Griselda's values? For example:

O noble wyves, ful of heigh prudence,
Lat noon humilitee youre tonge nayle.

'CIT' 1183–4

And why does the Host emphasise this implicit criticism of women still further by wishing that his wife could be more like Patient Griselda? 'The Clerk's Tale' has a complex and many-layered ending, which will be examined in Section VI, but it is important to note here that the conclusion clearly links Griselda to Chaucer's contemporary female audience. The focus on a female response, rather than on the provocative tests devised by Walter, suggests that it is feminine patience and humility which are being subtly advocated, not masculine brutality.

If we compare two passages, one from 'The Clerk's Tale' and one from Christine de Pisan, it becomes possible to perceive that patient suffering was a commonplace of female experience in the medieval period. When Walter is finally convinced of Griselda's constancy, he reverses all the trials, restoring her children and rightful position as his wife:

> 'This is ynogh, Grisilde myn', quod he;
> Be now namoore agast ne yvele apayed,
> I have thy feith and thy benygnytee,
> As wel as evere womman was, assayed,
> In greet estat, and povreliche arrayed.
> Now knowe I, deere wyf, thy stedfastnesse,' –
> And hire in his armes took and gan hir kesse.
>
> 'ClT' 1051–7

Griselda could almost have been following the advice Christine gives to wives in *The Treasure of the City of Ladies* (1405) where the historical woman advises:

> Suppose that the husband, of whatever class he may be, has extremely perverse and rude behaviour. Suppose he is unloving towards his wife or strays into a love affair with some other woman. If the wife cannot remedy the situation, she must put up with all this and dissimulate wisely, pretending that she does not notice it and that she truly does not know anything about it.
>
> (de Pisan, 1985, p. 64)

Christine concludes that if the wife follows this behaviour she will eventually be rewarded, for there are,

> three blessings that can come to you from conducting yourselves

well and wisely towards them, whoever they are, and keeping your promise to be faithful and loyal to them and holding your peace and in all things doing your duty. The first is the great merit to the soul that you acquire by doing your duties; the second is great honour in the world; and the third is, as one has often seen, that although many rich men of many and varied positions are and have always been remarkably cruel to their wives, when the hour of death comes their conscience pricks them and they consider the goodness of their wives, who have endured them with such a good grace, and the great wrong that they have committed against their wives, and they leave them in possession of their whole fortune.

(de Pisan, 1985, p. 146)

Chaucer offers a similar fairytale conclusion, with Griselda's Christian virtue triumphant and her material circumstances fittingly elevated in 'clooth of gold . . . / With a coroune of many a riche stoon' (1117–18). It seems that the Wife of Bath is not the only one of Chaucer's female characters to attain economic success. When patience and perseverance are the only choices open to women, then they must make those qualities into virtues. But even the noble and pious Christine de Pisan recognised that the worldly promise of monetary remuneration might be a necessary incentive to suffer silently, rather than extending the prospect of riches in a heaven where patriarchal values might still pertain.

'Experience' is the first word in the Wife's prologue and, as Mary Carruthers points out in her article 'The Wife of Bath and the Painting of Lions', 'Alisoun does not deny authority when authority is true . . . she does insist, however, that authority make itself accountable to the realities of experience' (Carruthers, 1979, p. 209). This is the process that we have initiated in Section II: examining the experiences of the female characters in the text and seeing how far they correspond to the realities of women's lives in the medieval period. Three important points have arisen, which will re-emerge in later discussions. First, that the Wife of Bath and Patient Griselda clearly belong to a view of women which existed in both literature and life; their experiences are those of medieval women in general. Secondly, that Chaucer uses the actual repression of women, linguistically and sexually, in order to develop the broader thematic concern of control over language and society. Thirdly, and perhaps most interestingly, similarities between Alison and Griselda have already started to emerge. If both characters belong to a 'cloven' view of women grounded in female experience, then we must ask ourselves how and why they have been seen as antithetical for so long, and in order to do this we must turn next to the critical 'authorities'.

III

'Chaucer, notwithstanding the praises bestowed on him, I think obscene and contemptible'

(Byron, 1978, vol. I., p. 249).

This attack on Chaucer by Lord Byron suggests both the Romantic poet's challenge to literary tradition and, more importantly for us, the authoritative position that Chaucer had already come to sustain in the canon of 'great writers'. In the first part of the fifteenth century, soon after his death, he was being given epithets such as 'fadir Chaucer' (Thomas Hoccleve, *The Regement of Princes* 1405) and 'maister Chauser' (John Lydgate, 'The Life of Our Lady' 1410). He was seen as the first poet to develop poetic writing in the English language and, as such, he became a revered, almost laureate, figure. There were few writers and, later, critics who followed Byron's example; Chaucer was universally recognised to have an unassailable position in English literature. His reputation remains intact today, as may be shown from the vast quantity of books being produced about Chaucer and, even, the numerous knick-knacks available from souvenir shops across the country. Still, while recognising Chaucer's continued importance, twentieth-century literary critics have approached his texts in several different ways.

Criticism at the beginning of this century concentrated upon tracing the historical, biographical and literary sources for the texts. Chaucer was perceived as a passive but wise observer of human events, which he recorded faithfully in his poems. This period is often classified under 'historicism' and it produced informative evidence which is still useful to modern critics. Its main exponent, and perhaps one of the most famous Chaucerian critics, was G.L. Kittredge; his work *Chaucer and His Poetry* (1915) advanced the idea that the tales were like dramatic monologues, expanding the characters of their tellers in a realistic manner. He also, as is mentioned in the Introduction, emphasised the importance of the Marriage Group as a coherent unit of tales and allocated the tales of the Wife and the Clerk formal positions within the

Group's overall thematic structure. For Kittredge the Wife represented the unorthodox view of marriage, an attitude which was due more to the aberration of her character than to Chaucer's own beliefs. Similarly, the Clerk was said to represent an extreme of suppression at the other pole of married relations, and as such balanced the Wife in the Marriage Group. The early historical criticism thus contributed to the 'cloven' view of women in *The Canterbury Tales*; it set up the Wife and Griselda as two opposing images, which were assumed to be valid historically due to Chaucer's supposed literalism.

New Criticism rejected all forms of background study and asserted that close reading was the only way to gain full access to the deeper meaning of the text. Initiated by I.A. Richards's *Practical Criticism* (1929), this form of approach became increasingly popular with Chaucerians. Chaucer seemed almost ideally suited to the search for ambiguity, his layering of narrative voices opened up a myriad of possibilities for ironic comment. In this way Chaucer the author could be seen to be making a subtle attack on the character of the Wife when she is made to include misogynist tenets in her own prologue. Still, by and large, the New Critics were more sympathetic towards the Wife, seeing her as a comic figure, manipulated by the author. The consequent admiration of Chaucer's wit and intellectual dexterity is seen most clearly in the writing of E.T. Donaldson, whose analyses of Chaucerian irony are still immensely influential. Probably the two most significant of Donaldson's works are 'Chaucer the Pilgrim' (1954) and *Speaking of Chaucer* (1970). Other useful New Critical approaches to Chaucer are: C. Muscatine's hugely informative *Chaucer and the French Tradition* (1957); R.A. Pratt's detailed treatment of the Wife in 'The Development of the Wife of Bath' (1961); and on the Clerk, J. Sledd's '*The Clerk's Tale*: The Monsters and the Critics' (1953). An awareness of irony remains an essential aspect for our discussions of Chaucer, and close reading, as long as it is not practised to the exclusion of other influences on the text, is still of great importance.

The 1960s saw a backlash to the exclusivity of the text, and once again readings were made more accountable to background sources. There were roughly two developments: the allegorists and the new historical critics (this was not the same as 'New Historicism' which I shall return to shortly). Allegory is a symbolical narrative, that is, a material story which is translatable into metaphysical terms; for example *The Canterbury Tales*, as a pilgrimage, can be translated into the

Christian idea of humankind's pilgrimage through life. The allegorists rejected any individualism or human experience in the tales, and instead emphasised the eternal and universal qualities of the characters. Hence Walter's cruelty and Griselda's patience ceased to be implausible, as they were read in terms of a greater Christian truth, not realistic human expectations. The Wife, too, was allegorised into a type, often that of treacherous Eve, as opposed to Griselda's virtuous Virgin Mary. Although the allegorists did much to reinforce the antithetical stereotypes of women in *The Canterbury Tales*, their scholarly research has done much to show how Chaucer draws on the spiritual archetypes of the medieval world. Well worth looking at are D.W. Robertson's *A Preface to Chaucer* (1962) and, specifically on the Clerk, E. Salter's *Chaucer: The Knight's Tale and The Clerk's Tale* (1962).

Interestingly, D.W. Robertson's *A Preface to Chaucer* is also implicated in the revival of interest in historical sources; its detailed account of medieval values led to a less formulaic approach, which suggested, among other things, that the Wife's view of marriage was not as aberrant as Kittredge implied. A. David in *The Strumpet Muse* (1976) pursued this more sympathetic approach, revealing that the Wife was in some ways close to her times. This liberal emphasis on the social and cultural context of *The Canterbury Tales* still exists in the informative texts of D.S. Brewer. However, in the 1980s a very different form of historicism developed.

The most recent historical enquiries have their origins in Marxist criticism, focusing upon the sociological and economic circumstances of Chaucer's literary productions. They include useful discussions of feudalism, the Peasants' Revolt and Lollardism, such as will be found in the Introduction to this book. M. Carruthers's 'The Wife of Bath and the Painting of Lions' (1979), S. Knight's *Geoffrey Chaucer* (1986), and D. Aers's *Chaucer* (1986) have all been ground-breaking works in this respect. Still more recently, and especially in Aers's writing and in H. Marshall Leicester's *The Disenchanted Self* (1990), the influences of New Historicism and Cultural Materialism have started to appear. The American New Historicism and the British, more radically Marxist, Cultural Materialism have similar emphases on the importance of historical context; as Aers writes in *Community, Gender and Individual Identity*,

> The generation of meaning and individual experience cannot be understood apart from the social relations of a specific community, its organizations of power manifest in the prevailing arrangements of

class, gender, political rule, religion, armed force, and, not in-frequently, race. So any reading that hopes to have relevance to a particular text must include an attempt to relocate it in the web of discourses and social practices within which it was made and which determined its horizons.

(Aers, 1988, p. 4)

At the same time, however, these texts are involved in creating cultural meanings, so that we are confronted with a reciprocal relationship between text and context, not one of passive reflection. For example, the Wife of Bath's prologue is no longer seen as Chaucer's careful account of the contemporary state of the *querelle des femmes*, but an integral part of that dialogue, reworking and revising assumptions about the nature of women.

If Chaucer's text may now be seen as a dynamic element in the debate about women, then it is feminism that has facilitated the awareness of this role through the detailed research undertaken recently on the material circumstances of women's lives in the medieval period. Within this canon, however, there are wide divergences. On one side, feminist historians claim that women had a considerable amount of freedom: E. Power's *Medieval Women* (1975), P. Labalme's *Beyond Their Sex* (1980) and B. Anderson's and J.P. Zinsser's *A History of Their Own* (1988) concur with this view. On the other, a restricted role for women is uncovered by S. Sharhar in *The Fourth Estate* (1983) and M.W. Labarge in *A Small Sound of the Trumpet* (1986).

A similar division may be seen in feminist literary criticism, although here the Wife and Griselda are suspended within a more complex set of judgements. The first, and still essential, contemporary feminist criti-que of women in medieval literature was A. Diamond's and L.R. Edwards's *The Authority of Experience* (1977), in which Diamond laid down the central paradoxes of the Wife and Griselda. Of the former she writes, 'There is a fundamental disparity between the manipulation of her to exorcise the image of the overpowering female through comedy, and the creation of a sympathetically perceived woman suffering the loss of youth and affection' (Diamond and Edwards, 1977, p. 71). And of Griselda, 'We are left with a paradox: women have no choice but to suffer, and therefore their greatest virtue lies in suffering well' (Dia-mond and Edwards, 1977, p. 74). Both women must encode a conven-tional male understanding of them – 'overpowering' and 'suffering' –

but it is equally possible to perceive them as individually self-determining female consciousnesses within these ideological confines. S. Delaney in 'Sexual Economics, Chaucer's Wife of Bath, and *The Book of Margery Kempe*' (1983) and in her more recent book *Medieval Literary Politics* (1990), E.T. Hansen in 'The Powers of Silence: The Case of the Clerk's Griselda' (1988) and J. Mann in 'Satisfaction and Payment in Middle English Literature' (1983) and in *Geoffrey Chaucer* (1991), all basically follow Diamond's problematised readings. The Wife has roused more vehement and personalised responses: Marxist feminists, such as M. Carruthers in 'The Wife of Bath and the Painting of Lions' (1979) and S. Schibanoff in 'Taking the Gold Out of Egypt: The Art of Reading as a Woman' (1986), tend towards vigorous defences; and L. Patterson offers a grudgingly negative view of Alison in ' "For the Wyves love of Bathe": Feminine Rhetoric and Poetic Resolution in the *Roman de la Rose* and *The Canterbury Tales*' (1983). From the first two sections of this commentary it will be clear that I have followed the general trend in feminist Chaucerian criticism by highlighting the dialogue between liberation and repression in the construction of female characters. But rather than remain locked in an analysis of gender, I also intend to allow the structure of the feminist argument to span the theoretical divides, thereby facilitating further, distinctive, readings.

Within Chaucerian scholarship there are numerous schools of thought, from the old historicists to the feminists, and from New Critics to the allegorists. It is interesting and indeed valuable to read some of the material I have outlined above, but none of it is a substitute for the text itself. In one form or another, each criticism – this one included – erects a new textual authority with which to confront the experience of reading the text.

IV

Who too much trusts in womankind,
Often leaves honor far behind;
Who loves or prizes womankind
Often ends up much maligned;
He who trusts them one or all
Drinks the hemlock tastes the gall.
                            (*Le Blasme des Fames*, 1989, p. 121)

Do not womankind malign,
For as wise men have made clear
Only fools at women sneer.
Who leaves their honor unsung, unsaid,
His own honor must be dead.
                    (*Le Bien des Fames*, 1989, p. 113)

The twentieth-century critical debate about Chaucer's female characters is, perhaps, not quite as innovative as its proponents might wish to believe. Compare the quotations above, which come from two fourteenth-century French *dits*, with the two following accounts both written within the last 30 years. First, James Winny's attack on the Wife of Bath comes from his edition, *The Wife of Bath's Prologue and Tale* (1965), which is still commonly used at 'A' level; he writes:

> It might be conceded that the Wife could tell a fairy-tale, but not that she should become involved in a serious philosophical debate on the nature of 'gentillesse'. The woman who becomes enraged when another wife precedes her during the offertory, who cheats and deludes her husbands, seizing their wealth by force of 'maistrie' and even exacting payment for their use of her body, shows not the remotest interest in the ideal of gentle behaviour which forms the hub of her Tale.
>
>   (Winny, 1965, p. 24)

For Winny, the Wife is clearly a shrew, a drink of 'hemlock' or a taste of 'gall'; she is vain, jealous, avaricious and, most damningly, she will not obey her husbands, sexually or economically. On the other hand, Jill Mann in one of the most recent feminist criticisms of Chaucer, *Geoffrey Chaucer*, explores the same material in a different light:

> Yet the surprise of this tale . . .is that these cynical answers to the question of what women desire are *not* introduced in order to be derided and dismissed. On the contrary, the tale legitimises the female desire for 'maistrye' which the anti-feminist writers view with such fear and hostility, by making it the just response to male 'oppressioun'.
>
>   (Mann, 1991, p. 91)

Mann, along with the anonymous author of *Le Bien des Fames*, suggests that attacks upon women are self-deconstructing, provoking female responses which are mirror images of the violence used upon them; the misogynists are indeed 'fools'.

The conventions appear hardly to have changed; certainly the argument of domineering harridan versus docile wife remains constant. But this implies that the position of women in European society has not altered since the medieval period, an assumption which common sense must confirm as mistaken. Indeed, the material experiences of medieval women have been shown, earlier in this Commentary, to be much harsher and more repressive than those of anyone, female or male, reading this text. While, therefore, it is important to perceive a continuity in human experience from Chaucer's day to our own – particularly as this provides the fourteenth-century writing with an immediate relevance – at the same time, we should be aware of the different social values and cultural traditions of the past. It might be perversely satisfying, or infuriating, to highlight the continued repression of women and the underprivileged classes, but this essentialist approach should be balanced with an active recognition of the complexities unique to the period in which the text was produced.

The two main loci for the discussion of women by fourteenth-century authorities were the *querelle des femmes*, which has already been discussed in the Introduction, and the cult of courtly love. Each system produced vast quantities of literature, both analysing and giving examples of the virtues and vices of women. In the *querelle* authors seem to line themselves up for a two-sided confrontation. Those who were 'anti', like the author of *Le Blasme*, called upon Ovid's *Ars amatoria* (first century BC), Jean de Meun's *Roman de la Rose* (c.1277) and the host of misogynistic literature cited in the Wife of Bath's prologue. Indeed, later contributors to the debate used Chaucer's description of

> the sorwe and wo
> That Socrates hadde with hise wyves two;
> How Xantippa caste pisse upon his heed.
> This sely man sat stille as he were deed;
> He wipte his heed, namoore dorste he seyn,
> But 'Er that thonder stynte, comth a reyn!'
> 'WBP' 727–32

Compare this with Joseph Swetnam's account in his *The Arraignment of Lewd, idle, froward, and unconstant women* (1615):

Socrates, when his wife did chide and brawl, would go out of the house till all were quiet again, but because he would not scold with her again, it grieved her the more. For on a time, she watched his going out and threw a chamber pot out of the window on his head. 'Ha, ha!' quoth he, 'I thought after all this thunder there would come rain'.

(Swetnam, 1985, p. 299)

The narrative details are equivalent, and Swetnam clearly interprets the earlier text as a pejorative attack on argumentative women; however, there is a slight, but significant tonal variation between the two. The anger and condemnation which characterises *The Arraignment* is perceived with ease, there are no secondary sensations to be uncovered. With the Chaucerian text it is impossible to determine a single dominant response: Xantippa's actions signify that she is a shrew, but the Wife's ridicule of Socrates' ineffectual behaviour cannot help but woo us into a collusion with her laughter and scorn. It appears that the Chaucerian text encodes both sides of the *querelle*, an attack against women, as well as a sympathetic response to them.

On the other side of the debate, those who wished to praise women, like the author of *Le Bien*, found themselves in alliance with a woman writer, Christine de Pisan, whose *The Book of the City of Ladies* (1404) was written in defence of women. Indeed, her description of the relationship between Xantippa and Socrates differs significantly from those of Chaucer and Swetnam; she writes,

The noble lady Xanthippe possessed great learning and goodness, and because of these qualities she married Socrates, the greatest philosopher. Although he was already quite old and cared more about searching for knowledge and researching in books than obtaining soft and new things for his wife, the valiant lady nevertheless did not stop loving him but rather thought of the excellence of his learning, his outstanding virtue, and his constancy, which, in her sovereign love and reverence, she considered to be a sign of his excellence.

(de Pisan, 1983, p. 130)

Although Christine de Pisan's choice, and character alteration, of two of the stock figures from the *querelle* was undoubtedly ironic, an ambiguity of tone is as absent from the feminist statement as it is from Swetnam's misogynistic diatribe. She plainly defends Xantippa. It is

133

Chaucer again, this time writing on the 'pro' side of the debate, who allows the construction of the argument to work on several levels of irony at once. In *The Legend of Good Women*, Queen Alceste and the God of Love accuse Chaucer, who has written himself into the poem as a character, of depicting only false women in his works, such as in the 'Rose or elles in Creseyde' (*LGW* 441; the texts Alceste refers to are *The Romaunt of the Rose* and *Troilus and Criseyde*). Chaucer tries to defend himself by claiming that he was simply following his sources, but Alceste is adamant, ordering that

> Thow shalt, while that thou lyvest, yer by yere,
> The moste partye of thy tyme spende
> In makyng of a glorious legende
> Of goode wymmen, maydenes and wyves,
> That weren trewe in lovyng al hire lyves;
> And telle of false men that hem bytraien,
> That al hir lyf ne don nat but assayen
> How many women they may doon a shame;
> For in youre world that is now holde a game.
>
> *LGW* 481–9

Chaucer's use of a double-self, which also occurs in *The Canterbury Tales*, enables him to exploit the difference between what he, as poet, might imply, and what he, as character, is actually allowed to say. While one appears to be staunchly supportive of 'goode wymmen', the other offers weak arguments in order to defend his earlier condemnation of them. Of course, we also have to recognise a further level of irony; however 'politically correct' (to use a much hyped-up phrase of the 1990s) Chaucer the author may seem to be in his support of Alceste, it was he, after all, who wrote the offending works. It is exactly this kind of dialogue that may be excavated from the prologues and tales of the Wife and Clerk. A juxtaposition of the shrew-like Wife and the utterly submissive Griselda leaves us, not with a warning and a paradigm of feminine behaviour respectively, but with an accomplice in humour and a remote and unbelievable paragon.

In *Le Bien des Fames* one of the virtues accredited to women is upholding 'the rules of *courtoisie*'; Christine de Pisan criticises Socrates for not 'obtaining soft and new things for his wife'; and Alceste demands that Chaucer 'Speke wel of love' (*LGW* 491). If the defenders of women wished to verify their argument, they had only to turn to the dominant cultural more of their age – courtly love. The idea of courtly love originated in the troubadour poetry of eleventh- and twelfth-century Provence, in France, and became closely associated with a classical sensuality. Desire was the central theme and determining force of these early works and their descendants, but the erotic material was combined with a recognition of the purifying powers of affection, to give an overall sense of eros and agape united. Within this formula women were presented as ideals of virtue and beauty, who wielded an absolute, almost feudal authority over the aspirants to their love. This concept of courtly love is expounded by C.S. Lewis in *The Allegory of Love* (1936) where he claims that it is an accurate portrayal of medieval life. The historical evidence would suggest, however, that Lewis's argument cannot be sustained, and indeed, E.T. Donaldson successfully challenged it in 'The Myth of Courtly Love' (1970), which argued for a literary interpretation, rather than a reflection of reality. As we have seen, women did not exert the kind of power described by courtly love, nor was adultery acceptable in an age in which dynastic succession was all-important.

Yet, since the ideal of courtly love persisted from the eleventh to the sixteenth centuries, it is necessary to ask how it could radiate such a powerful and resilient influence. The Wife of Bath's tale offers one possible explanation for this disparity between the material and fictional self-images of medieval European society. The rapist knight is presented to the queen in order for her to enact judgement upon him, rather than leaving him to be prosecuted, as the populace expect, by the king. When the knight returns with his answer he is confronted by:

> Ful many a noble wyf, and many a mayde,
> And many a widwe, for that they ben wise,
> The queene hirself sittyng as justise.
>
> 'WBT' 1026–8

The description resembles a legal case, in which the queen adopts the role of judge and the ladies of the court the jury. Even after the knight has presented his answer and been pardoned, the hag commences another 'action', this time identifying herself as a plaintiff on the grounds of breach of marriage. The knight's fate is again decided by the female assembly and he is forcibly wedded to the aged dame. Although marriage was the expected outcome of most rape charges in the noble classes, the fact that it is the queen and her ladies who perform the official court duties suggests that Chaucer is referring not only to the courts of law but also to the courts of love.

The most popular manual of courtly love was the *De amore* (*The Art of Courtly Love* c.1174) written by Andreas Capellanus, who is said to have been attached to the court of Marie de Champagne at Troyes, in France. There is little verifiable evidence about Andreas or the circumstances in which his text was produced, and there has been a considerable amount of debate in the twentieth century as to whether the work praises or condemns courtly love. What is important for later writers, such as Chaucer, is that Andreas depicted Marie's court as a centre of learning and culture which was dominated by women, and in which the Countess and her ladies presided over real-life courts of love. Andreas set out the rules of love, and described various decisions made in love cases; and as such, he provided a literary template for narratives like 'The Wife of Bath's Tale'. Thus it could be suggested that courtly love was simply a social game played by the aristocratic elite of the European courts. This explanation, however, isolates the ideal fictional women from their historical counterparts, and reinforces the traditional male hierarchy, by confining love and feminine concerns to a 'game world'. On the other hand, it is plausible to propose that the very existence of courtly love denotes a desire within medieval society for alternative social and moral codes. Courtly love might have been a cultural artefact, but it was at the same time an essential and persistent facet of the way medieval society constructed its own identity. The existence of plausible, yet unconfirmed, accounts of the love courts at Troyes allowed courtly love to remain, at one and the same time, a mystical ideal and a valid source of aspiration. The conclusion to the Wife's tale exists in the same veiled area of game and reality; the hag's pillow lecture to the reluctant knight includes arguments redolent of sense and rationality, but her transformation into a fair lady is pure romance.

However, 'romance' means more than the narration of an extravagant and imaginative occurrence. Romance is also a literary genre with its own rules and subjects. It is a genre which flourished in the medieval period alongside courtly love, and of which 'The Wife of Bath's Tale' is a perfect example. The genre is, as Gillian Beer writes in *The Romance*: 'a serene intermingling of the unexpected and everyday, a complex and prolonged succession of incidents usually without a single climax' (Beer, 1970, p. 10). Beer's short book is a useful introduction to romance, and it may be read together with Northrop Frye's still definitive 'The Mythos of Summer' from his *Anatomy of Criticism* (1957), and the most innovative of the critical works on the topos, Patricia Parker's *Inescapable Romance* (1979). All three texts focus on both the linking of a metaphysical ideal with social answerability, and on the romance structure which, as Parker points out, simultaneously quests for and postpones a particular end. These two ideas may be linked: a society might have a very clear sense of perfection, which it constantly works towards, but at the same time, because the world is far from perfect, it realises that this ideal is unattainable. Thus romance collaborates with a society by reflecting and sustaining that society's ideals. However, these literary manifestations constantly rework, and consequently perpetually refuel, the society's desire to attain perfection. This, in turn, ensures that the ideal remains *un*attainable, since the romance form is essentially, even blatantly, fictional and can offer only an insubstantial mirage of reality.

Courtly love is just such an ideal, seen as absolutely desirable by the medieval society which created it, but also recognised as an impossible goal. In the Wife's prologue and tale the same structure is replayed: the aged Wife wishes for a young and lusty husband; her prologue is a series of quests for the ideal partner, all of which fail; and her tale presents us with what seems to be a happy resolution, only to turn back upon itself, calling our attention to the fact that this was simply a story:

> And thus they lyve unto hir lyves ende
> In parfit joye; and Jesu Crist us sende
> Housbondes meke, yonge, and fressh abedde,
> And grace t'overbyde hem that we wedde;
> And eek I praye Jesu shorte hir lyves
> That noght wol be governed by hir wyves;
> And olde and angry nygardes of dispence,
> God sende hem soone verray pestilence!
>
> 'WBT' 1257–64

The Wife moves seamlessly from the traditional happy ending to a statement of personal desire, which remains unfulfilled because of the realities of the society in which she lives. Instead of the Wife's un-realistic ideal, husbands who are 'meke, yonge, and fressh abedde', she acknowledges the more likely situation – partners who are 'olde and angry nygardes of dispence'. Moreover, the references to 'Jesu Crist' imbue the Wife's plea with a prayer-like quality, which confirms the sense of a fallen and imperfect world, belonging equally to Christian ideology and the romance genre.

In romance and courtly love we return to the same apparent duality as in the *querelle des femmes*. In each case an argument is constructed about two issues, one of which appears to be unreal in its idealism (Patient Griselda, the docile wife, the virtuous adherents of courtly love, *De Amore*, the courts of love, the happy ending, unchallenged authority), and the other of which seems to spring from a sense of materialism (the Wife, the shrew, the validated accounts of medieval society, *Roman de la Rose*, the recognition of human flaws and failings, nonconformist experience). These are sketchily drawn parallels, and laid out in this formal manner they already appear inadequate. Indeed, at the beginning of the Commentary, Christina Rossetti's sonnet alerted us to the dangers of perceiving the world as 'cloven', of creating stereotypes, rather than complex characters. It is a pitfall which, feminists acknowledge, Chaucer avoids; as Jill Mann writes:

> Chaucer could not plumb the unrecorded secrets of woman's existence, but he *could* anatomise the literary stereotypes which set the terms in which male–female relationships were played out, and he could question the male writer's role as the 'auctoritee' that supports them.

(Mann, 1991, p. 83)

The authorities who govern the production of male and female identities in the *querelle*, courtly love and romance initiated the simple dualities detailed above, which have been exhumed and unquestioningly brought back to life by twentieth-century criticism. The next stage, inevitably, as Mann suggests, is a questioning of how different these images of women really are. How different are the Wife of Bath and Patient Griselda? Can the stereotypes be sustained?

V

Hir body was schort and thik,
Hir buttokes bay and brode;
More lykkerwys on to lyk
Was that scho hade on lode.
(Gawain Poet, 1976, p. 195)

After centuries of treating the Wife of Bath and Patient Griselda as

138

antithetical images of women, from the medieval authorities discussed in Section IV to the twentieth-century critics outlined in Section III, is it now possible to reconcile the disparate pair? On the other hand, perhaps they were never truly apart. 'Auctoritee' might attempt to divide Alison and Griselda, but their narrative experiences, which as we have seen bear a close resemblance to real-life female existence at that time, bring them together. A number of similarities between the Wife and Griselda have already been mentioned in the Introduction and in Section II of this Commentary. For example, both women see the sexual consummation of marriage in economic terms ('WBP' 131–2 and 152–3, 'ClT' 883–6); both suffer abuse from their husbands ('WBP' 634–6, 'ClT' passim); both are astute managers of supposedly 'male' business ('GP' 447–8, 'ClT' 435–41); and both have experience of marriage at twelve years of age, the Wife personally, Griselda through her daughter ('WBP' 4–6, 'ClT' 736). However, the convergence of seemingly opposite female types is more pervasive than these basic echoes in plot suggest, and exists not only in Chaucer's poetry but in the works of his contemporaries.

The quotation at the beginning of this section is taken from *Sir Gawain and the Green Knight*, a late fourteenth-century alliterative poem written in the north-west of England; thus, although it is contemporary with Chaucer's work, the language appears very different from the London dialect of *The Canterbury Tales*. It describes two women: the short, fat hag, and the beautiful woman who is with her, the latter being 'sweeter to the taste'. In the story the two women will together trick Gawain into betraying his sense of honour, although the seriousness of this betrayal is a moot point, much discussed in the poem itself and by later critics. What I wish to focus on is how the lines above suggest a link between the two women, placing them in close conjunction and allowing the words suggesting unity – 'on lode' meaning 'with her' – to occur right at the end of the stanza, thereby giving them greatest weight and significance. The two are like reverse sides of the same coin, the fair and the foul; and together they may be described generically as a 'loathly lady'. The knight in the Wife's tale, which is also, through its sources, part of the Gawain canon, has a parallel experience; as he journeys on his quest he meets a mysterious hag, described as a 'fouler wight ther may no man devyse' ('WBT' 999). At the end of the tale, after she has saved and wedded him, the old woman transforms herself into a lovely young maiden, causing the knight's heart to be 'bathed in a bath of blisse' ('WBT' 1253). There is, of course, a significant difference between the texts, as the two women remain separate in *Gawain* and the hag exerts a malevolent control over the lady, whereas in the Wife's tale the hag is in control of her own identity and the two are clearly the same person. Chaucer might be authenticating the Wife's independent nature by giving her a tale about a self-determining woman, but the individual freedom and 'maistrye' of the loathly lady have an undeniable impact wherever the authorial/narratorial control lies at this point in the poem.

The influence of Chaucer's hag over the knight originated in the power attributed to the loathly lady in medieval romance. She governs her own lands, which are often depicted as a fairy world, and she dominates over the male characters in the tale. As such, the hag inverts the accepted social structures of property and gender relations. Thus at the centre of the conformist romance convention lies an opposite world which reverses orthodox ideas like the negative of a photograph, and it is here that women can lay claim to an independent subject position. Although this challenge to accepted value systems remains within the fictional and transient world of the romance, the fact that the Wife chooses to present her imaginative self in this way allows the text to challenge our traditional assumptions about female identity.

By conflating stereotypical views of women the character of the loathly lady obtains both control over her own signfication in the text, as well as the power to disrupt conventional views of women. The similarities which exist between Patient Griselda and the Wife of Bath perform a similar function: rather than epitomising two oppositional female roles, they demonstrate that the differences are artificial constructs, developed by a society which suppresses female individuality. Their similar experiences, which most medieval women would have recognised, have been listed above, but there is a more unusual narrative resemblance – they both faint. When the Wife's argument with Jankyn over his book becomes physically abusive, he strikes her:

> And with his fest he smoot me on the heed,
> That in the floor I lay as I were deed.
> And whan he say how stille that I lay,
> He was agast, and wolde have fled his way,
> Til atte laste out of my swowgh I brayde.
>
> 'WBP' 795–9

It is Jankyn's fear that he has killed his wife that proves to be the turning point in their relationship, and it is from the moment of her 'swowgh' that Alison gains mastery over him. Similarly, in 'The Clerk's Tale' Walter's final revelation to Griselda that she remains his wife and that her children are alive before her, provokes the faint:

> Whan she this herde, aswowne doun she falleth
> For pitous joye.
>
> 'ClT' 1079–80

Once again it is the faint that proves to be the fulcrum of the tale, as from this point on she is able to assume fully her role as Walter's wife and lady of the manor.

The motif of a woman fainting is common to romance tales, as well as to literary representations as a whole; it is easy to recall pulp fiction stories where the heroine slumps unconscious into the strong arms of the hero. Usually, then, a woman fainting suggests feminine weakness and provokes sustenance from the dominant male persona of the text. This significance is certainly encoded in both Chaucerian tales: where the Wife plays upon Jankyn's sympathy – 'Er I be deed, yet wol I kisse thee' (802); and where the author clearly encourages our pity for Griselda:

> O which a pitous thyng it was to se
> Hir swownyng, and hir humble voys to heere!
>
> 'ClT' 1086–7

But there are disconcerting aspects to the 'swownyng' of both women. The Wife, while apparently unconscious, notes her husband's actions well enough to recount them to the Canterbury pilgrims later on, and it is perhaps not insignificant that she recovers at the very point at which Jankyn is about to leave. It is quite fitting that the dominant and self-assertive Wife should be able to manipulate her 'swowgh' in such a fashion, but the meek and pliant Griselda also exhibits independent desires while insensible. The confusing composite of Griselda's swooning and vocalised grief (she faints and recovers at least twice in thirty lines) leads to the anomalous authorial comment quoted above, where it appears as if the lady faints and speaks at the same time. Moreover, during her second swoon she holds on to her children so tightly,

> That with greet sleghte and greet difficultee
> The children from hir arm they gonne arace.
>
> 'ClT' 1102–3

Neither the Wife nor Griselda vacate the narrative completely when they faint; they combine a powerful and verbal presence in the text, with the image of insensible weakness and silence. The combination proves successful, for it is from these moments of what appears to be repression that the Wife will gain what all women want ('maistrey' in marriage), and Griselda will cease to suffer Walter's sadistic tests on her loyalty. But why should 'swownyng' have such a powerful impact?

Let us return briefly to the historical experience of women, the contemporary cultural environment, and one of the central themes of *The Canterbury Tales*, all of which reveal a society and texts that encourage men's domination of women. In the two tales examined here, the Wife engages in a perpetual battle as to which sex should have control in wedlock, but is herself the subject of male authorial irony in the prologue, while there can be no question about Griselda's total subservience to her husband, Walter. Women are presented as the excluded opposites of masculine identity; they are what men are not, whether shrew-like in their claims to equal power, or meek and obedient when conforming to their prescribed roles. By encoding and personifying this 'otherness', women can remind men of what constitutes male subjectivity; Griselda reveals Walter as puissant and implacable by embodying the opposite qualities of humility and tractableness. He rules, she is ruled. Both are part of the same creation of gender identity. Yet this leads to a paradoxical situation in which men and women are seen to be similar, but in which, since society has clearly benefited them, men wish to sustain a clear division between the sexes. Thus, in order to perpetuate this hierarchy, it becomes necessary to spurn women and to marginalise them. In the tales this results in Walter denying his marriage, and in Jankyn's blow, which acts as a gesture representative of the cumulative attempts by the Wife's husbands to suppress her. The dominant masculine ideology is cornered into a position of instability through the Wife's insuppressible personality and Griselda's Christ-like patience, so that Walter and Jankyn must resort to drastic measures. But Griselda can stand no more and the Wife is knocked unconscious; the male characters, in an effort to assert their supremacy, have spurned and excluded the central female personae to such an extent that the women are forced to vacate the narrative action of the text. When this happens, Walter and Jankyn cease to have any significance: the Marquis becomes silent and his children replace him as the focal point of Griselda's attention, his people's destiny and the authorial interest; and the clerk decides to absent himself from the text, as the only possible solution to his actions – 'He was agast, and wolde have fled his way'. Through the very act of asserting absolute 'auctoritee' over their wives, the male characters, and the dominant ideology which they encode, are shown to be meaningless without female co-operation. These two Chaucerian tales are constructed in narrative, character and ideological terms in order for the reader to become aware that an independent female presence is as necessary to the continuing stability of society as to the literary text.

VI

And every wight that I saugh there
Rouned everych in others ere
A newe tydynge prively,
Or elles tolde al openly
. . . Thus north and south
Wente every tydyng fro mouth to mouth,
And that encresing ever moo,
As fyr ys wont to quyke and goo
From a sparke spronge amys,
Til al a citee brent up ys.
The House of Fame 2043–6 and 2075–80

The faint motif functions on different levels: as we have seen, by vacating the narrative, the female characters prove their indispensability to the continuation of the tale, yet this gendered reading allows us to perceive further interconnecting interpretations. For example, the 'swowgh' also deprives women of language, a point which is high-lighted by the narratorial confusion about speech and silence during Griselda's faint. Inevitably, the absence of language brings about the conclusion of the text; it is, thus, in the author's self-interest to license these alternative voices. Both language and gender significations bring us back, however, to the central themes of 'The Wife of Bath's Tale', the Marriage Group, and, perhaps, of *The Canterbury Tales* itself, that is, 'soveraynetee' ('WBP' 818).

The exercise of power is a potent force in both tales. The Wife wishes for absolute control in her marriages, in her language and in the tale she tells. In her quest for mastery she resorts to physical violence, she

143

subsumes the language of her husbands by deftly reinterpreting their words, she reworks – to her own advantage – established literary, theological and philosophical texts, and, as the focus of her tale she chooses women's desire for dominance over their husbands. Similarly, 'The Clerk's Tale' is introduced by the Host imposing his rule over the content and style of the Clerk's contribution to the company's story telling. In the tale itself there is an interplay between how far Walter must obey his tenants and how far he may proceed in reasserting his feudal authority over them. In the same way that the gendered social structure is subverted by female silence, so the feudal hierarchy is challenged by the voices of the peasants, indeed, the Clerk makes a direct allusion to the Peasants' Revolt ('ClT' 995). Nevertheless, it is Griselda's unquestioning acceptance of Walter's mastery which constitutes the central allegory, and which conclusively foregrounds the theme of control. By highlighting the mutual significance of power, of gender and of social control, in these two tales, Chaucer simultaneously tempts the reader to locate the source of authorial control as well. Who controls the text? Who produces its meanings?

All stories must have a storyteller. Often there appears to be a single voice speaking throughout the text and we usually identify this as the 'authorial voice'. In *The Canterbury Tales*, however, there is such a rich mixture of voices that it becomes impossible to pinpoint any single fixed speaker. The whole poem is about tale-telling and most of the pilgrims have characteristics which coincide with the way in which their tale is told. The Wife is a graphic example of the perfect harmony between teller and tale. Chaucer even places himself amongst the group and causes his tale, 'Sir Thopas', to be interrupted because it is too boring. The pilgrims' voices appear to have individualised and legitimate claims to the text. However, Chaucer's authorial voice breaks through the bounds of his poetic second-self and of the other characters, to invade every tale and every teller. In the Wife's prologue it is impossible to determine whether her retelling of antifeminist lessons shows she is in control of her discourse, or whether Chaucer is mocking her, and women like her, by giving her speeches in which she damns herself. At the end of 'The Clerk's Tale' the authorial voice intervenes more openly with 'L'envoy de Chaucer' (1177–212), a song which is equally ironic. The short poem appears to disapprove of clerks for upholding Griselda's 'pacient and kinde' virtues, but actually ridicules and condemns the 'archewyves' for making their husbands 'wepe, and wrynge, and wayle!'. The presence of irony in a Chaucerian text often alerts us to the incursions of the authorial voice, but the method's double nature (saying one thing, but meaning another) necessitates a contemporaneous description of another's viewpoint. In practice, therefore, Chaucer's authorial intrusions open the text up to a multiplicity of voices, rather than dominating the text with a single dictatorial tone.

Of all the pilgrims' voices, the Wife's is the most cogent and lively. The control of language is of great importance to her, and she dominates the formal elements in the tale – such as its rhetoric – as well as the thematic and symbolic contents. Her elevation of experience over authority has implications for our own reading of the text, since we experience the story through an almost sexual process of arousal, postponement and fulfilment. Within this assertion of female sexuality and the superior quality of physical experience, numerous voices explode. The Wife, on her part ironically, cites many male authorities; she reworks the words of other storytellers; she is the wifely gossip telling us her husbands' secrets; she is the astute hag of her tale; and, finally, she is the moral voice preaching the worth of virtue and humility. In conjunction with the Wife's many voices run the reported speech of her husbands and the male authors whom she cites. Moreover, as we have noted, the irony present in her prologue also posits an authorial voice beyond her own, comically exaggerating her image so that she appears like a parody of herself.

The Clerk's tale has a more unified, if less emphatic, voice. The narrator's humble self-awareness allows the host to berate him for his silence, and in his tale he abdicates responsibility for the narrative by attributing it all to Petrarch. While the Wife asserts her individual voice, the Clerk negates his into the equalising tone of Christian allegory. Within the tale itself, Griselda echoes his silence; Walter dominates the text verbally until her final rebellion when she dramatically defends herself for eleven stanzas in comparison with the Marquis's two-line response ('ClT' Griselda: 814–89 and Walter: 890–1). Ultimately this imbalance is unsettling; it allows for a criticism of both Christian doctrine, and of an unquestioning acceptance of the Church's authority. When Griselda finds her voice, she undermines the accepted notions of gender, feudal and religious power structures. Two hundred lines later her 'swowgh' cuts away at more of the traditional fabric of medieval society, but the final threat of chaos, when 'al a citee brent up ys', occurs at the very end of the tale.

The quotation at the beginning of this section is taken from Chaucer's unfinished poem *The House of Fame*; it depicts the people of the house whispering continuously to one another and spreading reports, both true and false, around the world. The individual voices have the ability to become so numerous, so powerful in collusion, that they may cause the conflagration and destruction of that symbol of social order, the city. The political allegory is not difficult to see, especially in a period which had just witnessed the burning of the Savoy Palace in London by a mob with just such a multitude of angry voices. It is doubly interesting then, that the tale which foregrounds noble/peasant relationships should end with almost a babble of differing voices. If the Wife finds it difficult to begin her tale, then the Clerk finds it wellnigh impossible to end his. The conclusion of 'The Clerk's Tale' is perpetuated beyond the formal closure of the narrative: after being told that the children of Walter and Griselda succeed them (1135–41), the Clerk draws our attention to the Christian moral of the tale, that everyone should be 'constant in adversitee' (1146). Although Petrarch's original concludes at this point, the Clerk's tale continues with a series of further endings: another amplification of the moral (1149–62); a direct parallel between Griselda and contemporary women (1163–9); an ironic address to the Wife (1170–6); the antifeminist song 'L'envoy de Chaucer' (1177–212); and finally, the Host's laconic comment that if you can't have what you want then it is better to 'lat it be stille'. More like a stand-up comedian than a shy cleric, the Clerk offers us a confusing and, seemingly, never-ending series of conclusions. Surely it must be authorial irony that makes the character preface this morass with, 'But O word lordynges, herkneth er I go'. It is impossible to determine any precedence amongst the opinions outlined or between the voices which pronounce them. In such a situation, when value-systems break down and no social order exists, the threat of change, of rebellion, and of the burning of cities is palpable. The relationships between gender and social and linguistic order were, and are, so basic and tightly-knit that should chaos develop in one area, then each organ of the state would be similarly infected.

This Critical Commentary began with a view of the world as 'cloven', illustrated by Christina Rossetti's sonnet. Afterwards, I traced the ways in which the two tales examined here, their narrators, their central female characters, and their real-life medieval counterparts, have all been similarly divided. Authorities, from the *querelle* to the twentieth-century criticisms, have had an investment in retaining that division; as

146

was shown through the simple process of deconstructing the fainting motif, clear identities and neat sets of dualities are easier to understand, and, more importantly, easier to control, than the complex alternatives. Chaucer never allows his writing to slip into such simplistic patterns, and nor do a number of other authors whose work we have glanced at briefly in this book, Andreas Capellanus and the Gawain Poet, for example. Instead of trying to force the Wife of Bath and Patient Griselda into oppositional stereotypes, we must accept that both portray valid feminine experiences of the medieval world. They are not antithetical, not even 'cloven' – they are complementary. It is important to remember that, while 'The Wife of Bath's Prologue' initiates us into the, still containable, challenge of multiple voices, it is the conclusion to the, supposedly conformist, Clerk's tale which spells out the possible dangers of autonomous language. But Chaucer was no revolutionary; historically, his sympathies would have been with the noble Gaunt faction, and not with the rebellious peasants. Nor does he condone the myriad tidings in *The House of Fame*. But Chaucer does allow the echoes of other voices to reverberate about his works: the strident Wife, the meek Griselda, the populace of Saluces, the bawdy Miller, the noble Troilus, the feminist Alceste. For although he had no wish for his literary edifice to be undermined, Chaucer realised that, like the house of fame, his poems were built with words, and that to deny language was to demolish the very foundations of his art.

Notes

1   *auctoritee*: written statement of authority. Although Chaucer here echoes *RR* where La Vielle explains that love may only be learned through experience, he endows male characters with similar sentiments – 'KnT' I.3000–1, 'FrT' III.1517 and 'SumT' III.2057.

4   Twelve was the legal age of marriage in canon law. Griselda's daughter in 'ClT' is betrothed at the same age (736).

6   In the fourteenth century weddings were commonly performed in the porch of the church; only wealthy people were married inside the building.

7   *If I so ofte*: Jerome questions whether any husband after the first is legitimate (*Ep.adv.Jov.* 1.14), and the Wife follows his text closely in lines 9–24. However, the remarriage of widows was actively encouraged in the secular world, where property was seen to be more secure under male ownership. Jerome's text was a well-known refutation of Jovinian's argument in favour of marriage and as such it is included in the series of misogynist tracts which make up Jankyn's 'book of wikked wyves' (685).

9–24   The Wife's argument is taken from Jerome *Ep.ad.Jov.* 1.14, for example: 'the Samaritan woman in John's Gospel who said that she had her sixth husband was reproved by the Lord because he was not her husband. For where there are more husbands than one the proper idea of a husband, who is a single person, is destroyed. At the beginning one rib was turned into one wife. "And they two," he says, "shall be one flesh". Not three, or four; otherwise, how can they be any longer two, if they are several?' (Jerome, 1977, p. 424–5).

10–11   *Cane*: the town of Cana from John ii.1–11. and Jerome *Ep.ad.Jov.* 1.40.

12–13   The example is taken from Jerome *Ep.ad.Jov.* 1.40. where it is advocated that women should only marry once.

15–16   John iv.3–26. This refers to the story of Jesus and the Samaritan woman where he appears to condemn women who marry more than five times: 'The woman answered and said, I have no husband. Jesus said unto her, Thou hast well said, I have no husband: / For thou hast had five husbands; and he whom thou now hast is not thy husband.' The Wife clearly questions this statement.

20   A feigned innocence, but a common rhetorical device rather than a character trait.

23   Jerome *Ep.ad.Jov.* 1.15, where Jerome is discussing how many marriages a woman may make: 'if, after baptism and after the death of a first husband, a second is taken, why should not a sixth after the death of the second, third, fourth, fifth, and so on?' (Jerome, 1977, p. 425).

25   *Upon this nombre diffynycioun*: a precise statement of the number.

26   *dyvyne and glosen*: a detailed interpretation of the scriptures.

26–8   Genesis i.28: 'and God said unto them, Be fruitful, and multiply, and replenish the earth'. However, Chaucer is also using Jerome *Ep.ad.Jov.* 1.3 who quotes 1 Cor. vii.29, as does the Wife at 31.

30–1   *he*: Christ. Matt. xix.5: in a reply to the Pharisees Jesus commented, 'For this cause shall a man leave father and mother, and shall cleave to his wife'. This incident is also cited in Jerome *Ep.ad.Jov.* 1.5.

33   *bigamye*: marrying twice; *octogamye*: marrying eight times. The latter word comes specifically from Jerome *Ep.ad.Jov.* 1.15.

35–6   *Lo, here*: a colloquial phrase meaning 'look, listen' and implying 'consider'. Solomon had seven hundred wives and three hundred concubines (1 Kings xi.3). See also 'MerT' IV. 2242.

43   *so wel was hym on lyve*: such a good life was enjoyed by him.

44   At this point six lines are found in some manuscripts (I have used MS Camb Dd. 4. 24 at Cambridge University Library, which is the best source for this excerpt); they are almost certainly a later addition, but run as follows:

> Of whiche I have pyked out the beste,   44a
> Bothe of here nether purs and of here cheste.
> Diverse scoles maken parfyt clerkes,
> And diverse practyk in many sondry werkes
> Maketh the werkmen parfyt sekirly;
> Of fyve husbondes scoleiyng am I   44f

45   *whan that evere he shal*: whenever he shall come.

46   *sith*: 'because'; *Ell* has 'sothe' which means 'truly'. *chaast*: the Wife means chaste widowhood, that is a widow who does not remarry. 1 Cor. vii.9 and Jerome *Ep.ad.Jov*. 1.9.

47   1 Cor. vii.39.: 'The wife is bound by the law as long as her husband liveth; but if her husband be dead, she is at liberty to be married to whom she will; only in the Lord'. See also Jerome *Ep.ad.Jov*. 1.14.

49   *th'apostle*: St Paul, as always in the Wife's prologue. 1 Cor. vii.9 and 39.

50   *a Goddes half*: in God's name.

52   1 Cor. vii.28.: 'But and if thou marry, thou hast not sinned; and if a virgin marry, she hath not sinned. Nevertheless such shall have trouble in the flesh: but I spare you'. This idea, however, that it is better to have sexual intercourse within marriage than to burn in hell for the sins of lust and fornication, was a commonplace.

54–6   In the Bible Lameth was the first man to have two wives (bigamy), see Genesis iv.19–24 and 'SqT' v. 550–1. For Abraham having three wives and Jacob four see Jerome *Ep.ad.Jov*. 1.14.

56   *Ell* has 'fer forth as'.

59   *in any maner age*: at any time in history.

64–5   *Th'apostel*: St Paul. 1 Cor. vii.6 and 25. See also Jerome *Ep.ad.Jov*. 1.12. Both texts make it clear that there is no absolute command from God to remain a virgin.

67   A common idea – 'to advise someone isn't the same as

ordering them' – which the Wife uses to undermine the concept of virginity.

71–2   The Wife takes this idea from Jerome *Ep.ad.Jov*. 1.12: 'If the Lord had commanded virginity He would have seemed to condemn marriage, and to do away with the seed-plot of mankind, of which virginity itself is a growth. If He had cut off the root, how was He to expect fruit?' (Jerome, 1977, p. 421). However, Jerome is actually citing the argument of his opponent, Jovinium and turns immediately to a strident defence of virginity. As usual the Wife uses only those passages which agree with her argument.

73   *Poul*: St Paul.

75   Jerome *Ep.ad.Jov*. 1.12. where the dart would be offered as a prize to those who did not marry. See also 1 Cor. ix.24.

81   1 Cor. vii.7.: 'For I would that all men were even as myself', where St Paul refers to his virginity. See also Jerome *Ep.ad.Jov*. 1.8.

84   *nys . . . no*: a double negative was used for emphasis in Middle English. Paul was lenient to people who found unmarried life difficult; see 1 Cor. vii.6.

87   In 1 Cor. vii.1.: 'It is good for a man not to touch a woman'. See also Jerome *Ep.ad.Jov*. 1.7.

89   A piece of folk wisdom: it is dangerous to bring fire and flax (an inflammable substance) together.

91   Jerome *Ep.ad.Jov*. 2.22.

96   *bigamye*: here meaning marriage by or with a widow/er.

99–101 Jerome *Ep.ad.Jov*. 1.40 which echoes 2 Tim. ii.20.: 'But in a great house there are not only vessels of gold and of silver, but also of wood and of earth; and some to honour, and some to dishonour'.

103   1 Cor. vii.7: 'But every man hath his proper gift of God, one after this manner, and another after that'. See also Jerome *Ep.ad.Jov*. 1.8.

107–12 This originates in Matt. xix.21 where Jesus is advising a young man how to gain eternal life: 'If thou wilt be perfect, go and sell that thou hast, and give it to the poor, and thou shalt have treasure in heaven'. However, the Wife follows False Seeming's manipulation of this idea in *RR* 11375–9:

> Remember, when Christ told the rich young man
> To sell his goods, give alms, and follow Him,
> He meant not that he should in His service live
> By beggary. That was not His intent.
> Rather that he should labor with his hands
> He meant, and follow Jesus in good works.
>
> (de Lorris and de Meun, 1962, pp. 234–5)

See also Jerome *Ep.ad.Jov.* 1.34 and 2.6. Both major source texts for the Wife's prologue.

113   *the flour of al myn age*: the best part of my life.

114   *fruyt*: this should refer to children, but in the Wife's speech it suggests sexual pleasure.

115–23   Jerome *Ep.ad.Jov.* 1.36. and *RR* 4401–24. The Wife takes the question from Jerome, 'Why then, you will say, were the organs of generation created, and why were we so fashioned by the all-wise creator, that we burn for one another, and long for natural intercourse?' (Jerome, 1977, p. 429). However, she turns to the romance text for the answer which suits her purpose: in *RR* Reason tells the Lover that sexual intercourse has been made pleasurable in order 'to procreate / The tenement for an immortal soul' (de Lorris and de Meun, 1962, p. 97).

117   *And of . . . ywroght*: and made by so perfectly wise a being. The major MS variant occurs in *Ell* which has 'And for what profit was'; this was used in Robinson's edition. The *Hg* is preferable, the confusion probably arising from the abbreviations 'par' and 'pro'.

129–32   1 Cor. vii.3: 'Let the husband render unto the wife due benevolence: and likewise also the wife unto the husband'. However, the Wife perceives sexual intercourse in marriage as part of an explicitly economic contract, a conjugal 'dette'; she repeats this legal emphasis at 152–7 and 197–202. Although this interpretation of sexual relations is apt for the Wife's character, it is equally as important to remember that marriage, intercourse and the possibility of heirs were issues of property and inheritance rather than of love. Sex within marriage was essential and both Church and state upheld both partners' rights to this 'dette', so that marriages could

	be, and were, annulled on failure to make 'paiement'. See also 'ClT' 883–6 where Griselda makes a similar assumption.
132	*sely instrument*: sexual organ; although the Wife's use of 'sely' (happy/innocent) suggests a somewhat patronising description of the penis.
135–41	The Wife draws generally from Jerome's discussion of virginity in *Ep.ad.Jov*. 1.36.
144–5	*barly breed*: an inexpensive kind of bread. Not from Mark, but John vi.9.; this is one of the Wife's several 'errors' most of which are designed to reinforce her own opinions at the expense of textual authorities. Jerome compares white and 'barly' bread to chastity and incontinence (*Ep.ad.Jov*. 1.7). It is interesting to note that the Wife compares herself to something which may be commodified and consumed.
146	*refresshed*: suggesting sexual enjoyment.
147	1 Cor. vii.20: 'Let every man abide in the same calling wherein he was called'. See also: Jerome *Ep.ad.Jov*. 1.11.
152–7	See note to 129–32.
154–60	One of the Wife's 'errors'; she rewrites Paul (1 Cor. vii.4) in order to suggest that women will be the tribulation of their husbands, rather than be completely subordinate to them.
156	*tribulacion*: 1 Cor. 7.28, which refers again to the idea that the body will have 'trouble' in marriage (see note to 52).
158	1 Cor. vii.4: 'The wife hath not power of her own body, but the husband: and likewise also the husband hath not power of his own body, but the wife'. See also: Jerome *Ep.ad.Jov*. 1.13 and 16. However, the Wife ignores the first part of the Biblical verse which offers the unwelcome rule that a wife's body belongs to her husband.
161	Eph. v.25: 'Husbands, love your wives, even as Christ also loved the church, and gave himself for it'. The Wife again (see note to 158) leaves out the parallel statement which notes that wives should also love their husbands: 'Therefore as the church is subject unto Christ, so let the wives be to their own husbands in every thing' (Eph. v.24).
163–8	The system of pardons was open to a good deal of abuse. Pardoners were usually clerical officers empowered to give pardons for sins which were truly repented, on payment of a

certain sum of money, and they were able to marry as they were only in lesser orders.

170   The goddess Fortune was supposed to have two barrels of wine, one sweet and the other bitter, from which she served everyone. The Wife could be suggesting that the Pardoner must drink from the bitter barrel. The original source is *Iliad* 24.527. Chaucer, however, could have obtained the idea from a number of sources including *RR* 6813–54 or Gower *CA* 6.330–48 and 8.2253–58. See also 'ParsT' X.859. The note to 199 offers another explanation.

177   *abroche*: to open a cask, to broach.

180–1   *Whoso . . . be*: whoever will not be warned by the example of other men, will himself become an example used to correct others. The Wife cites Ptolomy's *Almageste* as her source, but the lines actually derive from a twelfth-century collection of apophthegms attributed to Ptolomy. The quotation in 326–7 is similarly misattributed.

182   Ptolomy was a Greek mathematician and astronomer.

183   *Almageste*: a treatise on astronomy.

184   *Dame*: the title given to aldermen's wives or widows, denoting social status. See 'GP' I. 378.

190   *fantasye*: fancy or desire, but also a reference to the faculty of the imagination which calls attention to the Wife's role as author of her text.

193   *sire*: which suggests that the Wife is addressing the Pardoner alone. Some MSS have 'sires' which would mean that she refers to the whole company.

198   *statut*: the conjugal debt referred to at 129–30. The Wife again uses the legal discourse to invoke the idea of an economic contract. As a source for 198–202 see *M.de Mar.* 1576–84; this is another of the main antifeminist texts used by the Wife in her prologue; see the Introduction.

199   The Latin gloss in *Ell* has a reference to the idea that priests in Athens drank hemlock in order to emasculate themselves (Jerome *Ep.ad.Jov.* 1.49), which might refer back to the bitter 'tonne' which the effeminate Pardoner is threatened with at 170.

207–10   From La Vielle's speech in *RR* 13269–72.

Most haughty she should be to those who try

The most to gain her love by serving her.
The ones who of her living set least store
Are those she must work hardest to attract.

(de Lorris and de Meun, 1962, p. 277)

213–16   *M.de Mar.* 1576–84, where Deschamps writes that women demand material payment before they are prepared to succumb to their husbands' desires.

215   *Ell* has 'hem so a werke', which is probably the more accurate since it gives the line five stresses.

217–18   At Dunmow near Chelmsford in Essex a side of bacon was awarded to those couples who had not argued for a year and a day.

224–378   The following section directly refutes the advice given to women in fourteenth-century books of instruction such as *The Goodman of Paris* and *The Book of the Knight of La Tour-Landry*; see the Introduction, p. 12.

225   *wise wyves*: the only women in the narrative audience are the Second Nun and the Prioress, which assumes that the Wife's advice is addressed to Chaucer's audience outside of the text.

227–8   Almost an exact translation from *RR* 18136–7 where Nature comments of women that 'More boldly will they lie and falsely swear / Than any man' (de Lorris and de Meun, 1962, p. 385).

231   *if that she kan hir good*: if she knows what's good for her.

232   *bere . . . wood*: deceive him by swearing. The line refers to the story of the talking chough bird which tells a husband about his wife's adultery. She, however, with the aid of their maidservant persuades him that the bird is mad.

235–47   This stereotypical picture of a shrewish wife originated with Theophrastus's *The Golden Book on Marriage* which was preserved only in Jerome *Ep.ad.Jov.* 1.47, and was repeated in *M.de Mar.* 1589–611. The Wife's description draws upon both sources.

246   An earlier version of the proverb was 'as drunk as a drowned mouse' which clarifies the Wife's seemingly nonsensical comparison.

248–75   The passage recurs in three antifeminist texts used by the Wife, *M.de Mar.* 1625–48, Jerome *Ep.ad.Jov.* 1.47. and *RR*

8579–600. The texts explain *how* men woo women, but the Wife subtly turns this into *why* men woo women. This provides another example of how she rewrites male-authored textual authorities.

252   *malencolye*: anger, which was due under the theory of humours to an excess of black bile.

253–6   *RR* 8587–92 where the Friend discusses how a jealous husband may verbally abuse his wife:

> If she be fair, all men will her besiege,
> Flatter, pursue, attack, torment, engage –
> Make battle for her, study to assist,
> Flock round her making prayers, her favor seek,
> So covetous of her that in the end
> They'll manage so that it small wonder were
> If her defenses, thus beset, should fall.
>
>   (de Lorris and de Meun, 1962, p. 174)

258   *shape*: figure, but also the genitals of either sex.

262   *by thy tale*: according to what you say.

263–4   *RR* 8595–6, where it is suggested that a woman who is besieged on all sides cannot help but be overcome.

265   *RR* 8597–8600, where the Friend recounts the words of a jealous husband speaking ill of his wife:

> If she be foul, she'll try to please them all;
> And how can one do this and yet be safe?
> She guards a jewel all are fighting for –
> Which every man desires who glimpses it.
>
>   (de Lorris and de Meun, 1962, p. 174)

268   *chepe*: do business with; a commercial manner of talking about sex, see also 521.

271–2   *Ell* has 'welde' rather than 'wolde', which seems more appropriate since it means 'control' rather than 'wish'; this would reinforce the Wife's argument about the control of women by men. See also Jerome *Ep.ad.Jov.* 1.47.

282–92   Jerome *Ep.ad.Jov.* 1.47 and *RR* 8667–82 and *M.de Mar.* 1538–59 and 1570–5. Each text carries the same message, that women will hide their faults until they are married and then

157

show them freely. The Wife predictably resents such insinuations.

291   *shrewe*: a scoundrel of ambiguous gender; however, 'shrew' is an apt term for the Wife herself. Possibly Chaucer's authorial irony at the expense of the Wife.

293–302   The Wife draws upon Theophrastus's misogynist text, *The Golden Book on Marriage*, in Jerome *Ep.ad.Jov.* 1.47: 'Our gaze must always be directed to her face, and we must always praise her beauty: if you look at another woman, she thinks that she is out of favor. She must be called my lady, her birthday must be kept, we must swear by her health and wish that she may survive us, respect must be paid to the nurse, to the nursemaid, to the father's slave . . .' (Jerome, 1977, p. 412).

302   There is a pun on lies (untruths) and lees (dregs).

303   Jankyn was a common name in Middle English literature for rustic lovers or clerks. *Ell* has 'Janekyn' which is probably more accurate since the metre demands a trisyllabic form; this is also the case at 383 and 595.

306   *Hg* has 'caught fals'; I have used *Ell*.

311   *oure dame*: the Wife refers to herself in the personal colloquial form.

312   *Seint Jame*: St James; the Wife has been on a pilgrimage to the shrine of St James at Compostela in Spain; see 'GP' 466.

316   *Hg* has 'and spyen'; I have used *Ell*.

324–7   See notes to 180–3. Once again the text is misattributed Ptolomy.

326–7   *Of . . . honde*: he who is happiest is not envious of others, who have the world in their control.

332   *queynte*: pleasant thing, but also the Wife's pudendum and/or sexual intercourse. Her direct use of the word would have been shocking to her fellow pilgrims.

333–4   This commonplace image has sexual overtones and suggests that a husband should not resent his wife's ability to inflame and satisfy other men's desires, since she will also continue having intercourse with him. A more precise source may be *RR* 7410–14.

337–9   *M.de Mar.* 1878–84. The whole debate of women's love of rich clothes moves beyond moral and religious condemnation; in the secular world dress was an important signifier of

	class and status. The sumptuary laws passed to regulate women's dress acted to contain both their sexuality and their economic independence (337–61).
348–54	The parallel drawn between cats and women originates from *M.de Mar.* 3208–15.
357–60	*RR* 14381–4 and 19393–4. Jove set Argos (his hundred-eyed son) to watch over his mistress Io, whom he had turned into a cow. The Wife suggests that even Argos could not watch over her successfully.
361	*I make his berd*: a proverb meaning 'to delude him'. *as mote I thee*: as I may prosper.
362	*things three*: the wastelands, fire and parasites of 371–8; the *ferthe* (364) might imply woman and her suggested perfidy.
373	Called 'Greek fire', this was a preparation used in naval battles because it could not be doused with water.
376	See Jerome *Ep.ad.Jov.* 1.28: 'Like a worm in wood, so a wicked woman destroyeth her husband' (Jerome, 1977, p. 427).
378	See Jerome *Ep.ad.Jov.* 1.28: 'For no one can know better than he who suffered through them, what a wife or woman is' (Jerome, 1977, p. 427).
383	*Ell* uses the trisyllabic form, 'Janekyn'; see 303 and 595.
387–92	*M.de Mar.* 3600–8, 3620–2 and 3629–32, where Deschamps describes how wives torment their husbands and how they always make the first complaint when they are in the wrong.
389	A proverb: first come, first served.
395	*I*: the Wife implies that it is she who pleases her husband; *Ell* has 'it' which suggests that her husband's heart is 'tikled' by his own belief that she loves him.
407–10	*RR* 9091–6, where the Jealous Husband describes how women mistreat men:

> And then at night, when naked in my bed
> You lie beside me, you must not be touched;
> For when I want to take you in my arms,
> A kiss or other solace to procure,
> You cool my heat with looks as black as hell,
> And spite of all my efforts turn your back.
>
> (de Lorris and de Meun, 1962, p. 184)

412	*nycetee*: satisfy his desire or lust, but since 'nycetee' also

means foolish and stupid in Middle English, we may assume that the Wife is mocking her old husbands' sexual prowess here.

414   One of the most commonly quoted lines used to illustrate the Wife's love of money – she even offers her sexual favours in exchange for financial gain. However, marriage was a profitable business in the medieval period through the acquisition of custodies over marriageable heirs; indeed, Chaucer made money in just this manner. See also 447 and 478.

415   Falconry was a popular sport in the medieval period, and in order to train hawks to return to their owner after catching the prey, a lure of dead meat was held in the gloved hand of the trainer.

418   *bacoun*: either old men, as in meat that has been preserved rather than fresh, or a happy marriage as in the story of Dunmow (218).

432   *Wilkyn, oure sheepe*: 'Wilkyn' is the diminutive of William, the name of the Wife's husband, while 'oure' suggests colloquial familiarity. The Wife uses both terms patronisingly rather than affectionately.

436   Still a proverb, 'the patience of Job'.

446   *Peter*: St Peter.

447   *bele chose*: beautiful thing, but really the Wife's euphemism for her pudendum.

457   *Ell* has 'Wel koude' which suggests the Wife's passionate nature, but *Hg*'s *How koude* aligns more with her skill in dramatic verbal play.

460   Val. 6.3. See also 642 and 647 which use the same text. Metellius killed his wife by hitting her with a staff because she had drunk some wine.

464   Ovid *Ars* 1.229–44, where Ovid suggests that drinking wine inclines men and women towards sex; for example: 'At such time often have women bewitched the minds of men, and Venus in the wine has been fire in fire' (Ovid, 1947, pp. 28–9).

466   The Wife suggests that those who like drinking to excess also enjoy a large sexual appetite. Although this connection became a commonplace in the description of debauchery, this is its first known use in English.

467–8   *RR* 13452–53, but the idea that a woman who is drunk will easily be persuaded to have sexual intercourse is a familiar enough notion even today.

469–73   *RR* 12932–48, where La Vieille tells the story of her life:

> . . . I now rejoice;
> When musing on the past that is no more,
> I am delighted with my thoughts; my limbs
> New vigor feel when good times I recall,
> And all the jolly life that pleased my heart.
> Rejuvenated all my body seems
> When recollections come into my mind.
> When I remember every little fact,
> It does me all the good in the world. At least
> I had my fun . . .
>
> (de Lorris and de Meun, 1962, p. 268)

483   *Seint Joce*: St Judocus/Josse, a seventh-century Breton saint.

484   A common idea, to pay back someone in their own kind, in this case by making him jealous. *Hg* has 'troce'; I have used *Ell*'s 'croce'.

485   *nat of my body*: the Wife asserts that, despite her love of male company, she has not committed adultery.

487   A common saying which has today changed slightly to become: 'to stew in his own juice'.

489–90   The Wife refers to the common idea that being married is like the state of purgatory, so that when her husband dies he can go straight to heaven. It was believed that all souls had to pass through purgatory before they could attain bliss.

492   A common expression meaning that if you are constrained by a situation which doesn't suit you (an ill-fitting shoe) then you will be unhappy (have a pinched foot), however, also see Jerome *Ep.ad.Jov*. 1.48. for placing this proverb in the context of marriage.

495   On the Wife's pilgrimage to Jerusalem see 'GP' I. 463.

496   *roode beem*: the beam between the chancel and nave of the church. Burial here signified a prosperous and important social position.

498–9   Appelles was a craftsman who was supposed to have made a

161

fine and rich tomb for Darius. It is recorded in Philippe Gualtier de Chatillon's *Alexandreid* (c.1200).

503–14   Recalls La Vieille's speech in *RR* 14472–546 where she also recounts how she fell in love with the one man who treated her badly: 'Beaten and dragged me, scratched and blackened my face, / And called me shameful names' (de Lorris and de Meun, 1962, p. 302).

516–24   A common idea that something which is easily obtained ceases to have any value. See also *RR* 13697–708.

521   Grudgingly we spread out all our merchandise. Here and in the following line the Wife uses commercial imagery. See also 268.

534   The idea that women cannot keep secrets is part of a stereotypical denigration of women; however, Chaucer could have found a more detailed source in *RR* 16347–75, for example, where Genius describes an avaricious wife:

> A man who trusts his secrets to his wife
> Makes her his mistress. None of women born,
> Unless he's drunk or crazy, will reveal
> To women anything that should be hid,
> Unless he wants to hear it coming back
> To him from others.
>
> (de Lorris and de Meun, 1962, p. 349)

552   Chaucer follows *RR* 13522–8, but could have also known the source text, Ovid *Ars* 1.99. or *M.de Mar.* 43. All suggest that women stroll through the streets in order that they may see others and be seen themselves.

555–8   *RR* 13522–8, where La Vieille describes to Fair Welcome how to make men fall in love with her, and one of the pieces of advice she offers is to go regularly to social gatherings, such as festivals and plays, in order to be seen by those likely to succumb to her charms.

556   *vigilies*: these were occasions which preceded festival days and were supposed to be nights devoted to fasting and contemplation. More often they were popular congregations of feasting and dancing.

558   *myracles*: plays on religious subjects drawn from the Bible;

they were performed before the common people and were immensely popular.

559   *upon*: is adverbial; 'had on' in modern English.

560–2   Matt. vi.19–20. *Hg* has 'moththes', I have used *Ell*'s 'motthes'.

561   *Upon . . . del*: I swear on the peril of my soul that they did not eat a bit. The 'they' of the next line refers to her clothes.

572–4   *RR* 13150–2, where La Vieille gives advice to Fair Welcome: 'And at great peril forages the mouse / Who has for refuge but a single hole' (de Lorris and de Meun, 1962, p. 272).

575–84 These lines are not found in the Hengwrt manuscript, but as they are almost certainly revisions I have followed the Ellesmere manuscript for this passage. Similar inclusions may be found at lines 609–12, 619–26 and 717–20.

576   *My dame*: several identifications are possible: La Vieille in *RR*, Dame Alys her friend, the Wife's mother, or the goddess Venus. It is not important to make a choice in this instance, but simply to note that all of the Wife's authorities are female. See also 583.

578   It is interesting to note that, after a fashion, the Wife's dream is prophetic since it appears at one point that Jankyn has indeed slain her (800).

593–9   The wife follows Ovid's advice to women (*Ars* 3.431) where he writes: 'Often a husband is sought for at a husband's funeral' (Ovid, 1947, pp. 148–9). See also *M.de Mar.* 1966–77.

595   *Ell* uses the trisyllabic form, 'Janekyn'; see 303 and 383.

602   By referring to the teeth of a young animal, the Wife suggests that her tastes and desires are those of a young woman.

603   *gat tothed*: the 'gat' comes from 'gate' and means set wide apart. In medieval physiognomy lore this meant that the Wife had a bold and lecherous nature.

604   *Venus seel*: a birth mark on or around the genitals.

608   *quonyam*: from Latin, 'since' or 'that'; used here, however, as a euphemism for the pudendum.

609–12 One of the four revisions taken from *Ell*; see note to lines 575–84.

609   *Venerien*: dominated by Venus, that is physical passion.

610   *Marcien*: dominated by Mars and therefore wrath and physical violence.

613   This refers to the astrological influences present at the Wife's birth; the combination suggests that she will be unchaste.

615   *inclinacioun*: the Wife defends herself by saying that her conduct is the inevitable result of a certain astrological configuration.

615–26   The Wife now catalogues for herself a series of characteristics that coincide perfectly with a misogynistic list of women's failings.

618   *chambre of Venus*: vagina. See also *RR* 13336: 'A maid should keep her Venus' chamber clean' (de Lorris and de Meun, 1962, p. 278).

619–26   One of the four revisions taken from *Ell*; see note to lines 575–84.

619   *Martes mark*: a reddish birthmark on the face.

624   The wife describes herself in the same terms as used by the Jealous Husband abusing his wife in *RR* 8516: 'You care not whether it is long or short' (de Lorris and de Meun, 1962, p. 172).

628   *hende*: courteous, but a term usually applied to the nobility; thus it suggests a class distinction between Jankyn and the Wife.

629   Although Jankyn is twenty and the Wife forty, it was accepted that a young man without property should marry an older widow with an estate, thereby ensuring economic sufficency for the man and continued male control of lands and money.

630–3   Because the Wife could claim the English common law position of *femme sole* which gave her economic independence, she was in no way bound to yield her property to Jankyn. Her action here reveals the extent of her love for him. See also *TandC* II.750–73.

642   Jankyn's Roman history is by Valerius Maximus, *Facta et dicta memorabilia* (c.500). Unlike her other husbands who are only able to use proverbs, Jankyn is familiar with classical and Biblical learning. As such, he is able to confront the Wife with the whole force of patriarchal textual authority.

647   *Another Romayn*: Sempronius Sophus; Jankyn has gleaned the name from Val. 6.3.

648   Possibly the Midsummer Eve's festivals.

651–7   *Ecclesiaste*: Ecclesiasticus from the Apocrypha. Ecclus. xxv.25–6: 'Allow no outlet to water, and no boldness of speech in an evil wife, / If she does not go as you direct, separate her from yourself'.

652   *he*: the author of Ecclesiasticus, who the Wife assumes belongs to the panoply of male authorities cited by Jankyn.

655–8   Probably a popular song but not recorded before this.

659   *hawe*: the hawthorn berry was a symbol of nothingness; rather like the modern saying 'don't give a fig'.

662   *RR* 9980 and Ovid *Rem.am.* 123–4: both sources affirm that women hate to have their faults corrected.

666   St Thomas of Canterbury, the goal of this pilgrimage.

669–70   *gladly . . . wolde rede*: like to read.

671   *Valerie and Theofraste*: Jankyn's book is a compilation of three misogynist tracts, which were popularly used by the Church to encourage celibacy. As a collection it is fictional. For a full discussion of medieval anti-feminist writing see the Introduction. 1. *Epistola Valerii ad Rufinum*, ascribed to an ancient Roman, but actually written in the twelfth century by Walter Map, the archdeacon of Oxford. 2. *Liber aureolus de nuptiis*, a virulent antifeminist piece written by Theofrastus, one of Aristotle's followers. This is only preserved in Jerome. 3. *Epistola adversus Jovinianum* (674–5), Jerome's strident and well-known refutation of Jovinian's argument for the sanctity of marriage. The Wife draws upon each of these texts throughout her prologue.

674   Jerome was not a cardinal, but is referred to as such in Nicholas Trevet's *Les Cronicles*.

676   Tertulian wrote several books with a gender theme, such as *De exhortatione castitatis*, which advises a friend against a second marriage.

677   Crysippus is referred to by Jerome as an antifeminist. Trotula: the identification is uncertain, but possibly a woman doctor who was supposed to have written about female passion. Heloise: the mistress and wife of the philosopher Abelard. After their forced separation, she became an abbess at Argenteuil near Paris and wrote to him propounding anti-matrimonial ideas. The letters of Abelard and Heloise were well known and their story is mentioned in

165

RR 8745–956, which is probably recalled in this reference.

679   The Book of Proverbs, but especially the description of the harlot: 'And, behold, there met him a woman with the attire of an harlot, and subtil of heart. /She is loud and stubborn; her feet abide not in her house' (vii.10–11).

680   *Ovydes Art*: Ovid's *Ars amatoria*.

685   *wikked wyves*: all the tales are of older women and were customarily used to illustrate that women are weaker than, and consequently a danger to, men. The Wife's exaggeration calls into question the nature and degree of their sin, while simultaneously personalising the tales to herself as a 'Wife'.

689   The antipathy between the clergy and women was a commonplace. Referred to again at 706 and 'ClT' 935.

692   Aesop's *Fables* include the story of how, on being confronted by a lion, the man shows the animal a painting of a man killing a lion. Whereupon the lion asks who painted it – a lion or a man. The Wife suggests that if women had written books then the result would have been very different. It is interesting to note that one of Chaucer's possible sources was a female author's – Marie de France – retelling of the tale in her *Fables* 37.

697   Venus favours lovers, especially women, while Mercury has scholars under his protection.

702   *exaltacioun*: the point in the zodiac where a planet was said to have most influence. When a planet was at its highest point in an astrological sign, its opposite planet was thought to be at its lowest position. Hence, women (the Wife) and clerks (Jankyn) must always be opposed and only one may be in the ascendancy. *Ell* has 'falleth' not 'faileth' both here and in 705.

704   Pisces is the astrological sign of the fish.

707–10   *LGW* 261–3.

711   This is the third time that the Wife returns to her initial intent, calling attention to the length of the Prologue and to its rhetorical structure of *dilatio*. For a discussion of Chaucer's rhetoric see the Introduction, pp. 20–1.

713   *oure sire*: my husband; the Wife uses the familiar colloquial form again, but perhaps with more affection.

715   *Eva*: often contrasted detrimentally with *Ave*, the salutation of Gabriel to Mary. This is part of a more pervasive and

	topical opposition between the sinful Eve, who caused the fall of man, and the blessed Mary who bore the saviour of all mankind.
717–20	One of the four revisions taken from *Ell*; see note to lines 575–84.
721–3	The story comes from Judges xiii–xiv
725–6	Deianira gave Hercules a poisoned shirt which burnt his skin so badly that he cast himself on to a pyre rather than suffer the pain. Deianira had dipped the shirt into a potion made from the blood of Nessus (the centaur Hercules had slain for attempting to abduct Deianira), which she had mistakenly believed to be a love potion.
728–32	An apocryphal antifeminist story told of the ancient Greek philosopher and recounted by Jerome (*Ep.ad.Jov*. 1.48) as are the next two tales.
733–4	Pasiphaë was in love with a bull and became the mother of the Minotaur. Jerome *Ep.ad.Jov*. 1.48. and Ovid *Ars* 1.295–326.
737–8	Clytemnestra murdered her husband, Agamemnon, in order to retain her lover, Aegisthus. Jerome *Ep.ad.Jov*. 1.48.
741–6	Amphiaraus was forced to fight against Thebes because he had been betrayed by his wife, Eriphyle. She had been bribed with a golden necklace and Amphiaraus was killed while fleeing from his enemies. The source here is Statius's *Thebaid* 4. *Hg* has 'Exiphilem'; I have used *Ell*'s 'Eriphilem' since it coincides with the sources.
747	Livia and Lucillia are mentioned in *Ep.Val.Ruf*. 4.3. Livia murdered her husband, Drusus, at the instigation of her lover, Sejanus. Lucillia unwittingly poisoned her husband, the poet Lucretius, believing that she was administering a love potion to keep him faithful. I have followed the sources, using the name hyvia, in order to to avoid confusion; *Hg* and *Ell* have 'hyma'.
757	A stock tale, but told of Latumius in *Ep.Val.Ruf*.4.3.
769–70	As Jael killed Sisera in Judges iv.21.
775–7	Ecclus. xxi.16. (from the Apocrypha): 'I would rather dwell with a lion and a dragon than dwell with an evil wife'.
778–9	Proverbs xi.9–10: 'It is better to dwell in a corner of the housetop, than with a brawling woman in a wide house. / The soul of the wicked desireth evil: his neighbour findeth no favour in his eyes'.

782–3	Jerome uses this quotation from Herodotus in his *Ep.ad.Jov.* 1.48.
784–5	Proverbs xi.22: 'As a jewel of gold in a swine's snout, so is a fair woman which is without discretion'.
790	In her two previous accounts of this event (635 and 667) the Wife refers to only one leaf being torn out of Jankyn's book.
792	*Ell* has 'took hym on'.
824	*Denmark unto Inde*: that is, the whole world.
828–9	*[Biholde . . . Frere]*: from *Ell*.
829–49	The enmity between Friars and Summoners was traditional and is borne out by their own tales. Friars were a mendicant order dedicated to self-induced poverty; they travelled the country preaching and begging for monetary support. The summoners were minor non-clerical officials of ecclesiastical courts. Both groups were commonly condemned as greedy and dishonest.
838	*pees*: MS variants are 'pace' and 'pisse'; the last one corresponds more closely to the Wife's colourful use of language and explicit terminology.
847	*Sydyngborne*: Sittingbourne is a town situated between Canterbury and Rochester about twenty miles from London.
866	The satirical attack made by the Wife on Friars was common in late fourteenth-century writings owing to the obvious corruption of the Church at that time. Chaucer expands on the criticisms in 'FrT', 'SumT' and 'GP' I. 208–69.
880	*incubus*: an evil spirit especially known for illicit sexual intercourse with women.
883	*bachiler*: young knight.
884	*fro ryver*: possibly hunting for water fowls. See also *TandC* IV.413.
887–9	The fact that the Wife could include the rape of a maiden by a knight in her tale suggests the general disillusionment with chivalric values which occurred at the end of the fourteenth century. The criticisms were largely occasioned by the disastrous expeditions of the English side in the Hundred Years War.
893	The rape laws of the late fourteenth century demanded that a proven rapist be either blinded, castrated or killed; in effect there were almost no convictions. If the woman was a peasant a fine sufficed, and if the man offered to marry the

woman then the charges were dropped. It is significant that the knight's life is spared at the end of the tale in conjunction with his marriage.

894–912　By allowing the queen to enact judgement on the knight, the Wife may be recalling the Courts of Love conducted by Eleanor of Aquitaine and her daughter Marie of Champagne in the early thirteenth century. These elaborate games of courtly love were recorded for Marie by Andreas Capellanus in *The Art of Courtly Love*, which was a popular work throughout the medieval period. See also 1028. This line is taken from *Ell*.

906　　*iren*: of the executioner's axe.

911–12　The queen asks for the knight to give her his pledge, or word of honour that he will return before he is allowed to leave.

929–30　Women's love of flattery is discussed by the Friend and the Lover in *RR* 9945–58. For example:

> . . . There's no maid
> Good, bad, young, old, religious, secular –
> Not even a nun, chaste in both body and soul –
> Who'll not delight to hear her beauty praised.
>
> (de Lorris and de Meun, 1962, p. 200)

934　　*ylymed*: caught as with bird-lime, a sticky substance used to trap birds. *moore and lesse*: whatever rank; this shows the Wife's awareness of the hierarchical structure of medieval society.

940　　*clawe us on the galle*: scratch on a sore spot.

948　　*rake-stele*: rake handle, that is, nothing.

950　　The Wife imitates Nature in *RR* 19220, where the character criticises men and excuses women:

> As I'm a woman, I cannot keep still
> But will tell all, for women naught conceal.
>
> (de Lorris and de Meun, 1962, p. 407)

951–82　The tale of Midas's ears is taken from Ovid *Meta*. 11.174–93; however, the Wife changes one important point: in Ovid it is a man, Midas's barber, who whispers the information, rather than a woman, Midas's wife. The alteration in textual material coincides with the Wife's disregard for masculine authority in her prologue. But as the story is changed so as to focus on women as gossips, it is possible to read the revision as Chaucer's ironic comment upon the garrulous nature of the female character he has created.

954   Midas was given ass's ears as a punishment for his greed.

960   *Hg* has 'diffigure', I have used *Ell*'s 'disfigure'.

961–3   The Wife here draws upon Genius's description of the avaricious wife who falsely promises to protect her husband's secrets; see *RR* 16521–30.

965–8   The Wife's speech again recalls the avaricious wife *RR* 16366–8:

> . . . Though none ask
> Her secret, she will tell it just the same
> Without an invitation; naught will keep
> Her silent.

> (de Lorris and de Meun, 1962, p. 349)

972   *bitore bombleth*: bittern, that is, a crane whose mating call has a booming ('bombleth') sound.

990–2   the traditional idea of fairies dancing in a ring.

992   *Hg* has 'xxiiij'.

1004   A common idea that 'old people often know best'.

1013   Chaucer closely follows Gower's description of Sir Florent's acceptance of a loathly lady as his bride; see *CA* 1.1587.

1018   *calle*: a net covering the hair, usually part of a noble lady's headdress with lavish ornamentation.

1028   See note 894–912.

1069   *disparaged*: degraded by a marriage with someone of a lower class. *Hg* has 'on morwe'; I have used *Ell*.

1081   Gower *CA* 1.1727–31 uses the same simile for a young knight hiding from an old and ugly woman: 'Bot as an oule fleth be nyhte' (Gower, 1980, p. 67).

1100   *loothly*: the 'loathly lady', common to romance texts; she is always ugly, possessed of magic powers and in some way associated with a fair young maiden whom she parallels. This connection may be one of transformation, as in the Wife's tale, or one of control as in *Sir Gawain and the Green Knight*.

1106–12   A mock Lollard sermon on the value of individual morality as opposed to inherited worth. For a discussion of Lollardism see the Introduction.

1109 *gentillesse*: gentility, that which comes from character and not from social position; the source is Dante *Con.* 4.3, 10, 14 and 15.

1110 The Wife belongs to the merchant classes whose wealth was created by individual effort rather than gained by inheritance; these groups were expanding rapidly at the end of the fourteenth century and clearly threatened the old feudal order. Thus, the Wife has a keen personal interest in confronting the values of the knightly classes, while at the same time wishing to be allied to their sense of continuity. The compromise is achieved through the persona of the hag, who asserts her values over those of the knight, but also attains a happy marriage.

1117–18 *RR* 6579–92, where the virtues of nobility are praised:

> Gentility is noble; her I love
> Because she will not enter villain hearts.
>
> (de Lorris and de Meun, 1962, p. 136)

1118–24 *RR* 18620–34, where Nature discusses how true nobility is achieved by individual effort and cannot be inherited; for example:

> Nobility comes from an upright heart;
> Gentility of birth is nothing worth
> If he who has it lacks good heartedness.
>
> (de Lorris and de Meun, 1962, p. 395)

1120 *Hg* has 'hir', I have used *Ell*'s 'heigh'.

1126 *Dant*: Dante; Chaucer follows *Purg.* 7.121–3. 'Rarely doth human probity rise through the branches: and this he wills who giveth it, so that it may be prayed for from him' (Dante, 1901, p. 83).

1129 *prowesse*: the second time the word is used it should probably be replaced with 'goodnesse' (*Ell*) since that is a more appropriate virtue for God.

1133–8 Dante *Con.* 4.15.19–38, where Dante points out the absurdity of arguing that 'a gentle son cannot be the offspring of a base father' (Dante, 1909, pp. 245–6).

171

1140	*Kaukasous*: the Caucasus mountain range, but implying anywhere at a far distance.
1148	*ne doon hir operacioun*: do not behave as they should.
1152–8	Dante *Con.* 4.7.87–92: 'And so he who is of noble stock through his father or any of his ancestors, if he does not persevere in nobleness is not only vile but vilest, and deserves more contempt than any churl' (Dante, 1909, p. 216).
1158	*RR* 2083–6 where the Lover is warned against Villainy, for 'Villainy breeds churls' (de Lorris and de Meun, 1962, p. 45).
1162–3	Dante *Con.* 4.20.24–8 and 47–57. The Wife takes her text from Dante who writes that 'those who have this "grace" that is, this divine thing, are wellnigh like gods, free from all stain of vice. And none can confer this gift save God alone, with whom there is no respect of persons, as the divine Sciptures declare' (Dante, 1909, p. 261).
1165–7	Val. 3.4. Tullus Hostilius was a legendary figure who was a peasant by birth but became the third king of Rome.
1168–76	Seneca was a Roman philosopher and dramatist; his *Epistles* xliv suggests that everyone may be virtuous regardless of their social station.
1170	*RR* 18802–5, where Nature asserts that it is necessary to behave in a noble fashion in order to be considered of noble rank.
1178	2 Cor. viii.9: 'For ye know the grace of our Lord Jesus Christ, that, though he was rich, yet for your sakes he became poor, that ye thrugh his poverty might be rich'.
1183–4	A proverb, but it appears in Seneca's *Epistles* xvii.
1187	*RR* 18566, where Nature discusses true wealth: 'The more he covets things the poorer he' (de Lorris and de Meun, 1962, p. 394).
1191	*Hg* has 'synne', I have used *Ell*'s 'syngeth', since it conforms to the reading from Juvenal at 1193–4.
1192	Juvenal: a Roman poet who is mentioned in Dante *Con.* 4.13.101–10.
1199	*Ell* has 'this' rather than *Hg*'s 'thyng'.
1203–4	*RR* 4949–56, where Reason explains that true friends will remain by you whatever your financial circumstances.
1212	*And . . . gesse*: and many written authorities shall I find to support this.

1230–5	Here the knight shows true courtly love values when he places himself fully within his lady's power.
1249	*cast . . . curtyn*: the hag asks the knight to draw aside the curtains which would have hung around their bed, in order for him to perceive the transformation in the morning light.
1264	*pestilence*: the plague or Black Death which had decimated the country several times in the fourteenth century; see Introduction, p. 9.

THE CLERK'S PROLOGUE AND TALE

5	*sophyme*: sophism, not a specious argument, but any dispute in logic.
6	Eccles. 3.1: 'To every thing there is a season, and a time to every purpose under the heaven'.
10	A French proverb meaning that if you decide to participate in a game then you must accept the rules.
12–14	The Host's criticism of Friars was part of a growing disillusionment with Church corruption in the late fourteenth century; see 'WBT' 866 note. The alternative, that of plain speech in English – rather than Latin – was advocated by the Lollards and their leader John Wycliffe; see the Introduction. It is possible that Chaucer had Lollard sympathies and, certainly, both the Clerk and the Parson conform to several Lollard ideals.
16	*termes . . . colours . . . figures*: the 'termes' of rhetoric, the 'colours' coming from figures of speech such as metaphors, and the 'figures' suggesting arguments and lines of thought. The use of rhetoric is discussed in the Introduction.
18	*Heighe style*: Medieval writers followed the rule of adopting a style – high, middle or low – to fit subject and audience. See also 41, 1141 and 1148.
26–7	*a worthy clerk*: Petrarch, who was archdeacon of Padua and lived in the city. This does not necessarily mean that Chaucer himself met Petrarch in Padua; the Clerk is a fictional character and the use of personal experience is a common literary device. However, within the narrative it is appropriate that the Clerk should have made this journey, since clerics often went to Padua to study.

31	Petrarch was created poet laureate in Rome in 1341.
34	*Lynyan*: Giovanni da Lignano (1310–83), an Italian professor of law whom Chaucer may have known for his support of Pope Urban VI.
41	See note 18; although almost certainly a mistranslation of Petrarch's original.
43–51	*prohemie*: prologue. Apart from 'Mount Vesulus' Chaucer gives all the places their French names, which suggests that he was probably using the French translation. See the Introduction.
49	*Ell* has 'sours'.
54	*inpertinent*: seems to suggest that Petrarch's prologue is too long, certainly Chaucer's/the Clerk's is much shorter.
58	*roote*: the land of Saluces at the foot of the mountain. Vesulus is not described as 'colde' in either Petrarch or the French version, but its height ensures that it is often covered with snow.
72	*Lumbardye*: not in Petrarch or the French version, but fourteenth-century Lombardy was known for its tyrants; see Gower *Mir*. 23233–6 and 23257–9.
85–91	The idea of commoners advising their lord carries echoes of the peasants' rebelling against feudal rule in the Peasants' Revolt, which is referred to at 995. But like the real rebellion, this is contained when Walter reasserts his authority.
96	*gentillesse*: see 'WBT' 1109–76.
106–7	*so wel . . . doon*: so well do you and all your works please us, and ever have done.
110–40	The idea of a prince marrying someone of a lower class, of the 'commonweal', was a metaphor for social harmony and unity in the medieval period.
114	The people use the language of feudalism to describe marriage; the thematic parallel between the relationship of a lord and his people and of a husband and wife is sustained throughout the tale.
136	*Ell* has 'if it so'.
137	*slake*: it was of paramount importance in medieval feudal society that the lord's familial line should not die out.
155–61	The discussion of the superiority of individual merit, rather than inherited worth, is discussed by the Wife, 'WBT' 1109–206.

157	The Clerk uses the example of a peasant woman to show that virtue is not necessarily linked to class; see 'WBT' 1109–76.
174–5	Chaucer's addition.
180	*Hg* has 'I may', I have used *Ell*'s 'he may'.
196–7	Petrarch did not divide his text, but the French translation is sectioned, and since Chaucer's first four breaks coincide with this version, it is likely that he was following the later text. The Latin phrases may be translated as: 'Here ends the first part', 'Here begins the second part' (similarly for the later parts).
207	*oxes stalle*: Luke ii.7–16 and Isaiah i.3. Griselda is thus linked to the Virgin Mary in her maternal role – at the annunciation and nativity; consequently, she takes on the Virgin's archetypal symbolism of perfect femininity. This is Chaucer's addition, which suggests that the idealisation of Griselda is an important issue in the tale. See also 291–4.
210	Chaucer often varies the names of his characters, although here Grisildis implies a personal form, while Griselde is the more formal version.
215–17	Chaucer's addition, perhaps contrasting with the Wife's liking for wine, 'WBP' 459–63.
219–20	*brest . . . virginitee / . . . rype*: suggest that Griselda is ready for marriage.
223	Possibly another reference to the Virgin Mary who was often depicted spinning or looking after sheep, but the image of women involved in clothmaking has a broader significance. Eve was the first woman to spin after her expulsion from Eden, and the Wife of Bath is her equivalent, as Griselda parallels the Virgin ('WBP' 401). But all are women involved in an archetypally feminine task.
227	The realistic details of the food are Chaucer's addition.
236	*Hg* has 'wit', I have used *Ell*'s 'with'.
239	*wommanhede*: femininity. Chaucer alters his sources, which suggest that Griselda is virtuous beyond the limits of her class and gender; instead, he embodies in Griselda a gender-specific ideal. She is a good woman above and beyond being a good Christian.
249–52	Chaucer's addition.

254	*asure*: lapis lazuli or blue enamel.
260–94	This section, which deals with Griselda's personal response, is expanded by Chaucer.
276–94	In folktales and romances wells or water often function as entries into another world, sometimes a magical one. The change which is about to occur in Griselda's life is just such a fairytale transformation.
291–4	See note 207.
336	*Hg* has 'eft'; I have used *Ell*'s 'erst', which in this instance is being used as a superlative.
350	*yow avyse*: the correct translation is 'consider it further', but Walter implies a refusal.
351–5	Walter demands total obedience from Griselda; this was a common expectation of husbands since wives were subject to their absolute rule in both secular and religious law. Indeed, legally women's identity was subsumed into that of their husbands.
365	*ynough*: of course Griselda's protestations are not 'ynough' as Walter will continue to test her throughout the poem. It is only when he repeats the phrase at 1051 that he fully accepts her true worth.
372–6	Griselda's clothing is dealt with in more detail by Chaucer than in his source texts. In terms of the narrative it is important that we remember she brought nothing of material value – except her 'smok' – to Walter when she married him. However, the use of clothing to signify women's love of luxury ('WBP' 337–57 and 'ClT' 1208) and the worthy abstinence of the Clerk ('GP' I. 290 and 296), suggests that a point about gender and morality is being made.
429	*humblenesse*: which suggests modesty and is a fitting quality for Griselda; some MSS have 'hoomlinesse' which implies a more domestic skill.
431	*commune profit*: that which is good for society as a whole; Griselda puts others first, while Walter has thought only of himself (78–84).
435–41	Noblemen were often away from their estates, either at court or at war, and their wives supervised the property in their absence.
441	Matt. i.21: 'And she shall bring forth a son, and thou shalt

176

call his name JESUS: for he shall save his people from their sins'.

452   *tempte*: Griselda is tempted by external factors, whereas Walter must face internal temptation.

455–8   The absolute rule which Walter exerts over Griselda was a topical issue in the late fourteenth century, since Richard II practised an almost arbitrary tyranny, which resulted in his overthrow in 1399. See also 619–21, 701–7 and 732–5.

459–62   Not in Chaucer's sources and meant to encourage our sympathy for Griselda and our condemnation of Walter's uncalled-for cruelty. Chaucer's increasingly positive treatment of female characters in the late fourteenth century (see also *LGW*) might have been the result of Queen Anne's influence; she had clearly expressed her dislike of the emphasis on female infidelity in *TandC*, and Chaucer would have been dependent upon royal patronage.

496   *Hg* has 'youe', I have used *Ell*'s 'youre'

500   Although twentieth-century readers find Griselda's meek acceptance of her children's fate almost incomprehensible, it is important to remember that motherhood had different connotations in the medieval period. Infant mortality, wet-nursing and sending children away for their education at an early age were all common and resulted in a much less intense parent–child bond. For example, the writer Christine de Pisan hardly mentions the deaths of her young children, but wrote numerous elegies for her husband.

519   *sergeant . . . privee man*: a servant who was used to enforce the law, a private retainer used to acting in confidence for his lord.

523   *Hg* has 'hem', I have used *Ell*'s 'hym'.

538–9   Isaiah liii.7: 'He was oppressed, and he was afflicted, yet he opened not his mouth: he is brought as a lamb to the slaughter, and as a sheep before her shearers is dumb, so he openeth not his mouth'.

554–67   Not in Chaucer's sources; an incident added in order to emphasise the pathos of the tale.

581   An authorial intrusion and possibly a contemporary political allusion to Richard II; see note 455–8.

590   *Panyk*: *Hg* has 'Pavyk' and *Ell*, 'Pavik'; the source texts

	however make it clear that the name is 'Panyk', which possibly refers to the castle of Panico near Bologna.
607	*accident*: an external sign of change.
610	*Hg* has '4'.
617–18	Noble ladies almost always gave their children to wet-nurses to feed.
621–3	Chaucer's addition.
647–9	Chaucer's addition.
651	Perhaps an allusion to morning sickness and the pain of childbirth.
736	*Hg* has 'xij'. Twelve years of age was the legal age for marriage; see 'WBP' 4 and note.
737–49	Walter, of course, invents the papal edicts; in reality the reasons he gives, 'rancour and dissencion' amongst his people, would not have been sufficient for an annulment. The acceptable causes were consanguinity, adultery, impotence and leprosy, but the use of political and economic influence could result in annulments on spurious grounds.
743	*contrefete*: in Middle English this means 'imitate' rather than 'fraudulently copy' as the modern usage suggests.
769	*Hg* has 'thgh', I have used *Ell*'s 'thogh'.
811–12	Chaucer's addition.
812	*aventure*: an event that is caused by chance rather than fated.
834–8	1 Cor. vii.1–4, where St Paul advocates that a woman should have only one husband. The Wife uses the same passage but reaches very different conclusions; see 'WBP' 89 and 129–32.
839–40	Chaucer's addition.
840	Griselda avows that she will not take another husband, which contrasts vividly with the Wife's five marriages ('WBP' 6).
851–61	Chaucer's addition.
857	*Love . . . newe*: love is not the same when it is old as when it is new.
867–8	Some MSS have 'your' instead of 'my' in both places, while the Petworth House MS 7 has '*your* clothyng' and '*my* weddyng ring' (emphasis mine). This last form would suggest that the secular finery is Walter's, but that the symbol of spiritual union belongs to Griselda.
871	Job i.21: 'And said, Naked came I out of my mother's

womb, and naked shall I return thither: the LORD gave, and the LORD hath taken away; blessed be the name of the LORD'.

880–2   Not in Chaucer's sources, but a common enough idea.

883   Griselda bargains for a smock in exchange for the virginity which she has already surrendered to Walter; for the economic value of sexual intercourse in marriage see 'WBP' 131–2 and 152–3.

902–3   Job iii.3: 'Let the day perish wherein I was born, and the night in which it was said, There is a man child conceived'; not in Chaucer's sources.

911   The preservation of Griselda's original clothes is part of the folktale discourse, where the fairytale is reversed from the world of magic back to real life.

915–17   Realistic details, probably Chaucer's addition.

916   *she moore*: which suggests that Griselda herself is older; some MS simply have 'moore' which would imply that it is her clothes which have aged. The former seems a more practical reading.

927   *No . . . delicat*: roughly meaning that she had no taste for fine food, nor caring for luxury or self–indulgence.

932–8   Job xxxxii.6; Chaucer's addition, although 'the patience of Job' is proverbial. See also 'WBP' 436 and note.

935   The Clerk expresses a self–awareness of the fact that clerks do not praise women; see 'WBP' 687–90.

958   *sittyng and servyse*: his place at the dining table and the attendance he received there.

960–80   The tasks Griselda performs, making beds and instructing the servants for example, are the appropriate duties for a medieval lady.

970   *feyntyng*: weakening, but also prefiguring Griselda's faint.

981   *undren*: about nine in the morning.

990–1   Chaucer's addition.

995–1001   Chaucer's addition (up to line 1008) and a common attack on the fickle nature of the populace (see also *Bo* 4.5.31–7). However, Chaucer might also be referring to the Peasants' Revolt of 1381.

999   *jane*: a halfpenny coin from Genoa, which gives the sense 'too dear at a halfpenny'.

1047	*constant*: recalls Constance in 'MerT'; both characters exemplify archetypal female passivity (see also 1146).
1079–160	Considerably expanded by Chaucer.
1080	In Petrarch's version Griselda does not faint.
1092	*No fors of deeth*: death does not matter.
1141–62	The moral is from Petrarch who is the 'auctour' referred to in the text.
1152	*For . . . wroghte*: for it is very reasonable that he should test that which he created.
1153–5	James i.13: 'Let no man say when he is tempted, I am tempted of God: for God cannot be tempted with evil, neither tempteth he any man'.
1163	Both Petrarch and the French version end at this point; Chaucer follows on with a direct and satirical response to the Wife, his own 'envoy' and the final stanza by the Host.
1164–9	Possibly a reference to the Golden Age with its fine values being sullied with a decline into the Age of Brass.
1170	*Wyves love of Bathe*: by including this direct reply by the Clerk to the Wife, Chaucer clearly indicates that the two tales are meant to be read together.
1171	*secte*: her kind or, perhaps, her sex/gender.
1177	Chaucer's song or 'envoy' belongs to the authorial (Chaucer's) rather than the narratorial (the Clerk's) voice; as was usual for this kind of verse letter, it stands as separate from the main poem and is used to direct the reader's attention to the relevance of the tale for everyday life. The form changes to a six line stanza with only three rhymes.
1188	*chichyvache*: literally a 'lean cow'; it fed only on patient wives and so remained thin.
1189	*Ekko*: Echo; therefore always answers back.
1191	*bidaffed*: fooled or deafened; the latter meaning would recall the Wife who 'weex al deef' ('WBP' 636).
1195	*archewyves*: quintessential women, but also implying ones in authority; *defense*: ready for battle.
1196	*camaile*: a camel, but also, continuing the military metaphor, the French name for ventaille, the piece of armour used to cover neck and chest. See note 1204.
1204	*aventaile*: the English name for the ventaille; see note 1196.
1207–10	'WBP' 253–6 and 265–70.

1210   *To gete . . . travaile*: do everything to make yourself popular.

1212–13   *[Bihoold . . . Hoost]*: not in *Hg*, I have used *Ell*.

1213–19   It is generally assumed that the Host's speech was written early on and removed when Chaucer completed the Merchant's prologue which follows; however, it is included in both *Hg* and *Ell*.

Glossary

This glossary provides an alphabetical list of words in Middle English with their equivalent in Modern English. The list is not comprehensive and is intended to translate those words which would not be familiar to modern readers, as well as to supplement the page glosses and the notes. All verb entries use the infinitive, except where indicated otherwise. Some variant spellings have been included.

ABBREVIATIONS

adj: adjective.
adv: adverb.
conj: conjunction.
interj: interjection.
n: noun.
num: number.

pp: past participle.
prep: preposition.
pron: pronoun.
pt: past tense.
sg: singular.
v: verb.

★ ★ ★

Abaissen (v): to embarrass, to disconcert.
Aboute (adv): go about, set out.
Abreyde (v): to awake.
Abroche (v): to open.
Abyden (v): to abide, to stop.
Accident (n): accident, outward sign, outward appearance.
Acorden (v): to agree.
Adoun (adv): down.

Afraye (v): to frighten.
After (prep): after, following.
Agaste (v): to upset, to frighten.
Agayn, agayns, ayeins (prep): towards, against.
Age (n): life.
Agon (pp): departed, dead.
Agreve (v): to annoy, to aggrieve.
Agrief (adv): to be upset, to respond with anger.

Al, alle (adj, conj): all, although.

Algate, algates (adv): always, anyhow, in every way.

Alite (adj, adv): a little.

Allge (n): compatriot, friend.

Alliance (n): alliance, marriage.

Alway, alwey (adv): always, continually.

Amblen (v): to amble.

Amenden (v): to mend, to improve.

Amendere (n): improver.

Ameve (v): to change.

Among (adv): among, all the time, meanwhile.

Angwyssh (n): anguish.

Anon, anoon (adv): immediately, forthwith.

Anyght (adv): at night.

Aournemente (n): ornament.

Aparaile, apparaille (n): garments, ornaments, dress.

Apaye (v): to please.

Aperceyven (v): to perceive, to observe.

Apert (adj): public.

Apperen (v): to appear.

Appetit (n): desire.

Arace (v): to free, to tear apart, to tear from.

Araye, Arraye (v): to order, to array, to dress, to arrange.

Archewyve (n): strong, powerful wife.

Arewe (adv): in succession.

Arn: see *Ben*.

Array (n): behaviour, dress, adornment, display, arrangement.

Art (n): art, skill, study.

Art: see *Ben*.

Arwe (n): arrow.

Assay (n): trial, test.

Assenten (v): to agree.

Assure (v): to assure, to trust.

Asterten (v): to escape.

Astologen (n): astrologer, astronomer.

Astoned, Astoneyd (pp): astonished.

Asure (adj): azure.

Aswowne: see *Swowne*.

Aton (adv): at one, in agreement.

Atones (adv): at the same time.

Atte (prep): at the.

Attendaunce (n): attendance, attention.

Atteyne (v): to attain, to achieve.

Auctoritee (n): authority, text.

Auctour (n): author, authority.

Audience (n): assembly, hearing.

Aught (pron): anything.

Auncestre (n): ancestry, ancestor.

Availen (v): to avail, to help.

Avaunten (v): to boast.

Aventure (n): adventure, chance, fate.

Averyll (n): April.

Avyse (v): to consider, to judge, to plan.

Axen (v): to ask.

Ay (adv): always, ever.

Ayeins: see *Agayn*.

Ba (n): kiss.

Bachiler, Bachilrye (n): young knight, knights.

Bacyne (n): basin.

Bad: see *Bidde*.

Bak (n): back.

Bar, Baar: see *Beren*.

Bareyne (adj): barren.

Barm (n): lap.

Bathe (v): to bask, to wallow.

Bede (v): to offer.

Beere (n): bier.

Ben (v): to be. *Arn, Art*: are.

Benedictee (interj): God bless us.

Benygne (adj): gracious.

Benygnely (adv): graciously.

Benygnyte (n): graciousness.

Beren (v): to bear, to possess, to take, to conduct, to conduct oneself, to accuse, to carry. *Bar, Baar*: carried, bore. *Bern*: carries, bears.

Bern: see *Beren*.

Berne (n): barn.

Best, beste (n): beast.

Bet (adj, adv): better.

Bete (v): to make better.

Beten (v): to beat.

Bicam (pp): became.

Bidaffe (v): to fool.

Bidde (v): to ask, to command. *Bad, Bode*: asked.

Bifalle (v): to happen.

Bifoore, bifore, biforn (prep, adv): before, in front of.

Bigonne (pp): begun.

Bigoon (pp): situated.

Bigylen (v): to deceive.

Biheste (v): to promise.

Biholden (v): to behold.

Binde (v): to bind. *Bonde, bounden*: bound.

Birafte (pp): took away.

Biseke (v): to beseech.

Biseye: see *Sen*.

Bishrewe (v): to curse.

Bisy, bisye (adj): busy, careful.

Bisynesse (n): industry, constant work.

Bitake (v): to trust, to entrust.

Bithynken (v): to imagine.

Bitore (n): bittern bird.

Bitwix, bitwixen (prep, adv): between.

Bityden (v): to happen.

Biwaillen (v): to regret.

Biwreyen (v): to confess, to betray.

Blisful (adj): happy.

Blisse (n): happiness.

Blyve (adv): quickly.

Bobaunce (n): boast.

Bode: see *Bidde*.

Bomble (v): to boom.

Bon (n): bone.

Bonde: see *Binde*.

Boote (n): good.

Bord (n): table.

Borel (n): poor cloth.

Bounde (n): boundary.

Bounden: see *Binde*.

Bountee (n): goodness.

Bour, boure (n): bedroom.

Bowen (v): to bow, to yield.

Boystously (adv): roughly.

Braunche (n): branch.

Brayde (v): to wake up.

Breed (n): bread.

Bren (n): bran.

Brennen (v): to burn.

Bresten (v): to burst.

Brydde (n): bird.

Bryngen (v): to bring, to encourage.

Bulle (n): papal bull, edict from the pope.

Burghe (n): borough.

Burthe (n): birth.

But, but if (conj): but, unless.

Buxomly (adv): obediently.

Byen (v): to buy, to pay for.

Byten (v): to bite, to cut.

Cacchen (v): to catch.

Calle (n): hair net.

Caren (v): to care, to grieve.

Cas (n): subject, chance affair, case.

Casten (v): to cast, to throw, to lift.

Caterwawe (v): caterwaul.

Certayn, certein, certeyn (adj, adv): certain, certainly, indeed.

Certes (adv): certainly.

Cessen (v): to cease.

Chacen (v): to pursue.

Chaffare (n): trading wares.

Chalenge (v): to claim.

Chambrere (n): chambermaid.

Charge (n): responsibility.

Chaumbre (n): chamber, room.

Cheepe (n): bargain.

Cheepen, chepen (v): to do business with, to bargain.

Cheere (n): expression, appearance, behaviour.

Chees: see *Chesen*.

Cherl (n): rough, uncouth person.

Chesen, chees (v): to choose.

Cheste, chiste (n): coffer, chest, coffin.

Chiden (v): to chide, to scold.

Chiertee (n): affection.

Chiste: see *Cheste*.

Cladden: see *Clothen*.

Clamour (n): noise.

Clappen (v): to chatter.

Clene (adj): pure, cleanly formed, untainted, chaste.

Clepen (v): to call.

Clere (adj): sparkling.

Clerke (n): cleric.

Clooth, cloth (n): clothes, clothing.

Clothen (v): to clothe, to dress. *Cladden*: clothed.

Cofre (n): basket.

Cokewold (n): cuckold.

Collacioun (n): discussion.

Colour (n): excuse.

Colours (n): fine phrases of rhetoric.

Come therby (v): to obtain.

Commune (n): common people.

Commune (adj): common, public.

Compaignye (n): company.

Comunly (adv): commonly.

Conclusion (n): purpose.

Condicioun (n): condition, nature, character.

Conseil (n): advice, counsel, secret.

Constellacioun (n): constellation of stars.

Constreyne (v): to constrain, to compell.

Contenance, contenaunce (n): appearance, demeanor.

Contraryen (v): to contradict.

Contrefete (v): to counterfeit, to invent.

Conveyen (v): to accompany, to introduce.

Coost (n): coast.

Corage (n): heart, courage, mind, desire.

Coroune (n): crown, wedding garland.

Corps (n): body.

Costage (n): expense.

Cote (n): hut, coat.

Cours (n): course.

Coveiten (v): to desire, to covet.

Coverchief (n): head covering.

Coy (adj): demure.

Crispe (adj): curly.

Croce (n): cross.

Cure (n): care.

Curteisye (n): courtesy, courtly behaviour.

Curtyn (n): curtain.

Curyus (adj): skilfully crafted.

Cutten (v): to cut. *Kitte*: cut.

Daliaunce, dalyaunce (n): flirtation, socialising.

Dampnacioun (n): damnation.

Dampne (v): to condemn, to damn.

Dar (v): to dare. *Dorste*: dared.

Daun (n): master.

Daungerous (adj): distant, disdainful, reluctant.

Daunten (v): to frighten.

Dawe (v): to dawn.

Dayerye (n): dairy.

Debaat (n): dispute.

Dede (n): act, deed.

Deed (adj): dead.

Deere (adj): dear, expensive, precious.

Degree (n): rank, status, respect.

Del (n): bit, part, share.

Delicat (adj): delicate, pleasing.

Delit (n): delight, desire.

Delitable (adj): delightful.

Delyveren (v): to deliver, to set free.

Demen (v): to deem, to decide, to judge.

Departe (v): to depart, to part, to separate.

Derkeste (adj): darkest.

Desolat (adj): lonely, without influence.

Despit (n): spite.

Despitusly (adv): spitefully.

Dette (n): debt.

Devyne: see *Dyvynen*.

Devysen (v): to imagine, to contrive.

Deyen (v): to die.

Deyntee (n): delight, pleasure, value.

Deynteuous (adj): delicious.

Diffame (n): bad reputation.

Diffynycioun (n): definition.

Dighte (v): to have intercourse with, to prepare.

Digne (adj): worthy.

Dignitee (n): dignity, rank.

Discord (n): disagreement.

Discrecioun (n): moderation, prudence.

Discret, discreet (adj): wise, discerning.

Discryve (v): to describe.

Dishoneste (adj): shameful.

Disparage (v): to disparage, to dishonour.

Dispence (n): extravagance, spending.

Disport (n): amusement.

Disposed (pp): decided.

Disposicioun (n): position.

Dispoylen (v): to undress.

Do, don, doon, doone (v): to do.

Doghter (n): daughter.

Doom (n): judgement.

Dore (n): door. *Out at dore*: outside.

Dorste: see *Dar*.

Dotard (adj): foolish.

Doun (adv): down.

Doutelees (adv): doubtless.

Dowaire, dowere (n): dowry.

Drad: see *Drede*.

Drawen (v): to draw near. *Drow*: drew near.

Drede (n): doubt, fear.

Drede (v): to dread, to fear, to doubt. *Drad*: dreaded.

Drery (adj): gloomy.

Dressen (v): to array, to set, to prepare, to array oneself.

Dreye (adj): dry.

Dronken (adj): drunken.

Droppyng (adj): damp, dripping wet.

Drow: see *Drawen*.

Duren (v): to endure, to last.

Dwellen (v): to dwell, to live. *Dwelte*: lived.

Dwellynge (n): dwelling, place to live.

Dwelte: see *Dwellen*.

Dynt (n): blow.

Dyverse (adj): different.

Dyvynen (v): to divine, to conjecture. *Devyne*: divines.

Ech (adj, pron): each.

Echoon (pron): each one.

Eek (adv): also.

Eftsoones (adv): again.

Elde (n): old age.

Eldre (n): ancestor.

Elenge (adj): wearisome.

Ellis (adv): else, otherwise.

Encressen (v): to increase, to get larger.

Enditen (v): to write.

Enforcen (v): to strengthen, to make an effort.

Enformen (v): to inform, to instruct.

Engendre (v): to engender.

Engendrure (n): procreation.

Enlumynen (v): to illuminate, to give lustre to.

Ensample (n): example.

Entencioun, entente (n): intention.

Entende (v): to hope for, to strive.

Entrayle (n): entrails.

Entremette (v): to interfere.

Envenyme (n): poison.

Envie, envye (n): envy, desire.

Er (conj): before, formerly.

Ere (n): ear.

Erst (adv): before, at first.

Erthe (n): earth, land.

Erys (n): ears.

Ese (n): ease, pleasure.

Espien, espyen (v): to spy.

Estat (n): condition, state, rank.
Eve (n): evening.
Evene (adj): tranquil, even.
Evere (adv): ever, always.
Everemo (adv): evermore.
Everich (adj, pron): everyone.
Expres (adv): expressly,
Eyen (n): eye.
Eyle (v): to ail.

Fader, fadre (n): father.
Faillen (v): to fail.
Fair, faire, feyre (adv):
   courteously, properly.
Faire, fayre (adj): fair, beautiful,
   good.
Fairnesse (n): beauty, loveliness.
Fairye (n): fairy, enchantment,
   magic.
Fallen (v): to happen, to befall.
   Fil, fille, fyl: happened.
Falwes (n): open fields.
Fame (n): report, fame, rumour.
Fantasye (n): desire.
Faren (v): to go, to behave. *Ferde*:
   went, behaved.
Faste (adv): hard.
Fawe: see *Fayn*.
Fayn, fawe (adj): eager.
Fecchen (v): to fetch. *Fette*:
   fetched.
Fee (n): property.
Feeld, feld (n): field.
Feend (n): fiend.
Feeste, feste (n): feast, honour.
Feet (n): feat, action.
Felawe (n): companion.
Fele (adj): many.
Fer (adj, adv): far.

Ferde: see *Faren*.
Ferme (adj): firm.
Ferthe (adj): fourth.
Ferther (adv): further, more.
Ferthermoore (adv): furthermore.
Feste: see *Feeste*.
Fet (adj): fat.
Fette: see *Fecchen*.
Fey (n): faith.
Feynen (v): to pretend, to avoid,
   to feign.
Feynten (v): to faint, to weaken.
Feyre: see *Fair*.
Figures (n): figures of speech.
Fil, fille: see *Fallen*.
Filthe (n): filth.
Fit (n): bout.
Fleeth: see *Fleten*.
Fleten (v): to flow. *Fleeth*: flows.
Flokmele (n): flock, crowd.
Flour, floure (n): flower.
Flouren (v): to flower.
Folwen (v): to follow.
Folye (n): lust, foolishness.
Fonden (v): to try, to strive, to
   endeavour.
Foore (n): footsteps.
Forbede (v): to forbid.
Forberen (v): to put up with.
Forgon, forgoon (v): to give up.
Fors (n): force. *Do no fors*: do not
   mind.
Foryelde (v): to forgive.
Fostre (v): to bring up, to
   support.
Foul, foule (adj, adv): ugly,
   disgraceful.
Fowele (n): bird.
Freletee (n): frailty, weakness.

Frere (n): friar.

Fressh, fresshe (adj, adv): fresh, lively.

Freten (v): to consume, to eat.

Fro (prep): from.

Fruyt (n): fruit, result.

Ful, fulle (adj): very, full.

Fulfillen (v): to fill, to fulfil, to satisfy.

Fulliche (adv): fully.

Furlang (n): furlong.

Fyl: see *Fallen*.

Fyn (adj): fine, pure, refined.

Fyne (n): end.

Fyr (n): fire.

Galen (v): to cry out, to exclaim.

Galle (n): sore spot.

Galwes (n): gallows.

Gan: see *Ginnen*.

Gat (n): gap.

Gay, gaye (adj): bright, merry.

Gemme (n): gem.

Genterye (n): gentility.

Gentil (n): noble.

Gentil (adj): noble, excellent.

Gentilesse, gentillesse (n): courtesy, nobility.

Gentileste (adj): noblest.

Gentrye (n): nobility, noble birth.

Gerdoun (n): reward for, return for.

Gere (n): apparel, belongings.

Gest, geste (n): guest.

Geste (n): story.

Geten (v): to obtain, to get.

Gilt (n): guilt.

Giltlees (adj): without guilt.

Ginnen (v): to begin. *Gan*: began.

Gladen (v): to gladden, to make happy, to be willing.

Gladly (adv): gladly, willingly, happily.

Glosen (v): to interpret, to flatter.

Good (n): belongings, property.

Goon (v): to go.

Goos (n): goose.

Goost (n): soul, spirit.

Goost: see *Goon*.

Gossib, gossyb (n): close friend, gossip.

Governance, governaunce (n): rule, control.

Grace (n): mercy, honour, favour.

Graunten (v): to grant.

Graven (v): to bury.

Grece (n): grease.

Greet, gret (adj): great.

Grene (adj): green, fresh.

Greten (v): to greet.

Greven (v): to grieve, to hurt.

Grinde (v): to grind.

Grisly (adj): horrible.

Grucche (v): to complain, to begrudge.

Gyde (n): guide.

Gyde (v): to guide, to lead.

Gye (v): to govern.

Gyte (n): long robe.

Habit (n): clothes.

Habundance (n): abundance.

Habundant (adj): abundant.

Halt: see *Holden*.

Halwes (n): shrines.

Han (v): to have.

Happen (v): to occur, to happen, to chance.

Hardily (adv): boldly, surely.

Hardynesse (n): boldness.

Harneys (n): equipment.

Hastif (adj): hasty.

Hastiliche (adv): hastily.

Hauke (n): hawk.

Hauken (v): to hawk.

Hawe (n): hawthorn berry.

Hede (n): heed. *Taken hede*: take heed, pay attention.

Heed, heved (n): head.

Heeld: see *Holden*.

Heer, heere, heres, herys (n): hair.

Heeste, heste (n): commandment, behest.

Heigh, heighe, hye (adj, adv): high, elaborate, great.

Helen (v): to conceal, to keep secret.

Hem (pron): them.

Hende (adj): courteous.

Henten (v): to take, to seize.

Herbe (n): herb, vegetable.

Herberage (n): lodging.

Heres, herys: see *Heer*.

Herknen (v): to listen.

Herte (n): heart.

Hertly (adj, adv): sincerely.

Heryen (v): to praise.

Heste (n): command.

Heved: see *Heed*.

Hevynesse (n): sorrow.

Hewe (n): hue, appearance.

Hight, highte: see *Hoten*.

Hir, hire (pron): her. *Hirselven*: herself.

Hir, hire (pron): their.

Holden (v): to consider, to deem, to hold to, to be obligated. *Halt, heeld*: considered.

Holour (n): lecher.

Honde (n): hand.

Honeste (adj): respectable.

Honestetee (n): honour, modesty.

Hool (adv): whole, complete.

Hoold (n): keeping.

Hoom (n): home.

Hoot (adj): hot.

Hors (n): horse.

Hoten (v): to be called, to promise, to be named. *Hight, highte*: was called.

Hous (n): house.

Housbond, housbonde (n): husband.

Housbondrye (n): household goods.

Humanitee (n): benevolence.

Humblenesse (n): humility.

Hyden (v): to hide.

Hye: see *Heigh*.

Hyre (n): hire, paid service.

Ilke (adj): same.

In (n): dwelling.

Incubus (n): evil spirit.

Infeere (adv): together.

Inpertinent (adj): irrelevant.

Insight (n): insight, understanding.

Inwith (prep): within.

Iren (n): iron.

Jane (n): coin of little worth.

Jangleresse (n): chatterbox.

Jape (n): trick.

Joly (adj): jolly, lively, lustful.

Jolyfnesse, jolifnesse, jolytee (n): pleasure.

Juggement (n): judgement.

Kan: see *Konnen*.

Kaynard (n): dotard, foolish old person.

Keepen (v): to notice.

Kembe (v): to comb.

Kepen (v): to take care of.

Kitte: see *Cutten*.

Knave (n): boy, servant, peasant.

Knele (v): to kneel.

Konnen (v): to be able, to know, to understand how to. *Kan*: knows. *Kouth*: knew. *Koude*: could, knew. The verb 'konnen' implies either 'to be able' or 'to grasp something intellectually'.

Konnyngly (adv): cunningly, skilfully.

Koude: see *Konnen*.

Kouth: see *Konnen*.

Kynde (n): stock, kindred.

Kyndely (adv): by nature.

Lappe (n): fold of cloth.

Large (n): liberty.

Lasse (adj, adv): less.

Last (adj): farthest.

Lat: see *Leten*.

Lauryat (adj): laureate.

Lavour (n): washing bowl.

Lechour (n): lecher.

Leden (v): to lead, to spend.

Leef (n): page.

Leef, leeve, leve, lief (adj): dear.

Leeren (v): to learn. *Lere*: learns. *Lerne*: learned.

Leeste (adj, adv): least.

Leet: see *Leten*.

Leeve, leve: see *Leef*.

Leeve, leve (v): to believe.

Leeven, leven (v): to leave, to depart.

Legende (n): story.

Lemman (n): mistress.

Lenger: see *Longe*.

Leonesse, leoun (n): lioness, lion.

Lere: see *Leeren*.

Lerne: see *Leeren*.

Lesen (v): to lose. *Lorn*: lost.

Lest, leste: see *Lust*.

Lest, leste: see *List*.

Lest (conj): for fear that, in case.

Leten (v): to let, to leave, to desist, to stop, to allow. *Leet*: lets.

Lette (n): delay.

Letten (v): to hinder.

Leve (v): to permit, to allow.

Leveful (adj): allowable.

Levene (n): lightning.

Levere (adv): rather.

Leye: see *Lyen*.

Leyser (n): leisure, opportunity, spare time.

Lief: see *Leef*.

Lige (adj): liege, vassal.

Lightly (adv): easily.

Likerous (adj): lecherous.

List, Liste (v): to wish, to want, to desire, to please. *Lest, leste*: wished.

Lith: see *Lyen*.

Lo (interj): behold.

Lok (n): lock.

Lond (n): land.

Longe (adj, adv): long. *Lenger*: longer.

Longen (v): to belong.

Looken (v): to look, to regard.

Loore (n): law, knowledge.

Looth (adj): loath.

Loothly (adj): ugly.

Lordynge (n): gentleman.

Lorel (n): scoundrel.

Lorn: see *Lesen*.

Lowe (adj, adv): low, lowly, humble, humbly.

Lowely (adj, adv): humble, humbly.

Lust, lest, leste (n): lust, desire, wish, pleasure.

Lusty (adj): lusty, pleasant.

Lye (n): lie.

Lyen (v): to lie, to lie upon, to reside. *Leye*: was lying. *Lith*: lies.

Lyes (n): dregs.

Lyf (n): life.

Lyke (v): to please.

Lyme (n): limb.

Lymytacioun (n): district.

Lymytour (n): begging friar.

Lynage (n): lineage.

Lyne (n): line of descent, lineage.

Lyst (n): ear.

Lyven (v): to live.

Lyvinge (n): living.

Maistrie, maistrye (n): control.

Make (n): mate.

Maken (v): to make, to form.

Malice (n): malice, wickedness, evil.

Manace (v): to menace. to threaten.

Maner, manere (n): way, manner, kind of.

Mariage, maryage (n): marriage.

Mark (n): image.

Markisesse (n): marchioness.

Markys (n): marquis.

Marys (n): marsh.

Matere (n): matter, subject.

Matyns (n): morning prayers.

Maugree (prep): in spite of.

Mayde (n): maiden, girl.

Maydenhed, maydenhede (n): virginity.

Maymen (v): to maim, to injure.

Mede (n): meadow.

Mede (n): reward.

Meeke (adj): meek.

Meeste: see *Mooste*.

Menen (v): to intend.

Mervaile, merveille (n): marvel.

Merveillen (v): to marvel.

Merveilous (adj): strange.

Merye, murie, murye (adj, adv): merry, glad, happy.

Meschaunce (n): misfortune.

Mescheef (n): misfortune.

Message (n): message, messenger.

Mesure (n): measurement, moderation.

Meten (v): to meet.

Metten (v): to dream.

Mis (adj): amiss, wrong.

Mo (n): more, others.

Mo (adj, adv): more.

Moder (n): mother.

Mooste, meeste (adj, adv): greatest, highest.

Mooten, mote (v): must.

Mordre (v): to murder.

Mordrere (n): murderer.

Morne (v): to mourn.

Morwe (n): morning.

Morwenynge (n): early morning.

Mote: see *Mooten*.

Mote (n): bit of dust.

Motthe (n): moth.

Mowen (v): to have power, to be able.

Muche, muchel (n): much.

Muche, muchel (adj, adv): much, many.

Murie, murye: see *Merye*.

Murmur (n): grumbling, rumour.

Myghte (n): power.

Myn (pron, adj): my, mine.

Myre (n): mire.

Myrthe (n): amusement.

Mysavyse: see *Mis* and *Avyse*.

Myschaunce (n): unlucky event.

Myte (n): insect.

Nacioun (n): nation, family.

Nam (v): from *ne am*: am not.

Namely (adv): especially.

Namo, namoore (adj, adv): no more.

Nat (adv): not.

Nathelees (adv): nevertheless.

Nay (adv): no.

Nayle (v): to nail.

Ne (adv): not.

Ne (conj): nor.

Nece (n): niece, kinswoman.

Necligence (n): negligence, laziness.

Nedelees (n): needless, unnecessary.

Nedely (adv): necessarily.

Nedes (adv): needs, necessarily.

Neighe: see *Ny*.

Nel: see *Nyl*.

Nempnen (v): to name, to mention.

Noblesse (n): noble rank.

Nobleye (n): nobility, noble rank.

Noght (adv): not.

Nolde (v): from *ne wolde*, would not.

Nones (n): occasion. *For the nones*: for this purpose.

Noon (adj, adv): no.

Noon (pron): none.

Norice (n): nurse.

Norice (v): to nourish, to bring up.

Nowche (n): jewel.

Ny, neighe (adj, adv): near, close, almost.

Nyce (adj): foolish, lustful.

Nycetee (n): foolishness, lust, desire, sexual intercourse.

Nygard (n): miser.

Nyl (v): from *ne wyl*, will not.

Nys (v): from *ne ys*, is not.

Nyste (v): from *ne wyste*, did not know.

O: see *Oon*.

Obeisaunce, obeysance (n): obedience.

Obeyen (v): to obey.

Obeysant (adj): obedient.

Of (prep): of, from, by, off, in.
Office (n): duties, service.
Ofte (adj, adv): often.
Oghte (v): ought to, should.
On: see *Oon*.
Ones, onys (adv): once.
Oon, o, on (num, adj, pron): one, the same, single.
Oore (n): ore.
Oppressioun (n): violation.
Ordynance (n): order.
Ouch (n): brooch.
Out (adv): out, without.
Outher (adj, conj): either.
Outrely (adv): completely, emphatically.
Outreste (adj): uttermost.
Overbyde (v): to outlive.
Owene (adj): own.

Pace: see *Passen*.
Palays, paleys (n): palace.
Parage (n): birth, lineage.
Paramour (n): mistress.
Paraventure (adv): perhaps, by chance.
Pardee (interj): certainly.
Parfit (adj): perfect.
Parfitly (adv): perfectly.
Passen (v): to pass, to depart, to step, to pace, to surpass. *Pace*: depart.
Pees (n): peace.
Penyble (adj): anxious to please.
Percen (v): to pierce.
Perree (n): precious stones.
Pestilence (n): plague.
Pistel (n): message.
Pitee (n): pity.

Pith (n): energy.
Pitous (adj): pitiful, mournful.
Pitously (adv): piteously.
Place (n): place, spot, rank.
Plante (n): cutting.
Playn, playne, pleyn (adj): plain, clear.
Plentee (n): plenty, abundance.
Plesance, plesaunce (n): pleasure, delight.
Plesant (adj): pleasurable, delightful, pleasing.
Pleye (n): amusement, game, rules of the game, dramatic performance.
Pleyen (v): to play, to amuse oneself.
Pleyn (adj): full, complete.
Pleyne (v): to complain.
Plighten (v): to pledge.
Plyght (pp): torn.
Point, poynt (n): point, condition.
Possessioun (n): possessions.
Povre (adj): poor.
Povreliche (adv): poorly, in poverty.
Powren (v): to gaze.
Poynt: see *Point*.
Praktyke (n): practice.
Pray: see *Preyen*.
Preambulacioun (n): making a preamble.
Prechour (n): preacher.
Prechen (v): to preach.
Precious, precius (adj): valuable, expensive, fussy.
Preente (n): imprint, mark.
Preesen (v): to press.
Preferren (v): to prefer, to choose.

Prescience (n): foreknowledge.
Preve (n): proof.
Preve (v): to prove.
Preyen (v): to pray, to beseech, to ask, to invite. *Pray*: prays.
Preysen (v): to praise.
Pridelees (adj): humble, without pride.
Priken (v): to afflict, to spur.
Privee, pryvee (adj): secret, private, personal.
Prively, pryvely (adv): secretly.
Privetee, pryvetee (n): privacy, secrecy, private business.
Profit (n): profit, good.
Profren (v): to offer, to request.
Prohemie (n): introduction.
Propre (adj): proper, special, own.
Proprely (adv): properly, appropriately, naturally.
Prowesse (n): excellence.
Prys (n): worth, praise.
Pryvee: see *Privee*.
Pryvetee: see *Privetee*.
Publisschen (v): to proclaim, to publish.
Pured (adj): refined.
Pursuen (v): to pursue.
Purveiaunce (n): foresight.
Purveyen (v): to prepare, to provide.
Putten (v): to put.
Pye (n): magpie.
Pyne (n): pain.

Quake (v): to quake, to tremble.
Queynte (n): pudendum, sexual intercourse.

Queynte (adj): strange.
Quod (pt, sg): said.
Quyten (v): to repay, to reward.

Radde: see *Reden*.
Rafte: see *Reven*.
Ragerye (n): passion.
Raunceon (n): penalty.
Realtee (n): royalty.
Recche, rekke (v): to care. *Roue*: cared.
Recchelees (adj): careless.
Reddy, redy (adj): ready, prepared, at hand.
Reden (v): to read, to advise, to understand. *Radde*: read.
Reed (n): advice, help.
Reed (adj): red.
Rekke: see *Recche*.
Relesse (v): to release.
Remenant (n): remainder.
Renden (v): to tear. *Rente*: tore.
Rennen (v): to run, to flow.
Renomee (n): renown.
Rente: see *Renden*.
Repaire (v): to return.
Repreve (n): shame.
Repreven (v): to reprove.
Requeren (v): to ask, to require.
Reste (n): rest, ease.
Rethoryk (n): rhetoric.
Revel (n): revelry.
Revelour (n): profligate.
Reven (v): to take. *Rafte*: took.
Rewe (n): row.
Rewen (v): to have pity, to be sorry.
Richeliche (adv): richly.
Richesse (n): riches, wealth.

Riden (v): to ride. *Rood*: rode.

Right, righte (adj): just, exact, direct.

Right (adv): exactly.

Riot (n): revelry.

Roghte: see *Recche*.

Rood: see *Riden*.

Roode (n): cross.

Roos (n): rose.

Roote (n): foot.

Roule (v): to wander.

Routhe (n): pity, sad or pitiful situation.

Rownen (v): to whisper.

Rubryche (n): rubric.

Rude (adj): humble, ignorant, rough, poor.

Rudely (adv): roughly.

Rudenesse (n): humble conditions.

Rumbelen (v): to rumour.

Rym (n): rhyme.

Rype (adj): mature.

Sad (adj): firm, serious, constant, steadfast.

Sadnesse (n): constancy, steadfastness.

Salwes (n): willow branches.

Sapience (n): wisdom.

Sauf (adj): safe.

Saufly (adv): safely.

Savoure (v): to taste.

Say: see *Seyen*.

Sclaundre (n): slander.

Seche: see *Seken*.

Secree (adj): discreet.

Secrely (adv): secretly.

Sect (n): company, group.

Seel (n): seal.

Seen (v): to see, to behold.

Seken, seche (v): to seek, to resort to.

Selde (adv): seldom.

Sely (adj): happy, good, innocent, blessed, simple, foolish.

Semblent (n): appearance.

Semen (v): to seem.

Sen (v): to see, to look. *Biseye*: looking.

Sengen (v): to singe.

Sentence (n): meaning, opinion, subject.

Sepulcre (n): tomb.

Serchen (v): to search, to haunt.

Servage (n): servitude.

Serven (v): to treat.

Servitute (n): servitude, subjection.

Servysable (adj): hardworking.

Servyse (n): service.

Sethe (v): to boil.

Setten (v): to set out, to set, to put.

Seyen, say (v): to say.

Seynt (n): saint.

Shapen (v): to form, to make, to shape, to plan. *Shoope*: formed.

Shenden (v): to destroy.

Sherte (n): shirt.

Shetten (v): to shut.

Shewen (v); to show, to present.

Shifte (v): to provide.

Shilde (v): to protect, to forbid.

Shipnes (n): stables.

Shoope: see *Shapen*.

Shorten (v): to shorten.

Shreden (v): to slice, to cut, to chop.

Shrewe (n): scoundrel, shrew.

Shrewednesse (n): malice.

Shrewen (v): to curse.

Sighte (n): sight, spectacle.

Siken, syken (v): to sigh.

Siker (adj): certain, sure.

Sikerly (adv): surely.

Sikly (adv): sickly.

Sire (n): master, sir.

Sith, sithe (adv): since.

Slaken (v): to fail, to desist, to assuage.

Sleen (v): to slay, to destroy.

Sleghte, sleighte (n): ingenuity, cunning.

Slyde (v): to slide away.

Smal, smale (adj): slim, slender, small, little, humble.

Smerten (v): to suffer, to feel pain.

Smiten (v): to strike, to smite. *Smoot*: struck. *Smyt*: strikes.

Smok (n): shift, undergarment.

Smoot: see *Smiten*.

Smyt: see *Smiten*.

Sobre (adj): sober, grave.

Sobrely (adv): soberly, gravely.

Sodeyn (adj): sudden.

Sodeynly (adv): suddenly.

Softe (adj): gentle, quiet.

Softely (adv): gently, quietly.

Sojorne (v): to remain.

Solempnytee (n): ceremony.

Som (pron, adj): some.

Somdel (adv): somewhat.

Somere (n): summer.

Sondry (adj): various, sundry.

Songen (pp): sung.

Sonne (n); sun.

Soore (adj): sore.

Soore, sore (adv): badly.

Sooth (n): truth.

Sooth (adv): truly.

Soothfastnesse (n): truth.

Soothly (adv): truly.

Sophyme (n): sophism, subtle thought.

Sorwe (n): sorrow.

Sorwefully (adv): sorrowfully.

Sory (adj): sad, sorrowful.

Sotilly: see *Subtilly*.

Souke (v): to suck, to breastfeed.

Soutiltee: see *Subtiltee*.

Sovereyn (adj): supreme, very high.

Sovereyntee (n): sovereignty, supremacy.

Sown (n): sound.

Space (n): some time.

Spak: see *Speken*.

Sparen (v): to refrain.

Spaynel (n): spaniel.

Spectacle (n): eyeglass.

Speken (v): to speak. *Spak*: spoke.

Spille (v): to waste, to destroy, to kill, to spoil.

Spitously (adv): cruelly, fiercely.

Spousaille (n): wedding, marriage.

Spousen (v): to marry, to wed.

Sprynge (v): to rise up.

Spyced (pp): over-particular.

Squyer (n): squire, escort.

Squyer (v): to escort, to serve.

Squyereth: see *Squyer*.

Stable (adj): steadfast.

Stalken (v): to creep, to stalk, to go quietly.

Stedefastly (adv): steadfastly.

Stedfastnesse (n): steadfastness.

Stele (n): handle.

Stente: see *Stynten*.

Sterre (n): star.

Sterten, stirte (v); to start, to move towards, to leap, to leap up.

Sterven (v): to die.

Stibourne (adj): stubborn.

Stifly (adv): strongly.

Stille (adj): still, silent.

Stirte: see *Sterten*.

Stonden (v): to stand.

Stoon (n): stone.

Stoor (n): account, store.

Stounde (n): time, moment.

Straunge (adj): strange, not natural.

Stren (n): strain, stock, as in a family.

Strepen (v): to strip.

Streyne (v): to constrain.

Stryven (v): to fight, to oppose.

Studien (v): to study, to think about.

Stuffed (pp): filled, supplied.

Sturdy (adj): harsh, stern, cruel.

Sturdynesse (n): cruelty.

Stynten (v): to prevent, to cease. *Stente*: ceased.

Subgitz (n): subjects.

Subtil (adj): clever, skilful.

Subtilly, sotilly (adv): skilfully, craftily.

Subtiltee, soutiltee (n): skilfulness, guile.

Suffisance (n): happiness.

Suffisant (adj): sufficient, capable.

Suffisen (v): to satisfy, to suffice.

Suffren (v): to endure, to suffer, to submit to.

Supposynge (n): belief.

Suretee, seuretee (n): security, safety.

Swal: see *Swelle*.

Swappen (v): to dash, to drop, to fall, to strike.

Swelle, swal (v): to swell.

Sweren (v): to swear. *Swoor, sworen*: swore.

Swete (adj): sweet, fine.

Swich (adj, pron): such.

Swoor: see *Sweren*.

Sworen: see *Sweren*.

Swowgh, swogh (n): swoon, faint.

Swowne, aswowne (v): to faint.

Swynken (v): to work.

Syk (adj): sick.

Syken: see *Siken*.

Syn (prep, conj): since.

Syngen (v): to sing.

Synne (n): sin.

Synnen (v): to sin.

Synful (adj): sinful.

Taken (v): to take. *Taken kepe*: take notice. *Token*: took.

Tale (n): account.

Talis (n): tales.

Taur (n): Taurus.

Tayle (n): tail, rear end.

Techen (v): to teach.

Tellen (v): to tell, to relate.

Tentifly (adv): attentively.

Terme (n): period of time.

Termes (n): literary terms.
Terys (n): tears.
Testament (n): will.
Thanne (adv): then.
That (pron): that, which, what.
Theef (n): villain.
Theen (v): to prosper.
Thenken (v): to think, to intend, to consider.
Thenne (adv): thence.
Ther (adv): there, where.
Thewes (n): morals.
Thilke (adj): that, that same.
Tho (pron, adj): those.
Thral (n): slave.
Thressfold (n): threshold.
Thrifty (adj): serviceable.
Throope (n): village.
Throwe (n): short while.
Thryven (v): to thrive, to prosper.
Thurgh (prep): through.
Thynge (n): affair, thing, goods.
Tidynge (n): news, account of events.
Tiklen (v): to please, to gratify.
Til (conj): until.
Tobreke (v): to break into pieces.
Togh (adv): though.
Token: see *Taken*.
Tonge (n): tongue.
Tonne (n): barrel, wine barrel.
Tooth (n): taste.
Tormentrye (n): pain, torture.
Tornen (v): to turn.
Toure (n): tower, castle.
Tow (n): flax.
Toward (prep): towards, in readiness for.

Translaten (v): to transform.
Traunce (n): trance.
Travaile (v): to work, to exert oneself.
Tree (n): tree, wood.
Tresoor (n): treasure.
Tresse (v): to dress, to braid.
Tretys (n): contract.
Trewe (adj): true, faithful.
Trewely (adv): certainly, truly.
Tristen (v): to trust.
Trouble (v): to disturb.
Trouthe (n): truth, troth, faithfulness.
Trowen (v): to believe.
Tweye, tweyne (adj): two.
Twiste (v): to torture.

Under (prep): under, near.
Undermelys (n): late mornings.
Undigne (adj): unworthy.
Undren (n): mid morning.
Unlyk (adj): unlike.
Unnethe (adv): hardly, with difficulty.
Unreste (n): distress.
Unright (n): wrong, injury.
Untressed (pp): unkempt.
Up (adv): up.
Up (prep): upon.
Upright (adv): face up.
Usage (n): custom.
Us-self (pron): ourselves.
Usen (v): to use, to use commonly, to become accustomed to.

Vanytee (n): foolishness, empty thoughts.
Variance (n): change, difference.

Verray (adj): true, real.

Verray (adv): truly.

Vertu (n): virtue.

Vertuous (adj): virtuous.

Vileynes (adj): villainous, sinful.

Vileynye (n): shameful act.

Visage (n): face.

Vitaille (n): agriculture, provisions.

Vouchen sauf (v): to vouchsafe, to permit.

Voyden (v): to vacate, to get rid of.

Voys (n): voice.

Vynolent (adj): drunken.

Walwe (v): to toss, to twist.

Wantowne (adj): wanton.

Warden (v); to beware, to avoid.

Wardeyn (n): guardian.

Wast (n): waste.

Wayten (v): to watch, to wait for.

Wedden (v): to wed.

Weddyng (n): wedding.

Wede (n): clothing.

Weel (adv): well.

Weex: see *Wexen*.

Weilawey, weylawey (interj): alas.

Wel (adv): well, correctly, many.

Wele (n): happiness, wealth, prosperity.

Welken (v): to wither, to languish.

Welkne (n): sky.

Welle (n): spring, well.

Wenden (v): to go, to depart.

Wenen (v): to think, to suppose. *Wenestow*: do you suppose. *Wende*: thought.

Wepen (v): to weep.

Weren (v): to wear, to carry.

Werk (n): work.

Werken (v): to work, to act, to make. *Wroghte*: made.

Werne (v): to refuse.

Werre (n): war.

Wey, Weye (n): way, path.

Weylawey: see *Weilawey*.

Weyven (v): to waive, to abandon.

Wexen, woxen (v): to become. *Weex*: becomes.

Wheither (adv): which.

Whennes (adv): whence.

Whete (n): wheat.

While (n): time.

Whilom (adv): formerly, once.

Widwe, wydewe (n): widow.

Wifhod, wifhode (n): womanhood.

Wight (n): person.

Wikke (adj): wicked.

Wilful (adj): willing.

Willen (v): to wish, to want, to desire. *Wol, wole*: wish. *Wolt, woltow, wostow*: you wish, do you wish. *Wolde*: wished.

Wirkyng (n): actions, behaviour.

Wise (n): manner, way.

Wisly (adv): surely.

Wisse (v): to instruct.

Wiste: see *Witen*.

Wit (n): understanding, judgement.

Witen (v): to know. *Wiste*: knew. *Wityng*: knowing. *Woot*: knows.

Withal (adv): moreover, indeed.

Withdrawe (v): to withhold.

Withoute, withouten (adv): outside, without.

Wityng: see *Witen*.

Wo (n): woe.

Wol, wole: see *Willen*.

Wolde: see *Willen*.

Wolt, woltow: see *Willen*.

Wombe (n): womb, abdomen.

Wommanhede (n): femininity.

Woned, wont (pp): accustomed.

Wood (adj): mad, angry.

Woot: see *Witen*.

Worte (n): cabbage.

Worthy (adj): excellent, of high rank, deserving.

Worthynesse (n): worthiness, excellence.

Wostow: see *Witen*.

Woxen: see *Wexen*.

Wrecched (adj): wretched.

Wreken (v): to avenge oneself.

Writen (v): to write. *Wroot*: wrote.

Wroghte: see *Werken*.

Wroot: see *Writen*.

Wrothe (adj): angry.

Wryen (v): to cover.

Wyl, wille (n): will, wish, desire.

Wynde (v): to turn, to wind.

Wynnen (v): to win.

Wys, wyse (adj): wise.

Wysdam (n): knowledge.

Wysly (adv): wisely.

Wyten (v): to blame.

Wyve (v): to wive, to marry.

Y: a prefix used with the past participle.

Y (pron): I.

Yaf: see *Yeven*.

Yate (n): gate.

Ydel (adj): idle.

Ye (pron): you.

Yelden (v): to yield, to pay.

Yen (n): eyes.

Yerde (n): authority.

Yerne (adv): eagerly.

Yeven (v): to give. *Yat*: gave.

Yfeere (adv): together.

Ygrave (pp): buried.

Yifte (n): gift.

Yis (adv): yes, indeed.

Yit (adv): yet.

Ylike (adj): alike, equally.

Ylymed (pp): trapped.

Ynogh, ynow (adj): enough, sufficient.

Yond (adv): yonder.

Yong, yonge (adj): young.

Yore, yoore (adv): of old, for a long time.

Yrekened (pp): counted.

Ytaille (n): Italy.

Yvel, yvele (adj): ill, evil.

Ywys (adv): certainly, truly.

Bibliography

EDITIONS OF CHAUCER

Benson, Larry D. (1988) *The Riverside Chaucer*, Oxford: Oxford University Press.

Blake, N. F. (1980) *The Canterbury Tales*, London: Edward Arnold.

Cigman, G. (1975) *The Wife of Bath's Prologue and Tale and The Clerk's Prologue and Tale from The Canterbury Tales*, New York, Holmes & Meier Publishers.

Donaldson, E.T. (1958) *Chaucer's Poetry*, New York: Ronald Press Co.

Manly, John M. and Rickert, Edith. (1940) *The Text of The Canterbury Tales*, Chicago: University of Chicago Press.

Robinson, F. N. (1957) *The Works of Geoffrey Chaucer*, 2nd edn, 1957, Oxford: Oxford University Press.

Ruggiers, Paul G. (1979–) *A Variorum Edition of the Works of Geoffrey Chaucer*, Norman, Oklahoma: University of Oklahoma Press.

Winny, James. (1965) *The Wife of Bath's Prologue and Tale*, Cambridge: Cambridge University Press.

MANUSCRIPTS OF 'THE CANTERBURY TALES'

Camb. Dd. 4. 24. at the University Library, Cambridge.

Ellesmere 26. c. 9. at the Huntington Library, San Marino, California.

— (1989) *The Ellesmere Manuscript of Chaucer's Canterbury Tales. A Working Facsimile*, ed. Ralph Hanna III, Cambridge: D. S. Brewer.

Hengwrt 154. Peniarth 392 D. at the National Library of Wales at Aberystwyth.

— (1979) *A Facsimile and Transcription of the Hengwrt Manuscript with*

Variants from the Ellesmere Manuscript, ed. Paul G. Ruggiers, Norman, Oklahoma: Oklahoma University Press.

Petworth House MS 7. at Petworth House, Petworth, Sussex.

PRIMARY TEXTS

Aesop. (sixth century BC) *Fables of Aesop*, trans. S. A. Handford, 1954, Harmondsworth: Penguin Books.

Augustine, St, bishop of Hippo. (c.400) *Confessions*, ed. and trans. H. Chadwick, 1990, Oxford: Oxford University Press.

— (427) *On Christian Doctrine*, ed. and trans. D. W. Robertson, 1958, Indianapolis: Bobbs-Merrill.

Le Bien des Fames and *Le Blasme des Fames* (c.1300) in *Three Medieval Views of Women*, ed. G. K. Fiero, W. Pfeffer and M. Allain, 1989, New Haven: Yale University Press.

Boccaccio, Giovanni. (1335) *The Decameron*, ed. E. Hutton and trans. J. M. Rigg, 1930, London: Dent.

Boethius. (522–4) *Consolation of Philosophy*, trans. V. E. Watts, 1969, Harmondsworth: Penguin Books.

Book of Hours: see R. S. Wieck, L. R. Poos and V. Reinberg. (1988) *The Book of Hours in Medieval Art and Life*, London: Sotheby's Publications.

Bryan, W. F. and Dempster, Germaine. (1958) *Sources and Analogues of Chaucer's Canterbury Tales*, New York: Humanities Press.

Byron, George, Lord. (1807) in *Chaucer: The Critical Heritage*, ed. D. Brewer, 1978, London: Routledge.

Capellanus, Andreas. (c.1174) *The Art of Courtly Love*, ed. and trans. J. J. Parry, 1941, New York: Columbia University Press.

Dante Alighieri. Relevant passages from the *Convivio* (1304–7) and the *Purgatorio* (1307–21) may be found in *Sources and Analogues of Chaucer's Canterbury Tales*, eds. W. F. Bryan and G. Dempster, 1941, New York: Humanities Press, pp. 264–6.

— (1909) *Convivio*, trans. W. W. Jackson, Oxford: Clarendon Press.

— (1901) *The Purgatorio*, trans. Paget Toynbee, London: Dent.

Deschamps, Eustache. (1406) *Miroir de Mariage* in *Oeuvres Complètes*, ed. G. Raynaud, 1894, Paris: Firmin-Didot.

Gawain Poet. (c.1375) *Sir Gawain and The Green Knight* in *Pearl, Cleanness, Patience, Sir Gawain and the Green Knight*, ed. A. C. Cawley and J. J. Anderson, 1976, London: Dent.

Geoffrey de Vinsauf. (c.1210) *Poetria Nova of Geoffrey of Vinsauf*, trans. M. F. Nims, 1967, Toronto: Pontifical Institute of Medieval Studies.

Goodman of Paris. (c.1393) *The Goodman of Paris*, trans. E. Power, 1928, London: Routledge.

Gower, John. (1376–9) *Mirour de l'omme*, repub. 1991, Woodbridge: Boydell.

— (1390) *Confessio Amantis*, ed. R. A. Peck, 1980, Toronto: University of Toronto Press.

Heloise and Abelard. (c.1132) *The Love Letters of Abelard and Heloise*, repub. 1933, London: Dent.

Hoccleve, Thomas. (1405) *The Regement of Princes* in *Chaucer: The Critical Heritage*, ed. D. Brewer, 1978, London: Routledge.

Homer. (eighth century BC) *The Iliad of Homer*, ed. and trans. R. Lattimore, 1951, Chicago: University of Chicago Press.

Jerome, St (c.393) *Epistola adversus Jovinianum*, trans. W. H. Fremantle in *St Jerome: Letters and Select Works*, ed. H. Wace and P. Schaff, 1893, Oxford: Parker.

Julian of Norwich. (c.1373) *Revelations of Divine Love*, ed. and trans. C. Wolters, 1966, Harmondsworth: Penguin Books.

Juvenal. (100–27) *The Sixteen Satires of Juvenal*, ed. and trans. P. Green, 1974, Harmondsworth: Penguin Books.

Kempe, Margery. (1436–8) *The Book of Margery Kempe*, trans. B. A. Windeatt, 1985, Harmondsworth: Penguin Books.

Langland, William. (1362–86) *The Vsion of Piers Plowman*, ed. A. V. C. Schmidt, 1987, London: Dent.

La Tour-Landry. (c.1371) *The Book of the Knight of La Tour-Landry*, ed. and trans. T. Wright, 1906, London: Early English Text Society.

Lorris, Guillaume de and Meun, Jean de. (1237–77) *Roman de la Rose*, trans. H. W. Robbins, 1962, New York: E. P. Dutton and Co. Inc.

Lucretius Carus, Titus. (first century BC) *Lucretius on the Nature of the Universe*, ed. and trans. R. Latham, 1951, Harmondsworth: Penguin Books.

Lydgate, John. (1410) *The Life of Our Lady* in *Chaucer: The Critical Heritage*, ed. D. Brewer, 1978, London: Routledge.

Map, Walter. (c.1181) *Epistola Valerii ad Rufinum* in *De Nugis Curialium*, ed. and trans. M. R. James, rev. C. N. L. Brooke and R. A. B. Mynors, 1983, Oxford: Clarendon Press.

Marie de France. (c.1180) *Fables of Marie de France*, ed. and trans. H. Spiegel, 1987, Toronto: University of Toronto Press.

The Marriage of Sir Gawaine (transcription c.1650) in *Sources and Analogues of Chaucer's Canterbury Tales*, eds. W. F. Bryan and G. Dempster, 1941, New York: Humanities Press, pp. 235–41.

Miller, Robert P. (1977) *Chaucer: Sources and Backgrounds*, New York: Oxford University Press.

Ovid. (first century BC) *Ars Amatoria* and *Remedia Amoris* in *The Art of Love and Other Poems*, ed. and trans. J. H. Mozley, 1962, London: Heinemann.

— *Metamorphoses*, trans. M. M. Innes, 1955, Harmondsworth: Penguin Books.

Petrarch, Francesco. (1373) *A Fable of Wifely Obedience and Faithfulness* in *Chaucer: Sources and Backgrounds*, ed. R. P. Miller, 1977, New York: Oxford University Press, pp. 136–52.

— (1380s) *Le livre Griseldis*, anonymous French translation of *A Fable Of Wifely Obedience* in *Sources and Analogues of Chaucer's Canterbury Tales*, eds. W. F. Bryan and G. Dempster, 1941, New York: Humanities Press, pp. 297–31.

Pisan, Christine de. (1404) *The Book of The City of Ladies*, ed. M. Warner and trans. E. J. Richards, 1983, London: Pan Books.

— (1405) *The Treasure of the City of Ladies*, ed. and trans. S. Lawson, 1985, Harmondsworth: Penguin Books.

Ptolemy. (c.150) *Ptolemy's Almagest*, ed. and trans. G. J. Toomer, 1984, London: Duckworth.

Rossetti, Christina. (1854) 'The World' in *A Choice of Christina Rossetti's Verse*, ed. E. Jennings, 1970, London: Faber & Faber.

Seneca. (63–4) *Seneca, Letters from a Stoic*, ed. R. Campbell, 1969, Harmondsworth: Penguin Books.

Statius, P. Papinius. (90–1) *Thebaid*, ed. A. Klotz, 1973, Leipzig: Teubner.

Swetnam, Joseph. (1615) *The Arraignment of Lewd, idle, froward, and unconstant women* in *Half Humankind*, eds. K. U. Henderson and B. F. McManus, 1985, Chicago: University of Illinois Press.

Tertulian. (200–25) *The Writings of Quintus Sept. Flor. Tertullianus*, eds. A. Roberts and J. Donaldson, 1870, Edinburgh: T. & T. Clark, Vol. III, pp.1–20.

Theophrastus. (third century BC) *Liber aureolus de nuptiis* in *Chaucer: Sources and Backgrounds*, ed. R. P. Miller, 1977, New York: Oxford University Press, pp. 411–14.

Trivet, Nicholas. (early fourteenth century) *Les Chroniques ecrites pour*

Marie d'Angleterre, fille d'Edward I, MS. Magdalen 45, Oxford.

Valerius Maximus. (c.35) *Valerii Maximi factorum et dictorum memorabilius libri novem*, ed. C. Kempf, 1888, rpt. 1966, Stuttgart: Teubner.

The Weddynge of Sir Gawen and Dame Ragnell (c.1450) in *Sources and Analogues of Chaucer's Canterbury Tales*, eds. W. F. Bryan and G. Dempster, 1941, New York: Humanities Press, pp. 242–64.

Wycliffe, John. (mid fourteenth century) 'Of Weddid Men and Wifis' in *Select English Works Of John Wyclif*, ed. T. Arnold, 1871, Oxford: Clarendon Press, Vol. III, pp. 188–201.

CRITICAL WORKS

Aers, David. (1980) *Chaucer, Langland and the Creative Imagination*, London: Routledge.

— (1986a) *Chaucer*, Brighton: Harvester Press.

— (ed.). (1986b) *Medieval Literature. Criticism, Ideology and History*, Brighton: Harvester Press.

— (1988) *Community, Gender and Individual Identity*, London: Routledge.

Alford, John A. (1986), 'The Wife of Bath versus The Clerk of Oxenford: What Their Rivalry Means', *The Chaucer Review* 21, 2: 108–32.

Anderson, Bonnie S. and Zinsser, Judith P. (1988) *A History of Their Own*, Harmondsworth: Penguin Books.

Barber, Richard. (1984) *The Pastons*, Harmondsworth: Penguin Books.

Beauvoir, Simone de. (1949) *The Second Sex*, trans. H. M. Parshley, 1972, Harmondsworth: Penguin Books.

Beck, Richard. (1964) *The Preamble and Tale of the Wife of Bath*, London: Oliver & Boyd.

Beer, Gillian. (1970) *The Romance*, London: Methuen.

Bennett, Judith M. (1987), *Women in the Medieval English Countryside*, New York: Oxford University Press.

Blake, N. F. (1985) *The Textual Tradition of The Canterbury Tales*, London: Arnold.

Boitani, Piero and Mann, Jill (eds.). (1986) *The Cambridge Chaucer Companion*, Cambridge: Cambridge University Press.

Bornstein, Diane. (1983) *The Lady in the Tower*, Hamden, Conn.: Archon Books.

Brewer, Derek. (1978) *Chaucer and his World*, London: Methuen.

— (1984) *An Introduction to Chaucer*, London: Longmans.

— (1986) 'Chaucer's Poetic Style' in *The Cambridge Chaucer Companion*, eds. P. Boitani and J. Mann, Cambridge: Cambridge University Press.

Burrow, J. A. (1982) *Medieval Writers and Their Work*, Oxford: Oxford University Press.

Carruthers, Mary. (1979) 'The Wife of Bath and the Painting of Lions', *PMLA* 94: 209–22.

Coleman, Janet. (1981) *English Literature in History*, London: Hutchinson.

Cooper, Helen. (1989) *Oxford Guides to Chaucer: The Canterbury Tales*, Oxford: Clarendon Press.

Crow, Martin M. and Olson, Clair C. (1966) *Chaucer Life Records*, Oxford: Clarendon Press.

David, Alfred. (1976) *The Strumpet Muse*, Bloomington: Indiana University Press.

Delany, Sheila. (1983) 'Sexual economics, Chaucer's Wife of Bath, and *The Book of Margery Kempe*' in *Writing Woman*, New York: Schocken Books.

— (1990) *Medieval Literary Politics: Shapes of Ideology*, Manchester: Manchester University Press.

Diamond, Arlyn and Edwards, Lee R. (1977) *The Authority of Experience*, Amherst: University of Massachusetts Press.

Dobson, R. B. (1983) *The Peasants' Revolt of 1381*, London: Macmillan.

Donaldson, E. T. (1970) *Speaking of Chaucer*, London: Athlone Press. 'The Myth of Courtly Love' (1965) may be found at pp. 154–63.

Duby, Georges. (1978) *Medieval Marriage*, trans. E. Forster, Baltimore: Johns Hopkins University Press.

Erler, Mary and Kowaleski, Maryanne (eds.). (1988) *Women and Power in the Middle Ages*, Athens: The University of Georgia Press.

Fries, Maureen. (1977) 'Slydynge of Corage: Chaucer's Criseyde as Feminist and Victim' in *The Authority of Experience,* ed. A. Diamond and L. R. Edwards, Amherst: University of Massachusetts Press.

Frye, Northrop. (1957) *The Anatomy of Criticism*, Princeton: Princeton University Press.

Gies, Frances and Joseph. (1978) *Women in the Middle Ages*, New York: Harper & Row.

Gist, Margaret A. (1947) *Love and War in the Middle English Romances*, Philadelphia: University of Pennsylvania Press.

Hansen, Elaine T. (1988) 'The Powers of Silence: The Case of the

Clerk's Griselda' in *Women and Power in the Middle Ages*, ed. M. Erler and M. Kowalski, London: The University of Georgia Press.

Hilton, R. H. (1976) *Peasants, Knights and Heretics*, Cambridge: Cambridge University Press.

Kanner, Barbara. (1980) *The Women of England*, London: Mansell.

Kaufman, Michael. (1973) 'Spare Ribs: The Conception of Woman in the Middle Ages and the Renaissance', *Soundings* LVI, 2: 139–63.

Kelly, Joan. (1984) *Women, History and Theory*, Chicago: University of Chicago Press.

Kittredge, G. L. (1911–12) 'Chaucer's Discussion of Marriage' in *Chaucer: Modern Essays in Criticism*, ed. E. Wagenknecht, 1959, New York: Oxford University Press.

— (1915) *Chaucer and His Poetry*, Cambridge, Mass.: Harvard University Press.

Knight, Stephen. (1986) *Geoffrey Chaucer*, Oxford: Basil Blackwell.

Labalme, Patricia. (1980) *Beyond Their Sex*, New York: New York University Press.

Labarge, Margaret Wade. (1986) *A Small Sound of the Trumpet*, London: Hamish Hamilton.

Leicester, H. Marshall. (1990) *The Disenchanted Self*, Berkeley: University of California Press.

Lewis, C. S. (1936) *The Allegory of Love*, Oxford: Clarendon Press.

Lucas, Angela M. (1983) *Women in the Middle Ages*, Brighton: Harvester Press.

Manly, John M. (1926) 'Chaucer and the Rhetoricians' in *Chaucer Criticism*, eds. R. J. Schoeck and J. Taylor, rpt. 1960, London: University of Notre Dame Press, pp. 268–90.

Mann, Jill. (1983) 'Satisfaction and Payment in Middle English Literature', *Studies in the Age of Chaucer* 5, 17–48.

— (1991) *Geoffrey Chaucer*, Hemel Hempstead: Harvester Press.

Morewedge, Rosmarie. (1975) *The Role of Women in the Middle Ages*, London: Hodder & Stoughton.

Muscatine, Charles. (1957) *Chaucer and the French Tradition*, Los Angeles: University of California Press.

Parker, Patricia. (1979) *Inescapable Romance*, Princeton: Princeton University Press.

Patterson, Lee. (1983) ' "For the Wyves love of bathe": Feminine Rhetoric and Poetic Resolution in the *Roman de la Rose* and *The Canterbury Tales*', *Speculum* 58, 3: 656–95.

Payne, Robert O. (1979) 'Chaucer and the Art of Rhetoric' in *Companion to Chaucer Studies*, ed. B. Rowland, Oxford: Oxford University Press.

Petroff, Elizabeth A. (ed.) (1986) *Medieval Women's Visionary Literature*, Oxford: Oxford University Press.

Pollock, F. and Maitland, F. (1898) *The History of English Law Before the Time of Edward I*, Cambridge: Cambridge University Press.

Power, Eileen. (1975) *Medieval Women*, Cambridge: Cambridge University Press.

Pratt, R. A. (1961) 'The Development of the Wife of Bath' in *Studies in Medieval Literature in Honor of Professor Albert Croll Baugh*, ed. MacEdward Leach, Philadelphia: University of Pennsylvania Press.

Richards, I. A. (1929) *Practical Criticism*, London: Routledge.

Robertson, D. W. (1962) *A Preface to Chaucer*, Princeton: Princeton University Press.

— (1980) ' "And for my land thus hastow mordred me?": Land, Tenure, The Cloth Industry and the Wife of Bath', *Chaucer Review* 14, 4: 403–20.

Rogers, Katherine. (1966) *The Troublesome Helpmate*, London: University of Washington Press.

Rowland, Beryl (ed.). (1979) *Companion to Chaucer Studies*, Oxford: Oxford University Press.

Salter, Elizabeth. (1962) *Chaucer: The Knight's Tale and The Clerk's Tale*, London: Arnold.

Schibanoff, Susan. (1986) 'Taking the Gold Out of Egypt: The Art of Reading as a Woman' in *Gender and Readings*, eds. E. Flynn and P. Schweickart, Baltimore: Johns Hopkins University Press.

Shahar, Shulamith. (1983) *The Fourth Estate*, London: Methuen.

Sledd, James. (1953) '*The Clerk's Tale*: The Monsters and the Critics', *Modern Philology* 51: 73–92.

Springer, Marlene. (1977) *What Manner of Woman. Essays on English and American Life and Literature*, Oxford: Basil Blackwell.

Toner, Barbara. (1977) *The Facts of Rape*, London: Arrow Books.

Traversi, Derek. (1983) *The Canterbury Tales. A Reading*, London: The Bodley Head.

Utley, Francis Lee. (1944) *The Crooked Rib*, Columbus, Ohio: Ohio State University Press.

Vinaver, Eugene. (1971) *The Rise of Romance*, Oxford: Clarendon Press.